D0212968

# RACE, SEX, AND GENDER
# IN CONTEMPORARY WOMEN'S THEATRE
## *The Construction of "Woman"*

Mary Brewer has written a timely and much-needed book, which draws out the important themes written about by the current generation of British and American women playwrights.

*Gayle Austin, Georgia State University*

Mary Brewer has done an excellent job in bringing together a rich mix of primary material and diverse critical perspectives in a book that takes the study of women's theatre into the next generation of (and for) feminist criticism.

*Lizbeth Goodman, University of Surrey*

# Race, Sex, and Gender in Contemporary Women's Theatre

*The Construction of "Woman"*

———

## Mary F. Brewer

Foreword by
*Professor Alan Sinfield*
THE UNIVERSITY OF SUSSEX

**sussex**
ACADEMIC
PRESS

*BRIGHTON • PORTLAND*

Copyright © Mary F. Brewer 1999

The right of Mary F. Brewer to be identified as author of this work has been asserted in accordance with the Copyright, Designs and Patents Act 1988.

2 4 6 8 10 9 7 5 3 1

*First published 1999 in Great Britain by*
SUSSEX ACADEMIC PRESS
Box 2950
Brighton BN2 5SP

*and in the United States of America by*
SUSSEX ACADEMIC PRESS
5804 N.E. Hassalo St.
Portland, Oregon 97213-3644

All rights reserved. Except for the quotation of short passages for the purposes of criticism and review, no part of this publication may be reproduced, stored in a retrieval system, or transmitted, in any form or by any means, electronic, mechanical, photocopying, recording or otherwise, without the prior permission of the publisher.

*British Library Cataloguing in Publication Data*
A CIP catalogue record for this book is available from the British Library.

*Library of Congress Cataloging-in-Publication Data*
Brewer, Mary F.
Race, sex, and gender in contemporary women's theatre : the construction of "woman" / Mary F. Brewer ; foreword by Alan Sinfield.
p.   cm.
Includes bibliographical references and index.
ISBN 1–902210–18–2 (hardcover : alk. paper). — ISBN 1–902210–19–0 (pbk.)
1. English drama—Women authors—History and criticism.
2. Feminism and literature—Great Britain—History—20th century.
3. Feminism and literature—United States—History—20th century.
4. American drama—Women authors—History and criticism.
5. American drama—20th century—History and criticism.   6. English drama—20th century—History and criticism.   7. Gender identity in literature.   8. Lesbians in literature.   9. Sex role in literature.
10. Race in literature.   I. Title.
PR739.F45B74   1999
822'.914099287—dc21                              98–53080
                                                  CIP

Printed by Biddles Ltd, Guildford and King's Lynn
This book is printed on acid-free paper

# Contents

# Contents

# Foreword by Alan Sinfield

When the women's movement was developing, prompted by the publication of Betty Friedan's *The Feminine Mystique* (1963), Germaine Greer's *The Female Eunuch* (1970) and Kate Millet's *Sexual Politics* (1971), theatre was already established in Britain and the USA as a place where avant-garde and political ideas might be explored. From the late 1960s British groups such as CAST, Red Ladder, General Will, 7:84, and Belt and Braces were playing working men's clubs, picket lines and tenants' associations, as well as art centres and student unions. Off Broadway between 1964 and 1967, Joe Cino's Caffe Cino put on gay plays such as *The Haunted Host* by Robert Patrick and *The Madness of Lady Bright* by Lanford Wilson, and *Moon* by Robert Heide.

Theatre is useful to such dissident groups because it can be relatively inexpensive and can target fairly precise audiences. Furthermore, small theatres may afford a distinctive experience of intimacy, immediacy and shared purpose. Elements of make-shift among the performers and physical discomfort among the audience contribute to a sense of integrity and authenticity.

Feminist theatre, alongside the consciousness-raising phase in the women's movement, began with recovery of the voices of women. By the mid-1970s, Helene Keyssar observes, companies such as the Women's Theatre Group and Monstrous Regiment in Britain and At the Foot of the Mountain and Omaha Magic Theater in the United States were creating their own dramas, "drawing on the performers' autobiographies and improvisational rehearsals as well as from collaborative historical research". Playwrights were challenging "conventional dramatic strategies and dominant beliefs about gender and violence, rights and responsibilities, individuation and community".[1]

It is sometimes said that politically-oriented theatre "preaches to the

---

[1] Helene Keyssar, "Feminist Theatre", in Martin Coyle, Peter Garside, Malcolm Kelsall and John Peck, eds, *Encyclopedia of Literature and Criticism* (London and New York: Routledge, 1990), p. 490.

converted", but this charge is entirely misplaced. Actually, there was no period of simple common purpose; all the main issues represented in feminist theatre were controversial *among women*. It is in feminist plays that the thought that women may be complicit with their own subjugation was broached; that the notion that women may share unitary identity was challenged; that the situation of women of colour is (eventually) recognized.

If theatre is right to explore such topics in stimulating ways, the task of critical commentary is not just to stand back and admire the elegance of the writing. Mary Brewer, with a shrewd grasp of theory and a comprehensive knowledge of British and American plays, homes in on controversial issues among women – pornography, rape, mothering, domesticity and work, and debates about the butch/fem model and gender-bending among lesbians. Most importantly, she addresses race, not just as a special issue but as a problematic aspect in feminist and lesbian theory and in very many playtexts. Brewer confronts the essentialism in mainstream feminism which locates women as white until proven otherwise. She is severe on theories and representations which collude with dominant ideologies, while clarifying the enabling positions that are being claimed by some bi-racial and lesbian women.

Most of the plays discussed here were produced in the most precarious financial circumstances with ruinous conditions for the dedicated practitioners. Most of the companies have made their contribution, struggled and died. These have been the terms on which serious and committed theatre has been possible. *Race, Sex, and Gender in Contemporary Women's Theatre* shows that the consequence has nonetheless been substantial – not just as performed drama, but as interventions in the lives of women.

*Alan Sinfield*
*Professor of English at the University of Sussex*

# Acknowledgments

—

The jacket picture (front) shows a scene from Caryl Churchill's *Top Girls* (Sarah Lam, Deborah Findlay, Lesley Sharp and Lesley Manville), performed at the Royal Court Theatre in 1991. Picture © copyright 1991, Douglas H. Jeffrey, photographer, whose permission to reproduce is gratefully acknowledged. The jacket picture (back) is from *Cabrini Green*, by Free Street Theatre – photograph by Martin Argles – The Guardian ©. The author acknowledges with thanks the assistance of Judith Caul of Guardian & Observer News Services in obtaining permission to reproduce these pictures.

Without the help of my teachers, colleagues, examiners and friends in several countries this book would not have been completed; individually and collectively they helped me to define and articulate many of the ideas expressed here. I have incurred many debts while researching and writing this book.

First and foremost, I am immensely grateful to Alan Sinfield, who supervised the doctoral research upon which the book is based. His generous and patient guidance has been invaluable. I appreciate the assistance and constructive advice provided by Sandra Freeman, who read chapters while they were in their formative stages. Thanks for copious suggestions and criticisms are also due to Carl Muckley, who read several drafts of the book.

Thanks also to the following, who helped me in different ways with the writing. Elaine Aston and Rachel Holmes examined my doctoral thesis and offered careful and serious critique of my work. Several people provided me with helpful advice on sources and criticism on specific chapters. Special thanks are due to Jonathan Dollimore, Lizbeth Goodman, Chris Hall, and Laura Salisbury. Harry Bennett and Angela K. Smith kindly acted as proofreaders.

I would like to thank the organizers of the Women's Studies Network Conference at the University of Hull (1998) for allowing me to present and discuss the ideas on representations of lesbian mothering. A special debt is owed to Judith Caul at *The Guardian*, who carried out the picture research for the cover. For their friendship and emotional support, warmest thanks to Carol Badilla-Bradford and Jenny Parsons. Finally, I wish to express my sincere gratitude to my editor, Tony Grahame, for his remarkable patience and his advice while preparing this manuscript. Of course, any errors and the opinions expressed here are my sole responsibility.

# Race, Sex, and Gender in Contemporary Women's Theatre

*The Construction of "Woman"*

*To my mother*
Elizabeth L. Rhodes

# Introduction: Women and Representation

After two decades of extensive feminist analysis of gender, one might expect feminist discourse to have moved beyond the notion that difference equals sexual difference. Yet, mainstream feminist discourse continues caught in the tension between a definition of gender in which gender functions as a category that delimits men and women, and one that captures gender's intrinsic instability by acknowledging its interconnectedness with race, class and desire.[1] Even that most sophisticated of feminist discourse, post-modern theory, continues to conceive its principles about women and women's position in the psycho-social order based on their "femaleness". This book is situated at the intersection of the aesthetic and socio-political representation of gender(s). Focusing on dramatic works by contemporary British and American playwrights in conjunction with feminist political and theoretical texts, I analyze the degree to which feminist constructions of the category "Woman" continue to reflect and reinscribe dominant racial and sexual biases, illustrating how the terms of feminist discourse require that a person be either a "Woman" (white, middle-class and heterosexual) or a female-other (black, working class, poor, and/or lesbian). Over and against representations of "Woman" in contemporary plays by women, I deconstruct the category "Woman" in order to reconstruct it as a more complex and inclusive set of representations. My main objectives are to problematize the notion that sexual difference is the fundamental form of difference; to map out the principal ways in which gender identities intersect with racial, class and sexual identities; and to demonstrate how the existence of distinct genders means that not all females will be culturally designated as "Woman," and thus accordingly some of them will be cut off from the resources accruing to those who fall within this category.

Starting from the position that representation is a process of semiosis or meaning-making, that representations construct with differing degrees of disclosure or distortion what is assumed to be true about any category, and that categories do not necessarily have to exist in a material sense in order to be represented, this book assumes that the category "Woman" does not exist as a specific socio-historical female space; rather "Woman" is a discursive space – a site upon which issues of class, race, sexuality and gender are constructed. However, whether or not the category "Woman" exists, the structural constraints under which women live, what women are able or allowed to be in society, are at stake in its representations. The field of representation is one of struggle not only between women and a male-dominated society, but also among different classes and races of women as well as women of diverse sexualities. How groups of women answer the question who or what is "Woman" can be used as a basic criterion for distinguishing among the various feminisms. Liberal, socialist, middle-class, working class, black, white, and lesbian feminists all acknowledge diverse representations of womanhood. Thus, there are a multiplicity of representations of "Woman" circulating at any one time, with each representation competing for a monopoly on meaning. Even though one story of "Woman" may predominate, the process of negotiation by which it is formulated means that it will necessarily embody the conflicts and coincidences that inhere within and among various feminist definitions as well as the normative. These contestatory representations of "Woman," formed in the margins of dominant discourse, also intervene in the conditions of women's lives. Teresa de Lauretis points out that gender is the *"product and process of both representation and self-representation."*[2] How different groups of women interpret the meaning of "Woman" helps structure the political field, determining to a significant degree the standards used for interpreting women's positions in the social structure and the strategies adopted for altering them.

It has long been accepted among feminists that control over images is central to the continuation of any form of domination: representations of "Woman" inform the material conditions of real women's lives by playing a crucial role in determining access to political and social power and economic resources. Although present-day feminism endeavors to sensitize itself to women's differences, it remains the case that it pays insufficient attention to the ways in which a representation considered transgressive or liberating by one group of women may be oppressive to other groups. What I term the "movement personality" operating at the center of mainstream feminist discourse remains a white, middle to upper middle-class, college-educated, consumer-orientated, heterosexual, wife-cum-mother-cum-careerist. Images that denigrate any group of women function to sustain a male-dominated social order that subordinates all women as well as perpetuating racial, class, and sexual hierarchies within the class of women. This book looks at why the category "Woman" remains the central subject of feminism as a series of social movements, an academic discipline, and an ideology both in the sense of a representational and performative term. It also examines how mainstream feminism asserts its portrait of "Woman" as the true narrative of womanhood and, in privileged reference to its attendant values, produces an exclusivist discourse.

## Contemporary Women's Theatre: The Plays

Historically, women's groups have recognized the importance of theatre as a means of disseminating women's issues. On both sides of the Atlantic, early second-wave activists formed women's street theatre groups in complement to their protests against women's objectification and exploitation. Feminists today also recognize that theatre can help alleviate one of the primary ways in which women are marginalized, by being denied access to public space and language, with the theatre continuing to play a significant role in the movement's efforts to raise the status of women. Gayle Austin identifies several advantages of studying women's plays for the feminist critical project. Given that they combine "verbal and nonverbal elements simultaneously", they allow questions of language and visual representation to be addressed at the same time and constitute a unique field of examples of women's representation.[3] Women's theatre has proven to be one of the most social forms of women's cultural production; performances have often worked as a form of group Consciousness Raising and have assisted women to develop political identities by providing a supportive context.[4] At its best, women's theatre has validated aspects of women's culture that have been / are disparaged by the dominant. It has furnished women with information about and analysis of their various situations, helped to strengthen feminist solidarity, and provided entertainment free from the sexism prevalent in so much of the mainstream media. The deconstructive mechanism of women's theatre has served to dismantle hegemonic representations of "Woman," thereby enabling women to find new ways of perceiving and presenting themselves, as well as to mitigate the contradiction between a woman's sense of self as subject and object.

While women's theatre has this affirmative potential, of course, it does not always live up to it. Critics have recognized the prescriptive nature of some plays that claim to articulate the true meaning of female identity, and thus camouflage the contradictions in women's identities and the dissension among groups of women. Women playwrights have not always questioned their own or feminism's relation to and possible complicity with the ideologies and institutions they examine. Some plays by heterosexual women have served to reinforce the dominant preoccupation with heterosexual relations, while white women playwrights have often failed to sufficiently challenge the prevailing racial hierarchy. One result has been a fragmentation of theatre audiences, with lesbian theatre attended primarily by lesbians, black women's theatre by black women and so on. Whether for good or ill, however, women's theatre has not only served women and the movement, it has helped to create them and it. This book works from the premise that stage personae are more than historical depositories of female images. They are eligible to claim a part in the making of modern womanhood by virtue of facilitating the propagation of feminist values, the translation of feminist images into social behavior, and the breakdown of sex-role stereotypes. Women's theatre may not be deemed culture with a capital "C," receiving little public subsidy and having no grand buildings dedicated to its preservation, but it has played an important role in the process of women's history.

Thus far I have spoken of women's theatre as a concept and a practice. I also endeavor to address it in the form of a body of literature. Since its inception, feminism has been writer-led to a larger degree than most other social movements, and it owes much of its success to the spread of its literature. Drama, what becomes of a play after performance, affords the basis of its meaning to succeeding generations of readers and viewers. Because only a small proportion of the population in the US and Britain attends theatrical productions, the dissemination of ideas and images generated by women's performances usually occurs through reading the play or reading what a critic/reviewer has to say about the play. With the growth of women's studies in recent years, most often this reading now takes place because the play and its criticism appears on a course syllabus. Knowledge of most of the plays featured here will be limited to specialist groups such as theatre practitioners and academics, although a few of the plays addressed are considered modern classics. Churchill's *Top Girls* and Wasserstein's *The Heidi Chronicles*, to name but two, have been produced by mainstream companies in the West End and on Broadway as well as adapted for radio and television. And several of the new playwrights covered also work as performers, moving between mainstream and alternative forms of entertainment in the realm of TV, film, etc. Consequently, the ideas expressed in their dramatic work should not necessarily be deemed obscure. All of the texts chosen are available in published form, and, with the exception of *Care and Control* (1979), all date from the 1980s and 90s. I read the plays primarily for how they negotiate between "Woman" as heteropatriarchal figure and woman as generator of black-, lesbian-, and mainstream feminist discourse. I have tried to maintain a balance between plays by British and American playwrights, black and white, lesbian and heterosexual women. However, the principal basis for inclusion is that each play provides an informative and distinctive slant on what social and political positions of power and privilege are at stake in the construction of the movement personality, and each sheds light on the consequences for the feminist movement of white women's monopolization of "femininity."

## Feminist Constructions of Difference

The dominant conceives of difference in terms of exclusion: difference forms the basis upon which power and privileges are distributed. I argue that difference in mainstream feminist thought is theorized in the same way. While mainstream feminists have been engaged in deconstructing images of femininity, black and lesbian women have continued to experience a crisis of self-definition due to white heterosexual women's monopolization of this category. Alice Walker has observed that white feminists often find it inconvenient and even mind straining to think of black women as *women*, "perhaps because 'woman' (like 'man' among white males) is a name they are claiming for themselves, and themselves alone. Racism decrees that if they are now women (years ago they were ladies, but fashions change) then now black women must, perforce, be something else."[5] Black and lesbian women are not the only ones to feel estranged from contemporary feminism or disappointed by "feminist spokeswomen." Notable feminist writers like Judith Butler, Diana Fuss, Zillah R. Eisenstein, Ruth. R. Frankenberg, Elizabeth V. Spelman and Wini Breines have offered valuable critiques of the movement's deficiencies and foregrounded its racist/heterosexist dimensions. Accordingly, I do not take a black vs. white, lesbian vs. straight approach to the subject or texts discussed; rather, I divide them according to whether or not they can be classified as progressive or non-progressive feminist works.

In mainstream or non-progressive feminist thought, difference is commonly understood as referring to race and class, with gender difference limited to a kind of difference between men and women. This position disavows the existence of a plurality of genders and reinforces the assumption that femininity is the province of one women's culture. Furthermore, the idea that all women are gendered as feminine expunges black and lesbian women from the narrative of "Woman" and its attached reward system. Elizabeth V. Spelman makes the point that feminism's "problem of difference" in reality signifies a reluctance among mainstream feminists to deal with the issue of privilege. When treating racial/sexual identities and issues, mainstream movement texts employ language that reflects and preserves black and lesbian women's status as outsiders. Movement overtures to these women continue to be proffered from a privileged position of insiders inviting others into the fold of feminism. This book contends that any effort to occasion truly multi-racial/multi-subcultural women's groups will be sabotaged unless feminism develops a discourse of race, class and sexuality that interrogates the status of its central personality.

## Defining Race

How to define race is a significant issue of contention among black cultural critics. Generally, critics can be divided into two camps: humanist Afro-centrists vs. poststructuralists. In its emphasis on individualism, the black humanist stance resembles that of traditional Anglo-European Liberalism. The stress placed on self-actualization and self-determination suggests that the individual can function as an autonomous entity, in some sense detached from her/his social circumstances. However, through its concomitant assertion of a common African-centered consciousness, alternately termed the "common spirit, power, or energy," Afro-centrism attempts to re-insert the individual within a black cultural milieu. A leading member of the Afro-centric school, Molefi Kete Asante, espouses the view that "to assume that one possesses more than one heritage is to suggest contradictions in the person's heritage. Actually our heritage might be composed of many backgrounds but in the end we inherit a unified field of culture, that is, one whole fabric of the past rather than split sheets or bits and pieces."[6] Contextualizing Afro-centric consciousness as the product of a single African heritage, which is and *only can be* uniquely expressed by black individuals, leads to an arcane theory of how black people come to consciousness. In a reversal of the liberal notion that the individual exists ontologically prior to society, Asante proposes a cultural totality that exists prior to black people and is somehow available for osmosis. Moreover, Asante's idealism essentializes blackness and posits a mythic mother-Africa from the histories of a variety of Afro-Caribbean cultures and backgrounds.[7] His reductive search for a sole determinant of black identity is disturbingly similar to imperialist and colonialist ideas that all blacks are alike – one color, one identity – which is the basis of cultural racism. Moreover, there is definitely no room at Asante's Afro-centric inn for black lesbians and gays.

In contrast, Henry Louis Gates Jr., one of black poststructuralism's principal adherents, argues that race should always appear in brackets to show that it is a "metaphor for something else and not an essence or a thing in itself, apart from its creation in an act of language."[8] Race is not a set of morphological or genetic traits or a composite history, but a trope of irreducible difference among peoples. While Asante's theory works to close off the meaning of race, thereby limiting the possibilities of black identity, some have argued that Gates' radically indeterminate concept may surrender too much. If Asante binds black identity too closely to blacks' African roots, Gates' deconstruction of race is in danger of severing black identity from black culture, of negating or at the very least diminishing the significance of race, as it calls into question the possibility of any epistemology of race.

Audre Lorde has objected to postmodern conceptions of race on the grounds that the fractured metaphors and ambiguous subjecthoods posited by poststructuralists render infeasible the unambiguous collective responses that assaults on human bodies require: political necessity dictates that black people hold certain identities and histories to be unproblematic.[9] Lorde recognizes the real effects of race and racism in society, but without recourse to any essentializing bio-cultural fictions. Invoking a unified black identity – as and when it proves politically expedient – also enables multi-racial alliances based on common political objectives rather than alliances made on the specious basis of skin-color.

This book starts from the premise that race is an index that refers to a set of discursive constructions of difference and the exploitative arrangements that produce them, that race is a marker of cultural, religious, and color difference mediated by class, gender and sexuality, and that these constructions and arrangements are variable. For any statement about race to be reliable, it must be qualified with the specific conditions under which it can be said to be true. My usage of race aims to honor the contingent nature of race while not denying its contiguity with black people and allow some meaning to be attached to race while ensuring that this meaning is central to contemporary black life and political reality.

## Organization

The book explores what "Woman" means in current feminist thought by tracing how its various roles or modes are developed and deployed in contemporary women's drama. It comprises six chapters with each devoted to a different aspect of the definition of "Woman."

Substantively, each chapter stands by itself; essentially each retains its basis in a close reading of the plays examined therein. The theoretical perspective of the book is wide-ranging. I draw upon the wealth of inter-disciplinary theories of sex, race and gender. The basis for selecting a particular theoretical methodology in any chapter is its effectiveness in providing insights into how and why mainstream feminist discourse continues to reinscribe dominant sexual, racial and class prejudices. However, the chapters are linked by a common purpose: to demonstrate the necessity for feminists to theorize and organize based on the exis-tence of a plurality of genders. As a whole, the book is meant to form a constitutive part of the ongoing progressive feminist project of breaching the boundaries of feminist ethnocentrism.

Chapters 1 and 2 present "Woman" as "Mother." Chapter 1 explores how social and legal institutions sustain the dominant pattern of family life, which has at its center the heterosexual wife/mother, and renders lesbians unfit mothers. It aims to demonstrate how mis-representations of lesbian sexuality and heterosexist biases in feminist theories of mothering collude with dominant ones in constructing motherhood as a category of sexual privilege, thereby reinforcing the biases which negatively effect lesbian mothers' chances of winning custody. Representations of lesbian motherhood in Michelene Wandor's *Care and Control*, Sarah Daniels' *Neaptide*, and Alison Lyssa's *Pinball* are compared with those in law reports and feminist psycho-logical/psychoanalytic analyses of mothering. Chapter 1 concludes by examining the effectiveness of current campaigns for lesbian mothers' rights and offering some alternative strategies for resistance. Chapter 2 extends the analysis of "Woman" as "Mother" to include the ways in which these categories are inflected by race as well as sexuality. Opening with a discussion of the parallels between the sex–gender and race–gender systems, this chapter engages critically with plays about black motherhood written by black women playwrights: Grace Dayley's *Rose's Story*, Breena Clarke and Glenda Dickerson's *Re/mem-bering Aunt Jemima: A Menstrual Story*, and Shay Youngblood's *Shakin' The Mess Outta Misery*. Issues addressed in chapter 2 include: the way that motherhood as a concept has been derived from the experiences and mothering practices of white, middle-class, heterosexual women and how the form and function of motherhood is one of the principal areas in which black feminist theory significantly differs not only from the dominant, but also from mainstream feminist theory; the historical underpinnings of negative representations of black motherhood; and the distinctly black ideology and practice of othermothering – a collec-tive approach to childrearing

By the time we reach chapter 3, it will have become evident that the categories "Woman" and "Mother," whether dominant, mainstream feminist, or alternative constructions, bear a dependent relation to the family and the way in which this institution is defined. Chapter 3 is divided into two parts. The first part deals with the extent to which the nuclear family remains a crucial site of women's subordination and how far "Woman's" traditional family role persists as a confining standard against which women's behavior is judged. Another related concern is the extent to which mainstream feminism, particularly the leading 1980s model, also worked to privilege the white middle-class nuclear family as the preferred space for the constitution of gendered subjects. I explore and develop further these arguments through a critical analysis of three plays by Wendy Wasserstein and Caryl Churchill's *Top Girls*. The second part of chapter 3 is concerned with how the changes and the opportunities for socio-economic advancement which second-wave feminism has brought about has affected different groups of women in different ways depending upon their position in the hierarchies of race, class, and sexuality. With regard to Cassandra Medley's *Ma Rose*, I explore how black women were used in the mainstream feminist backlash and the problems these "feminist" representations created for black women at work and within the black community.

Chapter 4 turns its attention to the third significant component of the category "Woman": its object status. In this chapter, I am concerned both with the general objectification of women and more specifically, women's sexual objectification and exploitation. I explore how representations of black and white women are linked through the theme of sexuality and, in turn, the ways in which this connection enables the elevation of white womanhood over black. These topics are addressed by way of two plays by black American women: Elaine Jackson's *Paper Dolls* and Kathleen Collins' *The Brothers*. I then move on to an analysis of how black and white women are objectified differently as regards the particular issue of rape. Chapter 4 argues that the way in which mainstream feminism represents rape has both directly and indirectly contributed to racist assumptions about black sexuality. I evaluate mainstream feminism's ideology of rape through the work of its two best-known theorists, Andrea Dworkin and Catherine MacKinnon. To help put their arguments in perspective, I consider Eve Lewis' *Ficky Stingers* and Robbie McCauley's *Sally's Rape*.

Chapters 5 and 6 focus on women writing the self; that is, woman – this time with a small "w" – as discursive subject. Chapter 5 further interrogates the notion of a unified category of "Woman" by virtue of exploring how women whose identities comprise a number of voices represent themselves as subjects, particularly how they negotiate their multiple identities using a conception of identity which necessarily operates with and through difference or hybridity. It also examines how contemporary feminist constructions of difference pose obstacles to bi-racial/sexual women who attempt to write the self in and through the terms of feminist discourse. These issues are addressed by means of Lisa Jones' *Combination Skin* and Jackie Kay's *Chiaroscuro*.

Chapter 6 highlights the lesbian subject, in particular the lesbian identities of fem and butch. The chapter explores the potential that the discourse of neo-butch/fem may harbor for the creation of a feminist subject position or at least the acceleration of its inception. Focusing on the work of the celebrated American theatre group Split Britches, the leading architects of fem and butch imagery, I attempt to negotiate between that vision of butch/fem held by theorists who would utilize these roles for more purely conceptual concerns and the view of those who live out these roles. I employ personal and historical accounts of butch/fem in conjunction with Split Britches' *Beauty and the Beast*, *Upwardly Mobile Home*, and *Belle Reprieve*, with the aim of identifying who created butch/fem roles, what historical factors have shaped their construction, and how they have been perceived by those women who identify with them. The chapter further aims to answer critics of butch/fem, who characterize these roles as a politically regressive eroti-cization of power difference, by highlighting the arbitrary relationship between butch desire and fem receptivity; to examine specifically how the fem role works to sever the ties that bind "Woman" to the impera-tive of male desire; and to discuss the relation between butch/fem and drag. It concludes by qualifying the conditions under which the discourse of butch/fem may function as a transgressive agency. The book's conclusion outlines where women of difference might locate themselves for resistance and how feminists might begin building a women's movement that is able to accommodate differences of race, class, and sexuality – both critical and urgent questions for a progres-sive feminist politics.

# 1

## Representations of Motherhood

Edie's hands, tendons tense as wire, spread, beseeched,
how she'd raised them, seven years, and now not even
a visit, Martha said she'd never see the baby again,
her skinny brown arms folded against her flat breasts,
flat-assed in blue jeans, a dyke looking hard as a hammer:
And who would call her a mother?[1]

### And Who Would Call Her Mother?:
### Carers Without Control

In 1921, Tory MP Frederick Macquisten attempted, unsuccessfully, to
combat social instability, while protecting women from neurasthenia
and insanity, by extending the Labouchere Amendment to women:
then, it was feared that bringing forward such cases would serve only
to broadcast practices of which few women were aware and thus, previously virtuous women might be encouraged to adopt them.[2] With the
advent of the second wave of the women's movement and Gay
Liberation, however, same-sex practices among women began to be
openly acknowledged and discussed. A wave of custody battles in the
1970s enabled lesbianism to speak its name for the first time in the
British courts. These early cases demonstrated a shift in the dominant's
strategy to contain lesbianism; if women could not be protected from its
taint, then they must me publicly warned of the grave social and legal
consequences that choosing to live as lesbians could entail.

This chapter aims to reveal the law's role in sustaining the dominant
pattern of family life that has at its center the heterosexual wife–mother.
It examines how British legal and social hegemonies work to render
lesbians unfit mothers, and it offers comparative analyses of the
construction of the category "Mother" in terms of dominant and feminist theoretical models in order to demonstrate how some strands of
feminist theory further misrepresentations of lesbian mothering.
Because representations of lesbianism for most of this century have been
confined to literary ones, these images have played a major part in the

construction of lesbian identities and have contributed to lesbian's understanding of their sexuality; accordingly, I draw upon literary representations of lesbian motherhood in three lesbian custody dramas: Michelene Wandor's *Care and Control*, Sarah Daniels' *Neaptide*, and Alison Lyssa's *Pinball*.[3] The plays are exercises in transforming the heteropatriarchal categories "Woman" and "Mother" from sites of cultural domination to ones of institutional resistance. I consider them as both historical and political texts, as being encompassed within the larger body of contemporary lesbian feminist work.

## Courts of Flaw: Representations of Lesbians and the Rights of Lesbian Mothers

*Care and Control*, the first British play about the rights of lesbian mothers in child custody cases, challenges the legal and social hegemonies which repress lesbian motherhood and questions the values according to which the functions of mothering are defined and organized.[4] Its origins are based specifically in the lesbian community. The theatre group Gay Sweatshop commissioned the play as a result of audience demand. Conceived collectively, it was scripted by Michelene Wandor (who does not identify as lesbian). First staged in 1977, it is still regularly performed and critically evaluated. Feminist playwright and critic Sandra Freeman attributes the play's continuing popularity to its basis in social fact.[5]

Act one follows three separate but parallel stories: (1) the deteriorating relationship of the young mother Sara and her non-committal live-in Stephen; (2) a developing lesbian relationship between Carol and Sue, both married but soon to be divorced; and (3) Elizabeth's feminist transformation and her husband's threatening reaction. Children are involved in all three of the scenarios. The question of legal custody is presented in act two. Here we switch to a courtroom setting, a sort of inquisitional paradigm in which the women's liberation movement, lesbianism, and the disintegration of the family are run together by the character Authority. In two out of three cases, custody is given to the father – though no "real" evidence is ever provided that he is the better parent.

The play suggests that while the courts are particularly prejudiced against lesbians, it is not only lesbian women who are viewed by the dominant as questionable maternal figures.[6] In their introduction to the play, Kate Crutchley and Nancy Diuguid argue that any woman who asserts a wish to live with her children independently of men may be regarded as suspect.[7] *Care and Control* not only protests against heterosexist representations of motherhood, but also illuminates the way that social institutions employ lesbianism as a scare tactic against women in an attempt to manage women's autonomy – sexual and otherwise. As a case in point, the play offers the custody battle between Elizabeth (a straight woman) and her former husband Gerald. Gerald need only imply that Elizabeth is a lesbian in order to effectively influence the judge in his favor. Carol's case also foregrounds how society can penalize women who deny men sexual and emotional access. One of the play's most chilling moments occurs during Carol's questioning when Authority makes the following pronouncement: "I would like to point out that there might be other women in similar circumstances who thought they might be justified in leaving their husbands . . . It must be brought home to them that there is a grave danger that they will lose their children, if they choose to behave in this way."[8] In Carol's case, we see lesbianism treated tantamount to a criminal offense, and once again, it is being openly employed as a patriarchal tool to police women's behavior. Significantly, Authority's statement is addressed directly to the audience, underscoring that there is little difference between the events portrayed on stage and what routinely happened to real women not only in the 1970s, but also for much of the 1980s.

The belief that women's sexual independence carries the potential to disrupt the status quo has been a western cultural constant. Like Macquisten in 1921, dominant culture in the 1970s equated the decline of public morality with unrestrained female sexuality; indeed, some conservative British as well as U.S. religious/political groups continue to voice this opinion.[9] The perpetuation of a capitalist system of male dominance requires the subjugation of women's sexuality (and women) to the reproduction of labor. One way in which this is accomplished is by harnessing women's sexuality to the institution of monogamous, heterosexual marriage. Radical lesbian–feminist Adrienne Rich refers to this system as the institution of compulsory heterosexuality.[10] This ideology operates to sustain and advance male dominance by representing heterosexuality as the "natural" form of sexual relations. In so far as compulsory heterosexuality functions as a key component of male dominance, the suppression of homosexual practice, especially lesbian mothering, is endemic to the system. The institution of compulsory heterosexuality complements that of motherhood. Rich isolates two meanings of motherhood: motherhood as experience – an individual woman's relation to her childbearing capacities and to her child/ren; and the institution of motherhood. She defines the latter as the system that ensures that women's potential relationship to their powers of reproduction remains under heteropatriarchal capitalist authority.[11]

Lesbians have always been the targets of particularly virulent forms of sexism and misogyny because they can threaten the stability of the traditional nuclear family, still the "backbone of society," as well as the roles of wife and mother that are preserved within it. Writing in 1993, Lynne Harne observes that lesbian mothers can teach their children that women don't have to be available to and can exist without men.[12] Leah Fritz contends that the political significance of the lesbian mother is that she threatens to undermine the notion that the penis is essential to a woman other than for purposes of reproduction.[13] Lesbian sexuality disrupts the naturalized signifying chain:

$$\text{biological sex: } \underline{\text{male}} = \text{gender: } \underline{\text{masculine}}$$
$$\text{female} \qquad \text{feminine}$$
$$= \text{desire: } \underline{\text{active}} \quad \text{[for the] } \overline{\text{OPPOSITE}}\ \underline{\text{sex}}$$
$$\text{passive} \qquad \text{SAME}$$

By virtue of replacing "opposite" with "same" in the equation, a lesbian woman falls into the category of "unintelligible genders." Gender theorist Judith Butler defines "unintelligible genders" as those which fail to maintain relations of coherence and continuity among sex, gender, desire and sexual practice.[14] Thus, lesbian women appear as logical impossibilities within the heterosocial domain, and the customary perception of lesbians as devoid of maternal feelings or possessed of abnormal ones may be attributed in part to the fact that the category "Woman" cannot accommodate lesbian sexuality.[15]

Motherhood is one of our society's most overdetermined concepts. It is almost impossible to mark any socio-linguistic distinction between what it means to be "Woman" and what it means to be a mother in our society. Femininity, the social construction of femaleness, has largely been absorbed into maternity or what Luce Irigaray terms the "maternal function"; metaphysically as well as materially women are not individuated: there is only *the place of the mother*.[16] Within heteropatriarchal discourse, "women" naturally desire to mother and naturally, mothers are "women." Reigning opinion dictates that children should be raised by their natural mothers, but there must be no mistaking who gets to define what constitutes this natural figure. Here natural connotes – in addition to the biological – a moral, economic, and politically prescribed role which requires that women be emotionally, economically, and sexually available to men. As runaways from this class of women, lesbian mothers may be sentenced to disappear by dominant social and legal discourses.

*Care and Control* depicts the effectual inseparability of motherhood and family life as responsible for the oppression of lesbian mothers. Repeatedly, the opinion is given that lesbian mothers are dangerous because they will subvert "family values" by socializing their children to accept, perhaps even desire, alternative family groupings. The judgment against Elizabeth presents this quite explicitly. Authority assumes that she will teach her son to have "little or no respect for the ordinary obligations of family life."[17] Moreover, he echoes the dominant fear that lesbian mothers may subvert traditional gender relations and roles, which are constructed and reproduced within the nuclear family. After the denial of the phallus, Leah Fritz identifies the "unmanning of boy children" as the second threat presented by lesbian motherhood, and one, I suggest, that has been a principal motive behind social services' removal of children from lesbian households.[18] However, when Authority declares that the social order will act to limit the dissemination of all doctrines about sexuality and sexual morality that could damage a "healthy aggressive little boy," the contradictory nature of dominant ideology is revealed.[19] Despite the fact that lesbians are conceptualized as non-women, lesbian mothers, it is feared, will feminize the social order itself by producing children who take up passive, non-aggressive roles, in other words, "Woman's" role.[20]

Authority also questions Carol regarding how she would encourage her children's sexuality. Her reply, "I don't know if you can. I wouldn't push them one way or the other," strides, without attempting to resolve, the nature/nurture controversy.[21] The first part of her answer suggests that one's sexuality is a function of nature or at least of a nurturing which occurs so early and is so complex it could easily be mistaken for nature. Alternatively, her resolve not to push one way or the other hints that one's sexual orientation is in part at least dependent upon the circumstances in which one is nurtured. Social constructionists such as Valerie Jenness maintain that "identities emerge from the 'kinds' of people it is possible to be in society."[22] If one accepts the constructionist position, lesbian parenting could signify a subversive practice. I would argue that it does constitute a positive threat to family life as we know it. While not evocative of hostility toward men or ruling out men's participation, it removes them from their traditional social position as head of the household, to what Hanscombe and Forster term "a position of de-institutionalized co-operation."[23]

## Fortunes at Low Tide

*Care and Control* probes the issue of lesbian motherhood through a rather formalized examination of how legal discourses within heteropatriarchal capitalist society consolidate power over women. Sarah Daniels' *Neaptide* offers a more in depth examination of lesbian mothering and its psychology.[24] Like *Care and Control* and Lyssa's *Pinball* (a discussion of which follows), *Neaptide* draws some of its material from the real experiences of lesbian mothers in the courts as well as the shared experiences of women in the lesbian community, and it comments on the effect of current legislative biases against women who choose to be mothers without also being wives. However, Daniels offers a more thematically complex representation of the controversies surrounding lesbian motherhood. *Neaptide* is woven out of a number of issue-based narratives. The first two themes I address question and seek to undermine society's allegiance to traditional family patterns by challenging stereotypes of lesbian mothers as well as the nexus of social values that inform people's prejudice against them. The third co-opts the phallocratic Demeter myth, emphasizing its matriarchal aspects. In *Neaptide*, Daniels manages to present a successful, albeit at times uneasy, synthesis of high cultural and sub-cultural discourses. She uses the psychology of the Demeter myth to illuminate the condition of lesbian mothers in relation to the prevailing sex–gender system and to displace the idea of patriarchal ownership of children.

In the first act, we are presented two sisters, Claire and Val. Val, as we discover at the outset, is in the midst of a psychological crisis. Claire is recently divorced and living with her platonic friend Jean. A sixth-form teacher, she becomes embroiled in a controversy at her school when one of the students insists on the right to publicly assert her lesbianism and is immediately censured. Unable to play the hypocrite during preliminary disciplinary proceedings, Claire makes a show of solidarity by openly declaring her own lesbian identity. Freeman notes that although "she could deny her sexuality as Peter denied Christ," Daniels' script makes clear that the only honorable choice available to her is to come out to her colleagues.[25] However, the play also makes clear that society will demand a high price for her honor. Her declaration precipitates the events of act two in which her ex-husband, on the grounds of her now public lesbianism, challenges custody of Claire's seven-year-old daughter. The result, award of custody to the father, is a foregone conclusion, but ultimately Claire finds a freedom of sorts by running away with her daughter to America.

In an interview with feminist critic Lizbeth Goodman, Daniels tells of the burden she felt when writing about lesbian motherhood:

> Claire always had to say the right thing, explain everything to her daughter perfectly . . . Society is so stacked against women that I felt I had to make her so good there wasn't a chink . . . I was speaking for a lot of women and I didn't want to blow it.[26]

The difficulties of speaking appropriately to and on behalf of lesbian mothers might seem at first to be exaggerated. But when one considers that her task is to challenge feminist mis-representations of mothering as much as men's, Daniels' response after all is not surprising.

Mainstream heterofeminist constructions of mothering collude with dominant ones in casting motherhood as a category of sexual privilege. Feminist psychological/psychoanalytic constructions of mothering are especially fraught with heterosexist biases. Anne Wollett and Ann Phoenix identify several commonalities between psychological literature and mainstream feminist texts: neither set recognizes the differences between mothers of social class, race, marital status or sexuality. And "failure to theorize these differences helps to maintain the status quo as normal mothers being white, middle-class married women and other mothers being deviant or aberrant."[27] Supposedly, mothering is an exclusively female phenomenon and is naturally dependent upon a heterosexual lifestyle. Psychologists and psychoanalysts regard mothers as the primary contributors toward their children's formative experiences, almost as if mothering determines one's consciousness. Among feminist theorists, Nancy Chodorow is the best known and most influential writer to uphold the traditional idea that it is principally the mother who mediates the gendering of children.[28]

Of Chodorow's work, *The Reproduction of Mothering: Psychoanalysis and the Sociology of Gender* has had the most influence on feminist theories of motherhood.[29] According to Lynne Segal, mother–daughter relations, along with rape and male violence, were a principal preoccupation of 1970s feminism in Britain and the US.[30] This general trend helps account for Chodorow's early popularity. Her continuing relevance to feminist studies may be attributed to the number of notable feminist theorists and literary critics who incorporate her ideas into their own work, such as Jane Flax, Sandra Harding, and Nancy Hartsock. Further, as Austin notes, her work continues to provoke discussion by virtue of providing the very ideas with which to disagree.[31]

*The Reproduction of Mothering* has invited a number of detractors to whom it also owes a measure of its celebrity. Pauline Bart's critique has been one of the more perceptive. The most important issue raised in her review draws attention to the problematical nature of Chodorow's "evidence." Chodorow ignores significant feminist analyses of motherhood such as Adrienne Rich's *Of Woman Born*. Instead, her theories rest "solely on psychoanalyst's reconstructions of patient's reconstructions of how their mothers treated them." There is no mention of the fact that people who enter into therapy, those who provide the clinical evidence upon which psychoanalytic writings are based, "differ on almost every important demographic point from the general population."[32]

Strong adherence to traditional psychiatric methodologies such as Chodorow's usually counts against lesbian mothers. From its inception, psychoanalysis has characterized lesbianism as a sickness, both in the sense of a psychological abnormality and a moral failing – therapists having largely usurped the place of priests as guardians of social morality. Lesbianism has been described as a crude separatism that is typified by a rejection of men that stems from hatred of them. Lesbians' presumed faulty personality development, it was argued, prevented them from providing good-enough maternal care, as did the greater instability of their relationships compared with heterosexual couples. Freud's theory that lesbians were pseudo-men and hyper-sexed beings was also used to suggest that lesbians would corrupt their children by influencing them to engage in premature and promiscuous sexual activity or to become homosexual themselves.[33] Some went so far as to suggest that lesbians were likely to sexually abuse their own or other's children. It was also held that the children of lesbians would suffer confusion about their gender identity, engage in inappropriate gender-type behavior, and were likely to suffer from depression and anxiety due to the social stigma attached to homosexuality.

These misrepresentations have trickled down to a host of related fields. Among the lesbian mothers interviewed by Gillian E. Hanscombe and Jackie Forster for their book on the role of social authorities in lesbian mother's lives, *Rocking the Cradle*, most women expressed a fear and suspicion of social authorities: the judiciary, social services, and medical professionals, in fact, all the "machinery of the Welfare State."[34] Their suspicions are well-founded: the "expert" testimony of general practitioners, teachers, social welfare workers and counselors, and court welfare officers, as *Care and Control* and *Neaptide* illustrate in detail, frequently mimic these stereotypical representations. Both plays high-light the crucial role these professionals play in determining the outcome of lesbian custody trials, lesbians' rights of access to their children, and whether women will be granted supervised or unsupervised visiting rights. An examination of case judgements from British trials recorded in the 1970s and 1980s clearly reflects an acceptance of these myths. Judges routinely ruled against lesbian mothers on the basis of the "unnatural," "abnormal", and "deviant" status of lesbianism and in the belief that the children of lesbians would be "blemished" and irreparably "scarred." An overwhelmingly male British judiciary defended the removal of children from lesbian mothers as being in the "public interest," arguing that for the courts to sanction lesbian moth-erhood would lead to the "decay of society."[35]

*Neaptide* attempts to dispute the notion that lesbians cannot help but fail to provide what Chodorow terms "good-enough" mothering – the kind of mothering that is capable of "socializing a non-psychotic child."[36] In narrative terms, much of the debate about the supposed pernicious effects of lesbianism takes place at Claire's work-place, a girl's sixth-form college, where the matter is discussed among Claire's colleagues, as much as within a familial framework. Claire's co-workers, who form a chorus of reactionary homophobes, hold contradictory views as to the "cause" of homosexuality. On the one hand, they espouse a view popular earlier this century, and one which has recently re-emerged as a significant strand among American gay activists, that homosexuality is an inborn condition, or as one of Claire's co-workers, Roger, puts it, there are "bent genes in the family tree."[37] At the same time, also voiced is the opinion that "there are ways to get round anything these days – even nature."[38] Those in the nature camp exhibit a great deal of anxiety inconsistent with something that is ostensibly dependent on biology. When two students are discovered kissing, one of whom then comes out as a lesbian, Marion insists that "it [homosexuality] must be stamped out, this sort of thing spreads like wildfire."[39] Seemingly, one is not born but rather one may become, or worse, be turned into a lesbian. And the principal figures capable of this kind of conjuring appear to be mothers.

Historically, mother-blaming has been rife in western culture and has proved instrumental in controlling the way that women mother. But regrettably, in contesting the stereotype of the destructive lesbian mother, Daniels creates another: the infallible lesbian mother. Goodman considers Claire a recreation of the earth–mother goddess. She interprets her as representative of womanhood and motherhood, rather than lesbian woman- or motherhood. She writes: "Her lesbianism is incidental to her other roles, but is the lens through which her situation is focused."[40] Given Claire's social and economic position, as set in the late 1980s, I would disagree. The aura of middle-class respectability with which Daniels endows her gives Claire a better than excellent chance of winning a custody fight – if it were not for her sexuality. Clearly, the issue is lesbianism, as revealed by her ex-husband Lawrence's threat: "The sordid details are going to make you look unfit to have a goldfish bowl in your care."[41] I do not mean to suggest that sexuality represents the key to one's being or even that lesbianism is the core of Claire's oppression. While sexuality is a primary locus of power in contemporary society, Foucault warns against thinking of sexuality as some kind of natural given which power tries to hold in check.[42]

Daniels is right when she says that society stacks the deck against women, but the deck is stacked in different ways against different women. Elizabeth V. Spelman, a progressive white feminist critic, suggests that the way in which one form of oppression is experienced is influenced by and influences how other forms will be experienced.[43] Gender oppression intersects with sexual oppression: that is, they are constantly in flux, experienced simultaneously. *Neaptide* should not be read as the story of a Woman or a Mother separated from her daughter, but as the story of a lesbian mother–woman bringing up her daughter alone in a heteropatriarchal culture that denigrates all women, where lesbianism is feared and despised, and in the midst of a backlash against single mothers. Together these constitute the catalysts that precipitate the court's decision to take Claire's daughter, Poppy, away from her.

*Neaptide* belongs to the developing pattern within radical feminism of gynocentric writing or what Mary Daly terms "Gyn/Ecology." As conceptualized by Daly, "Gyn/Ecology" involves the "dis-spelling of the mind/spirit/body pollution inflicted through patriarchal myth and language" and the speaking of "New Words."[44] Like Daly, Daniels believes in the necessity for women to reclaim mythic language, its power to symbolize and name, in their quest to define their experiences and re-configure the female subject.[45] *Neaptide* pursues this project through its reinterpretation of the Demeter Myth. Daniels takes a myth that for centuries has been read as revealing psychological reality and reveals how in fact it merely embodies established gender asymmetries that serve the interests of men.

The same sense of violation inherent in the Demeter myth also permeates the play. Just as Hades violates the mother–daughter bond between Demeter and Persephone, Lawrence, who has acquired a new wife to mother his daughter, threatens the bond between Claire and Poppy. In the play, the part of Hades undergoes a tri-partite division, with Lawrence, his Barrister, and the Judge enacting the role. These figures operate as an all-male criminal fraternity who, having already fixed the odds in their favor, approach the courtroom proceedings as a farce. A pre-trial conversation between Lawrence and the Barrister reveals the trial to be merely a hollow formality:

> B: When we win, will you take your little girl straightaway?
> L: Do you think it's actually a foregone conclusion?
> B: Everything's in your favor.[46]

The Barrister assures Lawrence that if they "throw the book" at Claire (meaning spotlight her lesbianism) their case is "watertight."[47] And seemingly in a matter of seconds, the next thing we hear is the Judge announcing that Lawrence has won. The dramatic compression of time reinforces the idea that the outcome has been rigged. The fact that Daniels does not dramatize the trial itself suggests that as far as the law is concerned the rights and welfare of lesbian mothers do not signify.

Claire's loss presents her with the dilemma of either surrendering her daughter to patriarchal captivity or becoming with her a refugee from patriarchy. She chooses to leave Britain for the US, thus ending the play on an equivocal note. I say equivocal because Claire's loss, like almost every incident in the play that depicts lesbian experience in a pessimistic light, is also shaded with some positive meaning. It is grossly unfair that Claire must separate herself and her daughter from family and friends, not to mention sacrifice her career; and, in one sense, Claire's flight implies an irredeemably patriarchal order. At times, reality in the world of *Neaptide* seems to be constructed according to male criteria. Throughout the play, one might argue that Claire is more acted upon than acting; her escape might be labeled a re-action rather than a self-affirming action. Read in this way, *Neaptide* replicates the hierarchical relations that society defines as natural. Yet, her chosen course also has its merits. Foremost, this way affords her the chance to raise Poppy according to her own feminist standards. The audience is provided with several instances of Poppy's ripening feminist consciousness. I think Daniels intends Poppy as a symbol of hope: at only seven years old, she refuses to subscribe to hierarchies, calling her adult relations by their given names. The stories that inform her consciousness are not the usual misogynistic children's tales, but unorthodox accounts of women's capacity for achievement. Raised on "Mrs. Plug the Plumber" and feminist re-writes of canonical texts, she can announce with great self-confidence that the Sun is "silly" to ask Demeter: "Why mourn the natural fate of daughters – to leave their mother's home, to lose their virginity, marry, and to give birth to children?"[48] Already, Claire has begun to instill in Poppy a transgressive potential, which, without the influence of her father, could well remain untamed. At the end of *Neaptide*, feminist values do not prevail outright, but neither are feminist alternatives completely obviated. One may hope that Poppy's generation will not mourn but resist, even re-shape, the "natural fate of women."

Furthermore, the trial's outcome provides Joyce, Claire's mother, with the impetus for defying her husband's judgment for the first time. Unlike the Demeter myth in which Demeter's mother collaborates with Zeus and Hades' attempt to pacify her, Claire's mother first takes it upon herself to find Claire a lesbian–feminist solicitor and then helps plan Claire and Poppy's escape to the US. Joyce's act marks a significant transformation in her character. For most of the play, she expresses distaste for all things lesbian, and her scenes with Claire are marked by confrontational disputes. However, her actions in defense of her daughter and granddaughter bring to the fore an underlying emotional bond between the women in this family. That bond is amplified by

Joyce's final gesture (also the play's final moment) toward Val. Represented as a traditional wife–mother figure, Val lives in a constant state of anger and frustration that she channels self-destructively, even attempting suicide. By successfully assisting Claire, Joyce has shown herself to be an effective agent; therefore, when she takes Val's hand, the audience can believe that things may yet turn out all right for her.

Paradoxically, just as patriarchy is being reinforced by the court's decision, it appears to be breaking down. The fissure can be traced to the possibility of woman-bonding being located within the conventional hegemonic discourse of motherhood as well as to the community of women, those family and friends both gay and straight who rally to Claire's support, which the patriarchal order is shown to harbor within itself. In another dramatic character reversal, Bea, the semi-closeted head mistress, undergoes a change of heart, offering to testify on Claire's behalf and announcing that she has reconsidered her decision to expel the two lesbian students. Through her exploration of how motherhood discourse underwrites patriarchal discourse, Daniels demonstrates that the points at which these two discourses meet are also the points at which their incoherences may be revealed and possibly exploited. Although some differences and conflicts remain unresolved among the women, their concerted efforts to resist patriarchal encroachment pose a viable threat to the established order. While Demeter never really gets her daughter back, having to relinquish her to Hades for three months of the year, *Neaptide* insists that "neither husband nor child nor stranger would ever claim her as his own. Persephone belongs to her mother. That was Demeter's gift to herself." This is also Daniel's gift to Claire, one that serves finally to counterbalance the view of an impregnable patriarchal order.

## The Politics of Lesbian Motherhood: Strategies for Resistance

Whereas *Care and Control* and *Neaptide* can be characterized as political plays with a small "p," Lyssa's *Pinball* has a more deliberate political design, providing yet another slant on lesbian mothering and the custody issue.[49] Of *Pinball's* first production in a mainstream Australian theatre in 1981, Lyssa remarks that "its heart was not quite understood." She prefers a theatre company for which "politics and political practice [is] the stated stuff of its life." One such company to perform *Pinball* has been Gay Sweatshop, whose 1985 UK production supplied the kind of environment where Lyssa need not explain her feminist principles or her vision of women "working together to change the world." *Pinball* is about many things. Society's outrageous treatment of lesbian mothers is used to introduce a whole canvass of Left concerns. Theenie's case serves as a paradigm in support of the argument for the socialist trans-formation of society. Instead of spot-lighting Theenie's struggle for personal autonomy as an individual lesbian mother, the action of the play revolves around Theenie and her women friends' invention of a collective agency capable of transforming the social conditions under which lesbian women mother. In addition to amplifying the play's polit-ical force, their position as communal protagonist functions to contest "Woman" and "Mother" as obvious and homogeneous entities, revealing them to be culturally bounded and historically constructed discursive categories.

In the same way as Daniels, Lyssa draws upon canonical texts to provide keynotes to her play. Father–daughter relations in Shakespeare's *King Lear*, and the *Old Testament* story of the two mothers and Solomon's wisdom, constitute the play's allegorical subtexts. Superimposed onto these narratives is the story of Theenie, a lesbian mother, and the battle she wages for custody of her seven-year-old son Alabaster, a child who is seen but never heard. Her bigoted brother Kurt, who convinces her reluctant, but weak, ex-husband Sylvester to take Theenie to court, challenges Theenie's parental rights. Kurt objects both to Theenie's having a woman lover and moreover, a black woman lover – Axis. Unlike its biblical counterpart, the wisdom of the heteropa-triarchal law, which awards custody to Sylvester and his new wife, Louise, is, in the end, shown to be contradictory, and the court is forced to reverse its decision.

From the outset, the women in *Pinball* act on the assumption that mainstream representations of lesbians and lesbian mothers are obvi-ously inaccurate and ludicrous. So confident is Lyssa in this belief that she creates in Theenie a realistic, well-balanced mother-figure, the opposite of Daniels' sugar-coated version. In *Gay and After*, queer theo-rist Alan Sinfield points out the way that les/bi/gay subcultural myths are fraught with the contradictions of their own histories and of their crucial positioning in the prevailing sex–gender system.[50] As a result, subcultural representations are just as apt to reinforce dominant arrangements as they are to subvert them. Daniels' construction of lesbian motherhood in *Neaptide* is at times so unrealistically conceived that no woman could possibly live up to her standard of mothering. The importance of and the need for positive and valid representations of lesbian mothers should not be underestimated. A 1993 study by lesbian–feminist critic Ellen Lewin found that many lesbians continue to think of themselves as unsuitable for mothering because they have internalized dominant images of homosexuals as "self-serving, immature, or otherwise not capable of the kind of altruism basic to maternal performance."[51] Lewin's research suggests that most women's accounts of becoming a mother focus on the power of the individual to construct or to imagine herself as a mother. She regards this sense of agency as singularly important for lesbians who decide to become mothers, especially for those who decide to become mothers once they have firmly identified as lesbian.[52] Because a woman's desire to become a mother is characterized as a *natural* desire, without the belief that she can re-negotiate her identity, many lesbian women would find it difficult to work through the equation of homosexuality with unnaturalness. Natural desires are, de facto, heterosocial desires – the traditional values, customary behaviors, attitudes, and gestures that are attributed to and expected from women in our culture. Motherhood must be disassociated from them if heterosexual women's monopoly of the category mother is to be broken. Separating mothering out from the traditional paraphernalia of femininity would eliminate the rationale for defensive images of lesbian mothers; lesbians could stop trying to make that which is culturally designated unnatural into the natural, which, as *Pinball* convincingly argues, merely reinstates rather than transgresses the natural/unnatural dichotomy.

Much of the focal point of *Neaptide* as well as *Care and Control* rests upon a heterosexual world-view; that is, lesbian stereotypes are confuted over and against a backdrop of dominant gender constructs, relations, and institutions. Using mainstream ideology as a foundation from which to argue for the legitimacy of lesbian practices may succeed in problematizing heterosexual constructs. In the end, however, heterosexuality will most likely re-assert itself as the "normal" version of sexuality, leaving lesbianism positioned as the deviant. Even more disturbing is that this strategy encourages a politics of toleration. In some respects, I think *Care and Control* and *Neaptide* foster this kind of politics – the latter undoubtedly less than the former. In each play, lesbianism itself goes on trial, not just lesbian motherhood. Each court case involves asking a figure of dominant authority to affirm the way that lesbian women live out their sexuality. Lesbianism is never affirmed within a lesbian community; indeed, neither play incorporates a lesbian community in its story lines nor accommodates any features of a lesbian sub-culture. For this reason, lesbianism emerges as little more than an alternative lifestyle – what kind of alternative is not entirely clear. This strategy, upon which lesbian mothers and their representatives often feel obliged to rely, necessitates trying to authenticate lesbian motherhood without, however, antagonizing the courts by placing homosexuality on a par with heterosexuality. The result is that lesbian mothers' rights to raise children remain precarious.

*Pinball*, on the other hand, recognizes that as things stand societal acceptance of homosexuality would demand that certain aspects of it be swept back into the closet. If lesbians and gays wish only to be tolerated or accepted, one could argue with American gay activist Andrew Sullivan that homosexuals should be granted equal rights because they are *virtually normal*; by this, he means that lesbians/gays are just like heterosexuals – except they sleep with people of the same sex.[53] Sullivan's argument for acceptance diminishes the political aspect of a homosexual identity. Actually, such arguments deny to gay/lesbian identities their political potential and, thereby, deny their power to challenge and contest social norms. In contrast, *Pinball* does not focus much on changing heterosexist views or explaining homosexuality within a heterosexual context; if anything, it celebrates the fact that lesbians violate society's "true" discourse of motherhood. Lyssa asserts the right and importance of lesbians to speak up for themselves drawing upon their specific subcultural perspectives, and this despite the fact that lesbian mothers in Australia have to navigate a legal system set up according to the British model, which means that custody decisions do vary according to an individual judge's attitude and biases.[54] At the same time, *Pinball* never downplays how risky it remains for a lesbian to "advertise what she is," or to seek support in struggle. Theenie's refusal to live in the closet precipitates Sylvester's bitter custody suit. Notwithstanding, Theenie, the play's counterpart to Cordelia, and her sisters, in the sense of feminist sisterhood, are imbued with an "iconoclastic fighting spirit that teaches the taking of risks."[55] For only in concert are the women able to raise the money and fight Kurt and Sylvester successfully, thereby demonstrating that the risks can be well worth taking.

Sinfield also makes the case that "there is no security in trying to join the mainstream." He contends that "subcultural groups gain more self-respect, more community feeling, and a better self-understanding by insisting on their own explicit subculture . . . "[56] I would add that they have a better chance of developing and accomplishing constructive political agendas as well. Rather than making overtures to the mainstream by downplaying difference, a better idea might be to explore similarities and differences within and among lesbian/gay subcultures and other marginalized groups. This way affords opportunities to learn more about how the way in which one group is oppressed bears upon the subordination of other groups. Outlining the connections among various forms of oppression can encourage the forging of activist coalitions. This is exactly what *Pinball* advocates. Lyssa sets her characters within a lesbian community, the cornerstones of which are political activism, cooperation and support. However, their mutual support is not presented in any way as facile. The play gives an honest, well-balanced view of lesbian community, even touching upon the sensitive issue of some lesbians' mixed feelings toward male children and the concern among others that lesbian motherhood itself may co-opt lesbian values and space.

In the courtroom scenes, *Pinball* refers to the way in which heteropatriarchy depends for its effectiveness not so much on raw power or legal authority, although these play a part, as on a general recognition of its cultural legitimacy. Without the imprimatur of those concerned, even raw power could not sustain the system for long. One way in which dominant groups exercise control is by presenting meaning as univocal. If subcultural groups are to effectively challenge dominant structures, it is essential to recognize with Gramsci that hegemony is a "process whereby a ruling group in capitalist society comes to dominate by establishing the cultural common sense."[57] Lyssa's understanding of language and identity is poststructuralist.[58] From its opening lines in which Solomon recounts God's words, *Pinball* construes male speech as representative of legitimate authority, as the verbalization of History, and as that which says "what goes without saying," referred to by Solomon as the "overall view."[59] Questioning the relation between "Woman," and Logos, she posits that women's limited access to power stems in part from their limited access to language and via language to legitimacy. She attempts to counterbalance this by endowing Vandelope with practical and effective powers of speech in the public realm. Vandelope appropriates the Word and uses it to question the will of men and the pedigree of heteropatriarchal authority by exposing its myriad connotations. She fights the ruling against Theenie – and wins – by using the sanctioned discourse of heteropatriarchal authority against itself. Disguised as a male doctor of laws, she gains control of the courtroom and proceeds to turn the logic of the law regarding father–mother–child relations upside down.

Her assumption of a masculine pose, though, raises one of the seminal concerns of contemporary feminist theory: does women's appropriation of masculine discourse signify more than an exploitation of masculine values which only momentarily effects a change in the distribution of power rather than a radical subversion of it? In so far as she must enact a male role in order to influence the court, *Vandelope's* power of women's speech seems to be contained within patriarchal ideology. To consider her courtroom speech-act in the light of a Foucauldian concept of transgression, however, opens up the possibility of an alternative scenario. In *Language, Counter-Practice, and Memory*, Foucault writes:

Transgression is an action which involves the limit, that narrow zone of a line where it displays the flash of its passage, but perhaps also its entire trajectory, even its origin; it is likely that transgression has its entire space in the line it crosses . . .

The limit and transgression depend on each other for whatever density of being they possess . . . Transgression carries the limit right to the limit of its being; transgression forces the limit to face the fact of its imminent disappearance . . . [60]

Foucault holds that transgression, while not necessarily subversive, always bears the potential to subvert, to shift discursive boundaries. Believing that power works not from above or beyond but through dominant categories and thus, is best contested through those same categories, he allows for the possibility of changing the social order by means of dissident behaviors. The extent of an action's effects does not correspond equally to and is not wholly determined by the scope of its causative agency. To Foucault's way of thinking, transgressive acts are like tiny acorns that are capable of producing – but not bound to produce – huge oak trees. If we accept that transgressive actions initiate a kind of rippling effect, which may eventually bear large fruits of change, one could argue that Vandelope's performance of masculinity destabilizes patriarchal ideology not only in the moment of its transaction, but also in the space it creates for more radical subversion in future. By linking Vandelope's performance of masculinity to the irruption of a counterhegemonic discourse into the Solomonic narrative, Lyssa exposes the relation between language, a masculine gendered subject, and power. And, if one reads her performance in the light of Butler's theory of gender as imitative and repetitious, then it is reasonable to suggest that her role-play discloses the constructed nature of masculinity and concomitantly femininity.[61]

Jonathan Dollimore describes how binaries hold in place more than they actually designate; a binary's displacement effects not only the binary itself, but also the "moral and political norms which cluster dependently around its dominant pole and in part constitute it" and which can only be separated for the purposes of analysis.[62] Because each binary intersects with a multiplicity of differential axes, not only is the validity of the masculine/feminine dichotomy called into question, but also its entire trajectory of meaning is complicated. If masculine/feminine is seen to be an unstable distinction and conceivably in some ways interchangeable, then there is no basis for framing an opposition that allies men or masculinity with, for example, mind and reason and women or femininity with bodily experience and irrationality, or for devaluing body/emotion/woman while valorizing mind/reason/man.[63] *Pinball* lays open to question the idea of femininity as necessarily an analogue of femaleness, heterosexuality as a corollary of woman-hood, and of maternity as inextricably conjoined to femininity. The audience knows that from beneath the doctor's robes issues the voice of Vandelope the dyke, a short-haired, loud-mouthed butch who has spent the entire play vandalizing billboards, organizing protests, and urging women to smash the State. By effectively managing to speak and read men as subject, Vandelope inverts the binary oppositions mascu-line/feminine, subject/object, and thereby calls into question the normative pattern of sex–gender hierarchies and relations. Thus, its production could prove an effective aid to lesbian women in their campaign to re-vision motherhood as an accessible role and as some-thing at which they may excel; it might also help lesbians to live more comfortably as mothers.

## Conformity or Rebellion: Lesbian Families at Risk

Although heterosexual women currently hold a monopoly on the cate-gory "Mother" and remain at the center of feminist analyses of motherhood, this chapter has argued that the category is susceptible to change by political activity. However, current feminist prescriptions for closing the parental power divide between men and women offer small hope for improving the position of lesbian mothers. Let us consider Chodorow's preferred solution: for men to fully participate in the care of infants and children and women to be fully integrated into the world of "meaningful, productive work." She considers that "women's continued relegation to the domestic, 'natural' sphere, as an extension of their mothering functions, has ensured that they remain less social, less cultural, and also less powerful than men."[64] This synopsis is hardly applicable to lesbians who, as I have shown, are denied any space within the "natural" sphere. Lesbians, by virtue of necessity, have always been more social and cultural, more integrated into the public sphere of work, than heterosexual women, despite which they remain less powerful. Further, as the plays under discussion indicate, when men participate in the lives of lesbian mothers and their children, the results are often far from desirable.

The treatment of lesbian mothers by the British legal system over the past two decades makes clear that the Freudian differentiation between private and public spaces based upon the sexual division of labor, which underpins Chodorow's theory of good-enough mothering, proves an unsuitable frame of intelligibility for lesbian subjects. In the first instance, it precludes an understanding of how the social intervenes in the family structure. The Child Support Act (CSA) 1991 represents a model instance of how British law can work to undermine autonomous motherhood by furthering women's dependency on men. The CSA, which primarily affects women and their children who receive state benefits, requires biological fathers to pay financial maintenance for both the child and the mother – regardless of the mother's wishes, and thus, it presupposes that women should look to men for financial support rather than the State. The Family Law Act 1996 also reinforces the primacy of the nuclear family through the introduction of "a period of reflection and consideration" for those considering divorce; for people with children, this period could last as long as two years. The belief that male role models are necessary for rearing "normal" children also forms the basis of The Children Act 1989, which sustains the presumption that ongoing father/child contact is always in a child's best interests; even in cases where domestic violence against the mother and/or the child has been proven, this law has worked to guarantee men access to children.[65] Lesbian accounts of mothering also depict the need to negotiate a variety of private and public terrains as a fundamental aspect of their parenting activities. Lesbian mothers who receive welfare benefits, for instance, must run a gauntlet of officials whom they describe as usually hostile to their sexuality in order to meet their children's basic material needs.[66]

In response to what Harne describes as a "depressing saga of discrimination" against lesbian mothers, lesbian–feminist activists have established a network aimed at developing more effective legal strategies for contesting lesbians' rights to mother. Activists have sought to foster research that could be used to refute stereotypical representations of lesbian mothers and to combat ignorance of the issues surrounding lesbianism and parenting as well as prejudice against lesbians on the part of solicitors and barristers.[67] The growing body of lesbian-centered research, which shows that no evidence – psychiatric, psychological, or educational – exists to suggest that lesbians are bad mothers, is working to lessen the discrimination lesbians mothers face.[68] Studies carried out by Fiona Tasker and Susan Golombok have persuasively refuted the view of lesbians as somehow deficient in mothering skills and the belief that children raised in lesbian households suffer detrimental effects. Their study of children who have grown up in lesbian households shows that neither lesbian mothers and their partners nor their children are more likely to suffer from mental health problems than heterosexual women and their children. Children of lesbians do not report experiencing any problems with their gender identity, nor are they more likely to engage in cross-gender activities or choose a gay/lesbian sexual identity. Further, lesbian mothered children do not relate instances of excessive teasing or bullying as a result of having grown up in a lesbian household.[69] By the end of the 1980s, these non-biased research findings combined with the campaigning efforts of lesbian–feminist activists meant that the chances of a lesbian mother winning custody was beginning to improve.

The good news now is that lesbianism in and of itself is rarely deemed to render a mother unfit. The bad news is that, when considering the best interests of the child, the mother's sexual identity is still held to be a significant factor by child welfare professionals and the courts. Although the British legal establishment and social service agencies may now be less overtly hostile toward lesbian mothers, this is not to say that lesbians have gained much mainstream support for their sexuality, lifestyle, or parenting activities. Consider the wording of the 1986 Education Act, which states that sex education, when taught, should encourage students to "have due regard to moral considerations and the value of family life." As Harne notes, models of family life other than heterosexual ones are implicitly excluded.[70] Consider also the disapproval of homosexual parenting reflected in the phrasing of Section 28, which prohibits the promotion of "pretended family relationships."[71] In the 1990s, dominant opinion has merely become less predictable and more contradictory, a fact borne out particularly in British social and legal practice concerning adoption and fostering. The law on fostering, contained within the 1989 Children Act, while not banning outright adoption by lesbians and gays, nevertheless, states that "the chosen way of life of some adults may mean that they would not be able to provide a suitable environment for the care and nurture of a child."[71] Therefore, although lesbians and gays may apply as foster parents, the law does not necessarily prevent discrimination on the basis of an applicant's sexuality. Indeed, a fear of adverse publicity motivates many local authorities to consider lesbian and gay foster parents only as a last resort when "more desirable" heterosexual families cannot be found for hard-to-place children. Furthermore, no precedent exists in British law to prevent adoption agencies from refusing outright applications from lesbians and gays; consequently, The Children Society, one of the largest agencies in the UK, may discriminate against gays/lesbians on the basis of Christian doctrine.[73]

Although the existence of unbiased research about lesbian mothering has made it more difficult to justify removing children from lesbian households, clearly room for discrimination still remains. Part of the problem is that most of the psychological research on lesbian mothering and their children is premised upon the assumption that heterosexual parents are preferable to lesbian or gay parents, and, in order for children to be considered psychologically healthy, studies imply that they must conform to conventional gender types. The strategy which lesbian mothers and their legal representatives tend to adopt in custody cases has also proven problematic. On the one hand, the practice of emphasizing the similarities between lesbian parenting practices and those of heterosexual women, and downplaying lesbian's sexual difference, has helped lesbian mother's win custody of their children. On the other hand, the price of success has been the tacit acceptance of the inferior status of lesbian motherhood.

In a 1994 report, Liberty, the UK's National Council of Civil Liberties, stated that lesbian mothers continue to live with the threat of losing parental control, lesbianism is still regarded as a relevant and negative factor in custody cases, and lesbian mothers are usually only awarded custody in cases where the father has been proven to be a totally unsuitable parent or the children "absolutely refuse" to live with him.[74] And the campaigning group Rights of Women (ROW) still hears from women who have been advised by their solicitors that they have no chance of winning custody because they are lesbians.[75] The outcome of any one lesbian custody trial largely hinges on the luck of the draw – depending on an individual welfare officer's/judge's personal inclination, a mother's lesbianism may be considered relatively unimportant, or it may be prioritized by the court. Recently, High Court judges have tended to take a pragmatic view of lesbian mothers; however, ROW reports that county court decisions continue to demonstrate ignorance and prejudice against lesbian mothers and that the Court of Appeal also remains "problematic."[76]

The victories which lesbians mothers have enjoyed in the courts in the 1990s have been double-edged. One mother who succeeded in winning Care and Control, known as a Residence Order since the 1989 Children Act, was awarded custody on the basis that her son's sexual identity would not be "adversely affected," meaning that he probably wouldn't grow up gay.[77] Some judges have also made disturbing distinctions between "private" and "public" or militant lesbians. One judge, ruling in favor of a lesbian mother, stated that he had considered it significant that the mother and her partner had previously been involved in heterosexual relationships. Most important, he underlined the private nature of their relationship; that is, they were women who did "not believe in advertising their lesbianism and acting in the public field to promote their lesbianism." In reaching his decision, the judge considered it a matter of principle that:

> what is so important in cases is to distinguish between militant lesbians who try to convert others to their way of life, where there may well be risks that counterbalance other aspects of welfare and are detrimental to the long-term interests of children either in relation to their sexual identity or corruption, and lesbians in private.[78]

Other "favorable" decisions have also made it clear that the nuclear family continues to represent the ideal model of family life and that the court's task is to choose the alternative that comes closest to it.[79] In these cases, lesbian mothers have been judged simply the lesser of two evils, winning custody only when circumstances prevented the father from providing for the children's material needs. And in almost all cases, lesbians have been reminded of the importance of a male role model and ordered to make provision for regular and continued contact with the father. Judges also remain free to impose conditions on Residence Orders. Lesbian mothers have been cautioned to behave "appropriately" in front of the children.[79] This can be interpreted to mean that the mother and her partner should abstain from physical contact or displays of affection in front of the children and even that they should occupy separate bedrooms. The plays discussed here then remain accurate in their portrayal of many of the problems lesbian mothers continue to face.

There is a good reason why lesbians are denied the right to call themselves mothers: lesbianism does constitute a threat to family life as we know it. Although proportionately, children mothered by lesbians do not grow up to be gay/lesbian in greater numbers than children mothered by straight women, the views of children raised in a lesbian context concerning what constitutes acceptable adult sexual behavior, in general, do tend to be much broader. And lesbian-mothered children, as adults, do appear more willing to consider becoming involved in a same-sex relationship. While lesbian-mothered female children do not display feelings of hostility toward men or necessarily rule out men's participation in child-rearing, they are more likely to form parenting relationships in which men do not take up their traditional social position as head of the household.

Although heterosexual women currently hold a monopoly on the category "Mother" and remain at the center of feminist analysis of motherhood, this chapter has argued that this category is susceptible to change by political activity. The plays discussed here aspire to assist lesbian mothers in politicizing their version of reality and in mobilizing around their own concerns by providing supportive representations of lesbian mothers, which women may draw upon to resist the closeting effects of dominant and mainstream feminist ideologies of mothering. Lyssa's *Pinball*, in particular, affords a powerful example of lesbian theatre that functions as an alternative space for self-definition and empowerment. This chapter has also argued that lesbian feminist practice in relation to lesbian custody issues, by virtue of supporting the natural/unnatural dichotomy, serves only to reinforce negative images of lesbian motherhood, which work in the material realm by limiting lesbians' chances to mother successfully. In the long term, a more advantageous approach might be for lesbians to openly claim their difference and use this as a base from which to develop the critical tools needed for understanding and contesting the social and political factors which produce the power divisions between subcultural groups and the dominant and among subcultural groups themselves. In this way, the difference of lesbian motherhood may come to signify other than exclusion within mothering discourse. With this goal in mind, I end with an invitation from *Pinball's* model heroine:

> But you never know what
> we could change
> if we risk it.
> Join hands friends
> and we can go home
> optimistic.[81]

# 2

# *OtherMothers*

I was once whipped, . . . because I said to my misses, my mother sent me.
We were not allowed to call our mammies mother. It made it come to near
the way of the white folks.

*New Orleans freedman*[1]

## The Sex–gender/Race–gender System

We have seen the ways in which "Woman" and "Mother" are
constructed as sexually exclusive categories. This chapter will present
an extended analysis of these categories to include their racialized
dimensions. Spelman contends that women mother in a social and political context in which they are not only distinguished from men, but are,
along with men of their same cultural background, distinguished from
men and women of other cultural backgrounds.[2] The idea expressed by
the freedman in the epigraph above reflects her thesis. The freedman's
recollection alludes to the way that dominant ideals of motherhood are
shaped and bounded by the absence of black mothers, and it makes
reference to how white culture views the conceptual terrain of motherhood as its property. Under slavery, black people who trespassed
against this property met with violent punishment. I maintain that
while dominant methods have changed, the essence of its program to
maintain "Mother" as a pure racial category has not: black women and
children still face penalties when they claim parity with white mothers
and families.

As a bridge to a discussion of heterosexualized patriarchy and
racialized patriarchy, I briefly return to Lyssa's *Pinball* and the connections it draws between lesbian and racial oppression and between
homophobia and racism. Solomon's questions to Vandelope in the
final courtroom scene allude to the existence of complimentary
sex–gender/race–gender systems: "How can you, a doctor of law, make
a plaything of our finest precedent? You invite the jungle to take over,
and blood to flow in the streets."[3] Solomon characterizes transgressive

sexual behavior as potentially infectious. He infers that should one class of people, women (particularly lesbian women), be allowed to get out of control, a general decline in the "civilization of centuries" (read white civilization) would necessarily follow. Though it is never made explicit, throughout the play the implication is that the character Axis is black, and I refer to her as such in chapter 1. And so the likelihood that the distinction drawn by Solomon between the rule of law and the lawlessness of the jungle contains an oblique racist image is hardly far-fetched.

This reading is supported by Kurt, the play's most outspoken sexist and racist character, when he draws a connection between "delectable milk white skin" and humanity.[4] Kurt subsequently elides blackness with subversive female sexuality by insisting to Theenie that "there is no basis for negotiation if you bring into my house, that . . . black witch."[5] Here, he is of course referring to Axis. Kurt makes it clear what kind of women he prefers: "I'll have my women white, and my coffee black" (note too the general objectification of women). And in act two, scene two, he exclaims: "Hey you! Where are you taking the kid? *They're kidnapping Alabaster* [my emphasis]. Harlots!" The pun on the boy's name, Alabaster, as well as references throughout the play to his developing black speech patterns, make the connection clear: white civilization is being stolen away. Kurt's reference to witchcraft provides additional confirmation. Typically, women accused of being witches were held accountable for the destruction of community: seminal witchcraft texts taught that "almost all the kingdoms on earth have been destroyed by women."[6] Solomon fears nothing less than this when he detects that Vandelope's ruse has provoked a decision in favor of a lesbian mother with a black partner: "For my children's sake I had an empire to hold onto, and I cannot have you telling me it's gone."[7] Axis appreciates this as the reason why she and Theenie and women like them face harassment and persecution: "Alabaster has to turn out perfect or their empire falls in ruins."[8] Again we see that if whiteness as well as conventional masculinity is compromised then all is lost.

De Lauretis defines the sex–gender system as a "system of representation which assigns meaning (identity, value, prestige, location in kinship, status in the social order, etc.) to individuals within the society.[9] Mae Gwendolyn Henderson extends this definition to include race. She explains the race–gender system as one in which a person is racialized in the process of experiencing gender as well as gendered in the experiencing of race.[10] This is not to say that the mechanisms of the race/gender system simply mimic those of the sex/gender system. Donna Haraway argues that discourses about sex, gender, motherhood, and race are co-produced, indicating that the meanings of race, gender, and sexuality intersect as cultural constructs.[11] Hence, what it means to be a straight woman in our society is predicated upon what it means *not* to be a straight woman. Likewise, what it means to be a black woman largely depends on what it signifies/does not signify to be a white woman. Bearing in mind Henderson and Haraway's comments, the way in which the category "Mother" may be inflected by race – by whiteness and blackness – and by the history of race relations, as much as it is inflected by heterosexuality, becomes clearer.

## Survival as Resistance: Black Women and the Family

Speaking of the ongoing struggle in the US to preserve motherhood for white culture, Barbara Christian describes three different ideas of motherhood: "the African-American community's view of motherhood; the white American view of motherhood; and the white American view of black motherhood."[12] Depending upon which construction of motherhood one takes to be central, the gender and status of black women who mother will widely differ, there being no reciprocity or true binarism. However, fundamentally, the solid ascendancy of the white cultural view has resulted in a diminution in the status of black women and black motherhood. In the US, negative images of single motherhood, mainly promulgated by conservative American politicians and their organs in the media, have focused intensely on black mothers, so much so that single motherhood is now practically synonymous with black motherhood. While racialized ideologies may be better linguistically disguised in British political discourse, Tracey Reynolds perceives the same dominant image in the British media and the public mind of the single parent as a young black woman.[13] The white British view of black single mothers, according to Reynolds, is of young, highly promiscuous women who are desperate and greedy for state benefits.[14] The plays discussed below – Grace Dayley's *Rose's Story*, Breena Clarke and Glenda Dickerson's *Re/membering Aunt Jemima: A Menstrual Story*, and Shay Youngblood's *Shakin' The Mess Outta Misery* – attempt to counter white views of black motherhood by presenting images of womanhood and motherhood that are informed by specifically black cultural concepts and practices of mothering. With reference to the above plays, the remainder of this chapter will explore the extent to which black women are able to successfully deconstruct and transform white meanings of "Woman" and "Mother."

In *Rose's Story*, a play about a fifteen year-old Anglo-African girl's experience of impending motherhood, Dayley interrogates the white British view of black motherhood.[15] The play refers to the way that the dominant's suspect view of black family life derives from black women's position as nucleus of the black family unit. It also returns to a topic of chapter 1: how the social stigma attached to alternative family units relates to the mother's exclusion from the category "Woman." *Rose's Story* convincingly argues that in a white supremacist society Motherhood is . . . what motherhood and children mean to white men and women. It also establishes that black women who mother, like lesbian women, are deemed incapable (but for different reasons) of adequately performing a nurturing role, and in the case of black mothers, even their motives for reproducing may be judged suspect.

Set in London in the 1980s, the play is based upon Dayley's own experience as a young black girl living in a Mother-and-Baby-home. Through the character of Rose, Dayley confutes many of the misconceptions surrounding black mothers, particularly single black mothers, and their families. The play draws a cause and effect relation between negative stereotypes of black mothers and social policies that are designed to harness black women's fertility to the needs of a changing political economy, in effect, to limit black women's reproduction. The cultural images that have grown up around black mothers as a result, for example, of the political wars over welfare, depict black women as being either too lazy or not intelligent enough to secure employment. Rickie Solinger relates how attacks on black mothers often employ tropes which draw on the language and concepts of the marketplace to characterize black mothers as consumers who produce nothing beneficial for society. Children, it would appear, like mothers, come in only one color.[16]

From their inception, western birth-control movements, both eugenicist and feminist in origin, have had racist underpinnings. Beverley Bryan, Stella Dadzie, and Suzanne Scafe, authors of *The Heart of the Race: Black Women's Lives in Britain*, link the dominant view of black women as a "high promiscuity risk" whose reproductive capacities are a "moral flaw," and, therefore, to be frowned upon and controlled, with the frequency with which doctors take it upon themselves to exercise control over black women's fertility – in the interests of white society: "The fact that we may not view our unplanned children in this way within our own culture is of no consequence . . . And such attitudes are reflected not only through our experiences here in Britain, but in our countries of origin, where myths about the need for population control are used as an excuse for the unleashing of mass sterilization and birth control programmes on Black and Third World women, often as part of the West's aid package."[17] *Rose's Story* reflects these feelings. Everyone in an official capacity responds negatively to Rose's pregnancy. Her doctor automatically assumes that she will not want the baby, and, when Rose refuses his patronizing advice, he briskly dispenses with her, committing her to the care of "someone from Social Services who knows about girls in your situation."[18] Miss Pickford, Rose's social worker, pressures her to have an abortion, telling Rose: "I've seen girls like you before and this almost always proves to be the best possible solution."[19] For whom this proves the best solution one may well ask. Pickford's knee-jerk reaction to Rose's refusal, her belief that Rose's child will necessarily suffer from an inadequate upbringing, is part and parcel of the negative stereotyping of young, single black mothers. If Rose won't abort the pregnancy, then she suggests adoption or at least fostering.

Rose, however, scoffs at the suggestion that she allow her child to be adopted or fostered by some "middle class white people who can't breed, and feel seh dem is doing my baby a great favor."[20] Rose's rejection of white middle-class "favors" for her child implies that she is aware of the kind of treatment a black child can expect in a racist society, and more important, how a woman's racial awareness or lack thereof will effect her mothering practices. This difference in knowledge, Spelman contends, cannot be dissociated from the differences in what it means to be a mother for a black woman as opposed to a white woman or in what a mother's love or method of nurturing means.[21] The main conceptual representation of motherhood through which the plays' figures of dominant authority interpret adequate mothering proves irrelevant to Rose because it ignores the issue of racism as a significant factor in maternal care.

Rose's attempts to make sense of her experiences with the social institutions she comes to inhabit as a result of her pregnancy rebuts the standard line that young black women choose to have children with the arrogant assumption that the State will provide. Rose is determined to continue her education after the baby is born so that she can find the kind of work that will enable her to support her child and avoid further contact with government agencies. Moreover, she anticipates that the baby's father, not the State, will provide support, giving the lie to the idea that single black mothers actively reject family life. Above all, she appears intelligent and level-headed regarding her future. She understands the implications of keeping the baby as well as the obstacles that she faces in a sexist and racist job-market. As she says, "its going to be hard."[22] Her decision to have and keep her child in spite of the pressurized situation in which she finds herself testifies to the way that choosing to bear and raise children can be, in itself, an act of political resistance for many black women. In the past, black women practiced self-induced abortion and even infanticide in the struggle against racist oppression, to keep their children free from a life of slavery. Now, as *Rose's Story* illustrates, a black woman's decision to carry her child to term can represent a challenge to institutional policies that encourage white, middle-class women to reproduce, while discouraging, even penalizing, poor and working-class black women from having children.[23]

In chapter 1, we have examined the commonalities between developmental psychological/psychoanalytic literature and feminist literature, how neither set recognizes the differences between mothers of sexuality, marital status, social class, or race, and thus, how these discourses help to maintain the racial and sexual exclusivity of the category "Mother." Ann Phoenix attributes the failure to recognize difference in mainstream feminist work on mothering and dominant thought to a fusion of culture with color or race when assessing the situations of black mothers. She points out that in mainstream studies of early motherhood culture is implicitly accepted as an influence on young black women, but not on their white counterparts.[24] Mainstream feminist writers generally accept the dominant explanation of black women's patterns of reproduction, attributing black women's having children outside of marriage to their African/Caribbean heritage and/or to patterns of life developed under the institution of slavery.[25] More interesting, however, are those cases which attempt an amalgam of cultural and biological rationales, with the unrestrained sexuality of young black women – considered to be an inbred tendency – placed paradoxically aside black women's African/Diasporic heritage. In contrast, the reasons most frequently offered for young unmarried white women who become mothers are based in psychology: they have babies because they want to feel needed or because they are searching for someone to love. Whether consciously or unconsciously, white women are understood as making emotional decisions to give birth, whereas black women are seen to be doing, without any thought, what comes naturally to them.

*Rose's Story* affords the audience an opportunity to witness a young black girl experiencing many ostensibly "white" emotions about childbearing. At one level, Rose views the baby as a means of escape from an intolerable, apparently loveless, home environment. Her pregnancy also serves as stimulus and reason for Rose to face and constructively cope with the history of emotional and physical abuse in her family. Rose tells her sister Elaine that the baby will force her to "become someone in my own right: I know this may sound silly, but me getting pregnant is not such a bad thing. I now answer back because I've got to . . . I can't really afford not to . . . " Her pregnancy has given her a "reason for living."[26] The play goes on to illustrate how preconceived racialized ideas about the psychology of young black mothers, when processed as social policy, result in different and unequal treatment for young single black mothers compared to their white counterparts. Miss

Pickford exemplifies the scant attention paid to the concerns and needs of black girls by social service agencies. Social welfare workers often make little effort to sympathize with the emotional make-up of young black girls, nor, as a whole, do they receive any training that might enable them to better understand how childbearing is viewed within a black cultural context. Whereas counseling is the remedy most often recommended for white girls, this kind of help is seen as a waste of time and money for black girls given that their pregnancies are just to be expected. Placed on "this list, that list and the other list," the answer to their "problem" is inevitably considered to be one form or another of birth control.

Chapter 1 made clear that objections to lesbian mothers are rooted in the belief that their children will be socialized in ways damaging to themselves. *Rose's Story* helps us to see that objections to black maternity are largely economic and not rooted in humanitarian concerns for black children. There is a dominant drive to reduce monies and social services used by black women who are seen as a drain on the State's resources. This effort is assisted by images of black mothers as social deviants who do not value marriage and the family because these representations mark as unnecessary and even threatening to whites' standards of living the fertility of women who are not white, married, and middle class. *Rose's Story* recognizes the connection between the dominant perception of the black family as a site for the reproduction of values which are antithetical to white culture and its particularly intense hostility toward young black mothers and their families. This is underscored by the contrast which the play sets up between the view of white culture held by those who grew up in the context of colonialism and as adults chose to emigrate to the United Kingdom and the present generation of black people who are more likely to share Rose's caustic opinion of white British culture.

Dayley creates Rose as the product of a traditional, religious upbringing, one which enacts in many ways the colonial view of how black people should behave. As Rose describes her childhood: "it was a miserable existence, nobody outside that house could understand. It was church, church, school, and more church, school." Rose only had the "freedom" to get pregnant when she ran away from home with Leroy. She describes this in terms of a flight from slavery: she laughs at her parents imagined reaction "when they realized that one of their slaves had absconded and this time she had taken her clothes."[27] Having internalized the values of the oppressor, "all [they] cares about is money and reputation and crap like that" – her parents' treatment of their children augments the dominant's police work. Mother treats Miss Pickford and the police officer called to investigate Rose's disappearance with deference and exaggerated respect, even after the WPC refers to Rose as an "abominable child." Black-feminist poet Zhana recounts her own mother's quest for acceptance in which her mother confused acceptance with power: "Like so many black women of her generation, she believed that all she had to do was to "prove" to white people how capable she was, and she could overcome their racism."[28] With this in mind, she tries to train her daughters to behave like ladies. Of course, Mother might believe that her daughters' safety and their chances for successful, happy lives depend upon mimicking the dominant ideal of womanhood. Zhana interprets some black mothers' obsession with propriety as a holdover from slavery when that which was unobtainable for black women, the title lady, became that which was most treasured.[29] But this venture has always been and remains an impossible task because black females do not meet the criteria for the title: remember that to be a lady, one must first be accepted by the dominant as "Woman." Of course, were more black women to share this goal, it would serve to keep them (from the dominant point of view) occupied and pacific. *Rose's Story* alludes to the way in which the sex–gender/race–gender systems slide into the discourses of nationalism and cultural imperialism. The pursuit of an approved cultural identity is shown as keeping black people, particularly black women, trapped between two worlds, too engrossed in striving to reconcile them that they lack the time, energy or resolution to contest white values and policies. It also suggests that all black family structures are in some way deemed a social problem because their values and loyalties bear the potential for producing a different set of political and cultural institutions, Rose's being the play's case in point.[30] For despite her quasi-conservative up-bringing, this young black woman, who equates police with pigs and the job of beating up youths, is unlikely to perpetuate respect for dominant white values in raising her child.

## Black Women and the Race: "Lifting as We Climb"

Having considered the primary contemporary representation of black mothers, it is now necessary to inquire into the historical genealogy of this image, in particular nineteenth-century constructions of black womanhood and motherhood. The most pervasive and enduring images of black women's maternity from this era have been the figures of Mammy or Aunt Jemima. Here I explore how these distorted images of black motherhood have served as the basis for the ideological hegemony which determines the relative worth accorded to present-day black mothers, especially in American culture, and I look at two black women playwrights' attempt to re-fashion this image to match black women's vision of black womanhood and motherhood.

Elizabeth Brown-Guillory's study of black women playwrights concludes that a principal concern of their work is the black family of the African continuum: those "persons linked by race, culture, heritage and shared ancestry."[31] Contrary to conventional black thought, Glenda Dickerson and Breena Clarke's *Re/Membering Aunt Jemima: A Menstrual Story*, first presented in 1992 at San Francisco's Lorraine Hansberry Theater, enjoins black women to celebrate Aunt Jemima as one of this family's most worthwhile figures.[32] This play, presented as a choral work, with its singing "menstruals," is a post-modern drawing of the Aunt Jemima of American commercial pancake myth into a strong black maternal figure, one who is represented as nurturing the black feminist movement. Dickerson and Clarke introduce their play by stating: "We decided that the bravest thing we could do would be to take on the stereotype of Aunt Jemima, tear it apart, examine it and put her back together as the archetype she originally was. . . . In doing so, we propose to rescue Aunt Jemima, and by extension our foremothers, from the stereotyping that makes us face our mirrors with fear."[33]

It might be considered odd, even a bit unsettling, that one should use a symbol of maternity which traditionally has been portrayed as more nurturing toward whites than blacks as an affirmative image of black motherhood: dominant representations of Mammy depict her as more interested in taking care of her white charges than her own children and as more devoted to protecting white culture than her own.[34] This aspect of the Mammy image has some basis in fact, what Sau-li C. Wong describes as the phenomena of "diverted mothering." Historically black women's time and energy for mothering has been diverted from those who, by kinship or communal ties, were their more rightful recipients.[35] Hence, many would assert that Mammy/Aunt Jemima cannot be salvaged as a representation of black motherhood. Granted, within the confines of a white cultural context, representations of Aunt Jemima have operated as a symbol of race and gender oppression insofar as the image has been propagated as a means of enhancing the image of white womanhood/motherhood. K. Sue Jewell describes Mammy/Aunt Jemima as the antithesis of the dominant conception of "beauty, femininity and womanhood."[36] However, Dickerson and Clarke's point is that the image of Aunt Jemima, in and of itself, does not disparage black women; that is, representations of her are detrimental only when judged solely in terms of white cultural definitions of black womanhood and motherhood.

Clarke explains the play as an

attempt to show that African people used to revere the qualities for which she [Aunt Jemima] is now denigrated. Aunt Jemima has big lips; she is fat; she wears bright colors; she is smiling. We have been taught to fear all those qualities. Voluptuous lips are ugly only when measured by European standards; the same with steatopygous buttocks. . . . It was somebody else's culture which told us we look stupid in bright colors. If we look to our Motherland, we see the lie in that idea. We think she smiles without cause and that this is somehow shameful. But how do we know why she smiles? The smile of Aunt Jemima is no less enigmatic than the smile of Mona Lisa.[37]

Re/membered, Aunt Jemima proves a fruitful figure through which to explore the development of the maternal function in black culture and for advancing our knowledge of how black constructions of mother-hood differ from white constructions of both black and white motherhood.

Although the image of Mammy arose over a century ago, it continues to effect contemporary meanings of black motherhood. Even today, there remains an aura of unexamined romance about Mammy, some-times inadvertently invested by those who are intent on correcting such mis-perceptions. Take, for example, Rich's description of being cared for by a black woman from her otherwise outstanding work on motherhood *Of Woman Born*:

As a child raised in what was essentially the South, Baltimore in the segre-gated 1930s, I had from birth not only a white, but a black mother. This relationship, so little explored, so unexpressed, still charges the relation-ships of black and white women. We have not only been under slavery, lily white wife and dark, sensual concubine; victims of marital violation on the one hand and unpredictable, licensed rape on the other. We have been mothers and daughters to each other . . . [38]

Note how Rich assumes that black women feel the same sense of fond nostalgia for a time when, typically, black women mothered the chil-dren of middle-class white women at their own children's expense. Even giving the title of Mother to the woman who minded her as a child is a suspect gesture. For it presumes that black women who worked as domestic servants in white homes perceived their employer's families as their own, thought of the white female children in their care as their daughters, and experienced meeting the needs of these children not as a form of paid labor but as embodying an ethic of mothering.

Rich mistakenly imputes symmetry to black and white women's circumstances under slavery and segregation. While slavery was a capi-talist patriarchal institution that subordinated white women to white men, nevertheless, black women were the victims of white men *and* white women. Her assumptions only insure that the racial dynamics which inform representations of black mothers remain unspoken, and if unspoken, they will remain unchallenged. Spelman points out that while there are similarities between black and white women they exist in a context of old differences. How those differences effect the similarities is an ongoing debate – a debate in which not everyone's opinion is given equal weight.[39] Certainly, in Rich's statement, what black motherhood means remains firmly defined according to a white woman's point of view.

The appearance of the dark, sensual concubine in the passage is perplexing given that the most significant aspect of Mammy's construction in dominant race–gender ideology is her asexuality.[40] She is never depicted participating in the natural process of conceiving or bearing a child. In nineteenth-century racist discourse, Mammy could not be granted children of her own *and* remain a figure of comfort for whites – her central function – because black mothers were routinely separated from their children. Alice Walker identifies a continuing split between black motherhood and sexuality in some strands of mainstream feminist thought that is more in tune with nineteenth-century representations than is the contemporary stereotype of hyper-sexuality described in *Rose's Story*. This split results from a strategy whereby white feminists try to dissociate themselves from their role in the system of white supremacy and the feelings of guilt brought about by the privileges it affords them:

> Perhaps it is the black woman's children, who the white woman – having more to offer her own children, and certainly not . . . a slave heritage or poverty or hatred, generally speaking: segregated schools, slum neighborhoods, the worst of everything – resents. . . . She fears knowing that black women want the best for their children just as she does. But she also knows black children are to have less in this world so that her children, white children, will have more (in some countries, all).
>
> Better then to deny that the black woman has a vagina. Is capable of motherhood. Is a woman.[41]

Here, the tactics of mainstream feminists differ from the dominant. Sexual purity and moderation being essential for membership in the cult of true womanhood, the dominant represents black women as sexually unrestrainable in an effort to justify containing their reproduction and limiting black mothers and children's access to material resources. While its strategy of un-sexing black women may differ, however, the result of mainstream feminist representations of black women is the same: "Woman" and "Mother" are rendered as racially as well as sexually exclusive categories.

Dickerson and Clarke aim to re-endow Aunt Jemima with a sexual and maternal nature, one that is orientated toward black men and children. While she is revealed to be a victim of forced sexual relations with her owner, Aunt Jemima is also shown as electing to have sexual/emotional relationships with several black men. She has three children with a slave named Two Ton and two more with another slave on the plantation, Uncle Ben. And Karo, a "smooth brown man of mystery" from Dominica, gives her three more.[42] However, the attempt to re-claim Aunt Jemima as a mother-figure for blacks of the Diaspora is complicated by the apparent absence of men from the concept of black community – except for immediate purposes of sexual reproduction. The lack of male agency is further puzzling given that the play does include male characters; these characters are not depicted in a negative light, and the play does not seem hostile toward men in general. Nevertheless, Dickerson and Clarke seem to consider neither men nor masculine roles significant enough to be represented. Even black men's role as biological progenitors, at the end of the play, is supplanted; the last of Aunt Jemima's children is not conceived with a man, but instead grows from a watermelon seed. Moreover, because Aunt Jemima has only female children, most of whom grow up to become leading figures in the black community, the sense that black men have no agency in the construction and maintenance of community nor any role to play in "race-uplift" is increased. As a result, one is not entirely sure for whom Aunt Jemima is preserving and defending black culture.

In part, I think black men's absence may be attributed to the play's idealization of the mother–daughter bond. Dickerson and Clarke do not treat the mother–daughter relationship sentimentally; they do, however, designate it as *the* fertile ground upon which women may realize their full potential. In this sense, the play bears a separatist outlook, but, unlike the standard white radical feminist stance, it is separatist without also being anti-male. I don't get the feeling that Dickerson and Clarke mean for men to come off badly, and, if men receive curt treatment, this marks the inevitable result of a privileged focus on women and their needs. Black feminine gender could be expected to take uppermost place in a play that aims to provide models of black female liberation. Black men share race and often class oppression with black women, but heterosexual black men do not face gender bias. Although the play contains a restricted definition of community, there is nothing wrong per se with it or any play that is more relevant to black women than black men. And if *Re/membering Aunt Jemima's* primary concern with black women still seems surprising, this may be due to white feminism's assumption that black women do not want a voice in gender issues, but only wish to concern themselves with questions of racism. Recall how Alice Walker reads white feminism in the same way, when she relates how it is inconvenient for white women scholars to think of black women *as women*.[43] Fixed attitudes about what is and is not of interest to black women arises more from mainstream feminist bias, which denies that black women possess a gender, than from anything in black feminist thought that is aimed at prohibiting black women from engaging in political movements or creating theoretical discourses apart from black men.

If Dickerson and Clarke's success at re-orientating Aunt Jemima toward black men is somewhat limited, their objective of dispelling the myth of her sterile maternity succeeds beyond a doubt. The play represents Aunt Jemima as loving toward her thirteen children, caring for them on a day-to-day basis, and fighting to keep them near her, to gain "simple title to the bodies of her daughters ."[44] She also struggles to instill in them a sense of pride in being black that will help them to resist white cultural representations of black womanhood. Despite her best efforts, five of her children remain ashamed of their blackness and live out their lives trying to pass as white. These daughters also internalize white cultures' disparaging opinion of their mother. Sapphire, for instance, can only see Aunt Jemima through the white gaze, as someone "sitten up on a goddamn box flipping pancakes for some white man!"[45] Lacking self-esteem themselves, they cannot comprehend Aunt Jemima's positive sense of self and comfortableness with her African appearance: "Mammy, how come you ain't 'shamed of the way you look. How come you always so happy?" Still, most of Aunt Jemima's daughters emerge as exemplary models of what bell hooks calls "loving blackness as resistance."[46] They express their feelings of self-worth outwardly through the work they perform for the benefit of the black community: Anna Julia, "a woman who risqued all to learn to read" goes on to found the National Association of Colored Women; Rebecca, "called by the thunder to preach the gospel," becomes an itinerant preacher who ministers to freed slaves; and Bondswoman, who runs away to freedom, returns to the South to lead others to freedom along the Underground Railroad.[46] To these are joined Susie-Fay, who becomes president of the Planned Parenthood ConFederation of America, and Freedom Fighter, who becomes "involved in so many slave revolts and shootouts, she [is] on the FBI most wanted list."[48] By creating a distinguished black feminist lineage for Aunt Jemima, drawing links between her birth-children and the founders and members of modern black political organizations, the play re-constructs Aunt Jemima as a special link between black mothers of the past and present and, most important, creates a space for her in the seminal black cultural narrative of race-uplift.[49]

The theme of "race uplift," which hooks characterizes as the "philo-sophical core of black women's dedication to home and community," is one of the most significant to emerge when the ideas and experiences of black women are taken as central to a theory of mothering, and one that is in marked contrast to mainstream feminism's preoccupation with all-powerful mother figures, who act as conduits of gender oppression and who unconsciously work to undermine their daughter's self-esteem and success.[50] Thus Aunt Jemima inspires, even sometimes drives, her daughters to succeed. One may also attribute black women's personal and political allegiance to this idea to the symbolic connection that exists between racism and black motherhood in dominant culture. Patricia Hill Collins traces black women's unwilling implication in the repro-duction of race as a dominant social and cultural entity to slave times, when children followed the condition of their mothers.[51] Another main-stream feminist assumption that is upset by placing black mothers center stage is the idea that all women presume to "see themselves primarily as individuals in search of personal autonomy instead of members of racial ethnic groups struggling for power."[52] Black women's understanding of self is grounded more in a concept of black commu-nity, and, historically, their mothering practices have been predicated upon a sense of connectedness among black people as a whole. Dickerson and Clarke's re/membered version of Aunt Jemima stands witness to the legacy of resistance to oppression and self-oppression which black mothers have left to their daughters, and she offers a rebuttal to white cultural definitions of feminine beauty, self-worth, and womanhood. Aunt Jemima teaches her daughters that "fore we come across de water, everybody look lak me. I ain't ugly. You just thinks I is: I got pretty black skin, I got a beautiful, long neck, I got a fine, rounded shape. I got plenty to smile about."[53] Such passages as this challenge another principal aspect of the Aunt Jemima stereotype by making the defense and affirmation of black looks and culture an essential part of Aunt Jemima's "motherwork."[54]

However, if Aunt Jemima is to be re/membered as an effective symbol of black women's liberation, she needs to appear as more than icon or archetype; women should be able to identify with her in some way as a flesh and blood kinswoman. For most of the play, Aunt Jemima appears to be endowed with unimpeachable self-confidence, and in keeping with the dominant image of her, she is always smiling and apparently satisfied with her life's circumstances. Though always cognizant of her own and her children's subjugation, she does not vocalize her resistance until the close of the play; nevertheless, when she finally speaks out, it does give some necessary flesh to her character. Following the acquittal of the men who rape her daughter Marie and her own complicity as a jury-member in this decision (being unaware that the plaintiff and Marie are one and the same), she gives vent to a plethora of grievances about how she and all black women suffer under white supremacy. But, in the world of the play, her outburst proves too little too late, and the National Association for the Advancement of Colored People (NAACP) calls for a boycott of Aunt Jemima Pancake Mix due to her "disgraceful behavior" on the jury.

This incident serves to draw attention to the field of representation as one of struggle between competing black views as well as between black and white views, a struggle in which Aunt Jemima finds she must engage on both fronts. She writes a letter to the NAACP President complaining that blacks should liken her name to something ignominious and asserting that it would be impossible for anyone "to be more proud of being a Negro than I."[55] She is equally vehement in defending her image to whites. When she becomes an embarrassment to the Quaker Oats Corporate Partners, she adamantly refuses their injunction to "dress for success":

Ah ain't havin' no skin peel. I ain't takin' off my head rag. And Ah ain't havin' my naps pressed. Ah'm a real woman, not a composite like Betty Crocker.[56]

Her refusal to assimilate leads to her eviction from the front of the pancake box and thus, from her place as the leading capitalist symbol of black womanhood. She loses her battle to stay atop the pancake box to a caricature of herself – her daughter Tiny Desiree – "who had no compunction about skin peels and pearl earrings."[57] Casting Desiree in Aunt Jemima's place typifies once again the way that the dominant will move to co-opt black motherhood and retain it as a symbol which fosters the very system that oppresses black women.

In discussing the ways in which the construction of black motherhood that emerged from the institution of slavery functions as another seminal structural intersection of race and gender, and seeing how Dickerson and Clarke's re/membered figure redresses racially exclusive constructions of mother (as well as their attempts to articulate a racially specific concept of motherhood with this figure as foundation), we can begin to see that an effective strategy of resistance to the institutional barriers that significantly limit black women's life chances must include a program to redefine the belief systems that are housed within dominant representations. Foucault maintained throughout his writings that there is always the possibility of resistance regardless of the relations of power in place. The tension between the re/membered Aunt Jemima, contextualized within the stream of black feminist thought, and the dominant representation, constructed from an alien white code, reaffirms his thesis, disclosing a margin for resistance, a space for a black feminist agency to begin the process of deconstruction. The ensuing process of reconstruction would hopefully provide black women with liberating models of black womanhood and motherhood, which they could draw upon in developing further strategies of resistance against racism and sexism.

## Re-constructing the "Chitlin-Circuit": Race, Representation, and OtherMothers

Rarely have black mothers been able to replicate the patterns of child-care typical of white, heterosexual, middle-class women. Like lesbian mothers, black mothers have usually needed to hold a job outside as well as inside the home. Frequently, black women's work-places were the homes of white women for whom they acted as maids and/or nannies. Their availability as a source of cheap labor helped many white families to maintain their middle-class status; this, in turn, helped maintain the class component in the dominant construction of motherhood. White culture still holds work to be incompatible with white mother-hood: working mothers are frequently cast as inferior caregivers. This is discussed in more detail in chapter 3. Within black communities, working mothers have not been stigmatized in this way. Because white society perceives black women as less threatening than black men, often it has been easier for them to find jobs. Consequently, their wages have been vital to the well-being of their families which has led to their work being considered a valuable aspect of their mothering. Black women's need to work at a time when paid child-care was non-existent for them gave rise to the practice of othermothering – the sharing of motherwork among a group of women who may or may not be blood-related.[58]

Whether or not othermothering continues as a typical social practice in contemporary black culture, however, is a contested subject among black scholars. bell hooks situates othermothering as part of the "chitlin-circuit:" an extinct network of black folks who knew and aided one another. Othermothering was largely an aspect of a Southern agrarian black lifestyle and, since desegregation, this practice has steadily eroded."[59] Pace hooks, Patricia Hill Collins believes that othermothers remain central to black life. She credits a continuance of "women centered networks of community based child care [which] often extend beyond the boundaries of biologically related individuals and include fictive kin." Further, she contends that "nurturing children in Black extended family networks stimulates a more generalized ethic of caring and personal accountability among Black women who often feel some responsibility toward all the Black community's children."[60] I agree with hooks that urbanization hampers the development or progression of extended kin networks. And while the traditional Southern agrarian lifestyle has certainly died out, nonetheless, neighborhoods across the US continue to be divided primarily according to the race and class of their inhabitants. Outside of the minority suburban black middle-class, most black and white people still live largely segregated lives, with a significant number of black people concentrated in sizable inner-city housing projects/estates. Conditions favorable to the establishment of networks of othermothers still exist in enough black communities to infer that these extended maternal networks endure as a standard form of parenting in black culture. The next play discussed supports the idea that the tradition of othermothering is a vibrant one that continues to be transmitted.

Shay Youngblood's *Shakin' The Mess Outta Misery*, first presented in 1988 at Spelman College in Atlanta, Georgia, aims to provide a space in which the oppositional practice of othermothering can be affirmed.[61] The play opens with its central character, Daughter, returning to her childhood home on the day of Big Mama's burial, the woman who has had the greatest hand in caring for her. The familiar surroundings spark many childhood recollections. These remembrances, a series of vignettes each of which features a different story about one of her Big Mamas – the group of women who have collectively raised her – constitute the play's pattern of action. The focus of the play is the nature of Daughter's relationship to these women: Daughter's guardian, Big Mama herself, Aunt Mae, Miss Corine, Miss Mary, Miss Tom, Miss Lamama, Miss Rosa, and Miss Shine, some of whom are blood relations, others not, but each of whom teaches her something about "living and loving and being a woman" in a white supremacist society where loving being a woman, especially being a black woman, is seen as threatening to the dominant order.[62] Youngblood's play provides the strongest contrast yet between dominant and mainstream feminist constructions of "Mother" and the forms and functions of mothering in black communities. In what follows, I examine the most significant differences between the political and psychological dimensions of these constructions.

One important difference between black and white cultural definitions of motherhood emphasized in the play is the way that public and private space is seen to be related. Historically, those women upon whom dominant definitions of womanhood and motherhood are based worked primarily as domestic laborers and child-rearers within their own biological family units. Relegated to the private domain, their social position was dictated by a relation to capital mediated by a relation to a family, wage-earning husband. Even though today most white women of all classes go out to work, my critique of Chodorow in chapter 1 demonstrated that the association between motherhood and the private sphere remains a strong residual component in both dominant and mainstream feminist constructions of motherhood. Rigid distinctions between the public and private realms, so characteristic of white western culture, simply do not register as much in black life. As mentioned above, black women's motherwork has always necessarily straddled the private/public divide. The doctrine of "race uplift" associated with black motherwork amplifies this intersection of public and private realms. While dominant culture insists that a woman should bear the full responsibility for mothering her biological children, the idea of "race uplift" embodies the belief that in some sense all black women are the mothers of all black children; that is, all black women are perceived as having some kind of motherwork to perform in the black community.

Another important difference between black and white discourses on mothering is black culture's construction of mothering as less Oedipal than white cultural patterns of childrearing. *Shakin' The Mess Outta Misery*'s exploration of the distinctive bond between black female children and their mothers underscores this. Daughter never shifts her allegiance to men. She experiences herself as subject through experiencing her resemblance to the Big Mamas. Her emotional energies remain directed toward these women and, in the political sense of the term, toward her sisters. The play picks up that strand of black feminist thought that conflates the mother–daughter bond with the political bonds of sisterhood. Alice Walker writes: "We are together, my child and I. Mother and child, yes, but *sisters* really, against whatever denies us all that we are."[63] Walker expresses a dynamic idea of black sisterhood, one which directs itself toward overcoming that which relegates black women to the place of the Other. This same dynamic informs the way in which black women bond over and through children. The most important facet of the Big Mama's personalities is that their primary allegiance is to other women: theirs is an ethic of community which holds that every woman is accountable to all the community's women and their children. Youngblood is careful to demonstrate that this allegiance is not based upon a belief in some particular female essence (frequently the case for white women-identified-women); rather they bond across a shared social and political value-system. The view that an individual black woman would be unable to preserve, much less pass on, a sense of self-worth unmarred by racist oppression without a feeling of group solidarity, without knowing the place of her people, particularly women, in history as well as how this lineage appertains to their future, reflects the way that black feminism welds together the empowering of the individual and the empowering of the black race. "Don't you never forget where we been, or that we got a long way to go" is a much repeated maxim in the play.[64]

The tendency to divide the comradely relationship from the familial and to elevate the former over the latter, which marks another point of divergence between mainstream and black feminisms, has meant that motherhood as experience and agency also differs dramatically for black and white women. In its collective aspect, motherwork emerges as a political as well as personal liberating experience for black women. As Patricia Hill Collins recognizes, black women's experiences as other-mothers lie at the heart of their political activism. In the nineteenth century, white feminists also held up motherhood as the basis of their activism, but second-wave feminists have largely severed the connection between women's rights and the experience of motherhood.[65] Mainstream feminism has tended to focus its analysis on the "problem" of motherhood, and it inclines toward casting maternal figures in extreme terms – either as all-perfect and all-knowing or all-powerful and destructive, with the latter theme predominating. Popular feminist texts, in particular, such as Nancy Friday's *My Mother/My Self*, and Judith Arcana's *Our Mother's Daughters* helped set the tone for the mainstream movement's attitude to mothering.[66]

Feminist's motives for declaring the negative aspects of motherwork may have been sound in the context of middle-class, married women's position in the 1960s and early 1970s. Nevertheless, rather than challenging those aspects of motherhood which they felt to be oppressive to women and children, many, perhaps inadvertently, have appeared to support the idea that under current conditions all mothers cannot help but act as the middlewomen of patriarchy. Consider Dorothy Dinnerstein's psychological analysis of motherhood in her best-selling book, *The Rocking of the Cradle and the Ruling of the World*.[67] According to Dinnerstein, motherhood is bad for men, women, and children, turning women into pliable objects and men into tyrannical beasts. Her list of charges against mothers is lengthy and harsh. Motherhood gives us boys who will grow up into childish men and girls who will grow up into childish women, "unsure of their right to full worldly status." It makes woman into a quasi-human supporter and deadly quasi-human enemy of the human self. It disables woman from nurturing her own self and so, creates in her a desire to debilitate her children's sense of self by sabotaging their autonomy. It is responsible for male rule of the world and the perpetuation of masculine values; and, more ominously, because it is these values which determine our propensity for destroying the natural and social environment, indirectly it is responsible for human's potential to destroy themselves.[68] Dinnerstein posits that when women act as the first or sole parent they suffer adverse psychological and social effects as do those children who are raised primarily by women. Female children, especially, will develop disabling personality traits similar to their mothers'. Women's maternal role, she argues, makes them into "It"s as opposed to male "I"s: "I"s make history and "It"s are acted upon by history.

Among black feminists, motherhood is perceived as raising the status of women. Much has been written of black women as captive adversaries of history; yet, even when slaves, through the nurturing of children black women have understood themselves to be participating in the creation of their own and their people's histories. Black women perceive themselves performing history through their performance of motherwork, particularly the practice of othermothering. Daughter tells us that "My Big Mamas had well prepared me for the river . . . I keep their gifts in my heart, and I know to pass them on."[69] The metaphor of going to the river refers to the transmission of womanist Afrocentric values. The Big Mamas promote a counter-hegemonic set of values designed to enable Daughter to resist conforming to dominant notions about gender and race, about the relation between mothering and family life and family life and community.

The play represents woman in the role of nurturer as occupying a position of strength. The Big Mamas clearly set the boundaries of family and community. They hold the power to determine who is allowed into and who is ostracized from the community. The idea that black men have no role as agents in developing black community, that we witnessed in *Re/membering Aunt Jemima*, surfaces here as well. However, whereas men are merely absent from the community in Dickerson and Clarke's play, Youngblood's play is more dismissive of men. Men function either as objects of ridicule or contempt for the Big Mamas. They are characterized as shiftless, dishonest, adulterous, and debauched – given to excessive drinking and gambling. Johnny Earl Davis deserts Maggie for another woman on their wedding day. Miss Lamama's first husband wanted to take a second wife (while still married to her), and her second husband, Mr. Otis, refuses to give her any money, claiming he uses it to pay his mother's medical bills as opposed to gambling it away, and cheats on her. A butch lesbian, Miss Tom, represents the play's sole respectable image of masculinity. She is the only paternal influence in Daughter's life. The Big Mamas perceive the presence of men as being neither beneficial nor desirable for themselves or their children.[70]

Black feminists incline toward representing motherhood and

mother–child relations as creative and energizing. *Shakin' The Mess Outta Misery* illustrates this by means of unifying the maternal role with that of the storyteller. According to Genevieve Fabre, the oral tradition remains an important practice in black culture. Black dramatists often emulate not only the artistic techniques of the storyteller, but also the storyteller's social function – "that of recording and reformulating experience, of shaping and transmitting values, opinions, and attitudes . . . [71] Telling stories, Sinfield points out, is merely a more accessible way of referring to cultural production, and "just as societies need to produce materially to continue so they need to produce culturally."[72] The intent behind re/membering Aunt Jemima was to render Aunt Jemima as an instrument for the production of sub-cultural resistance. In a similar move, *Shakin' The Mess Outta Misery* names the mother–daughter alliance as a site of refuge from the dominant and as a place where black cultural production may occur. In both plays, the knowledge needed for survival – both personal and cultural – is shown to pass matrilineally: from mother to daughter, sister to sister, black woman to black woman.[73] Youngblood's play, however, goes one step further and presents the extended spaces in which motherwork may occur as locations where the idea of blackness itself is produced. The stories that circulate among black mothers and daughters serve as vehicles for the relay of collective wisdom, and they are a means of promoting black political awareness.

The import of stories or cultural production is, Sinfield explains, that stories are lived:

> They are not just outside ourselves, something we hear or read about. They make sense for us – of us – because we have been and are in them. They are already proceeding when we arrive in the world, and we come to consciousness in their terms.
>
> Stories, then, transmit power: they are structured into the social order and the criteria of plausibility define, or seem to define, the scope of feasible political change.[74]

Viewed in the light of Sinfield's comments, the stories of the Big Mamas – all woman-focused and conveying the theme of "black women surviving with dignity" – function as a sort of cultural coinage: their exchange is perceived as keeping alive not just blacks' heritage, but the race itself.[75] One example is Miss Shine's tale. Narrated by Miss Lamama and punctuated with the subject's comments, it draws a connection between the socio-economic subordination of blacks and their cultural and psychological impoverishment. Shine, who works as a servant in the Governor's mansion during Southern apartheid, kills the Governor and his wife by mixing ground crystal with the sugar she serves them for tea. She is incited to this act by the Governor's humiliation of a group of black children who come to the mansion to perform Christmas carols; after the children's performance, only the white children are invited inside to the Governor's party, black children being deemed unfit for polite (white) company.

Miss Lamama and Daughter interpret the story as one that bequeaths a legacy of pride to Miss Shine's nominal descendants. There is pride in her having outwitted her oppressors and in her courage to directly refute white ideas about black intellectual inferiority: "Nobody knows how the master get sick. Nobody knows how he die."[76] Thus, Miss Shine's behavior is more than just an act of revenge. It also functions as an act of empowerment for herself and other black women. She reflects that "Folks say things changed, but it's still like slavery times."[77] Casting her mind "way, way back," she hears the whispers of enslaved ancestors and Africans: "Blood, boil thick, run red like a river, slave scream, wail, moan after they dead. Daddy lynched, Mama raped, baby sister sold down river." She credits her recollection of their pain with teaching her what "she has to do to save the race."[78] Informed by the historical landscape of slavery, her action becomes comprehensive in scope: it becomes a gesture of resistance to the whole racist apparatus that objectifies and dehumanizes black people. The violent nature of her action, besides being the most effective form of resistance available to a woman in her position at the time, ensures that her story will be so compelling that it is bound to be repeated. And it is the repetition of her story that contributes most to safeguarding the race; for it preserves black women's psychological ability to make the words that create the reality of the race, an ability without which one cannot empower oneself or others.

As mentioned in chapter 1, one of the principal objects of dominant cultural production is to influence those whom it subordinates to accept certain belief systems so that they will be led to behave in prescribed ways. With this in mind, Audre Lorde writes that programs for revolutionary change must go beyond a focus on oppressive situations. Subordinate groups must uproot that "piece of the oppressor . . . planted within them, which knows only the oppressor's tactics, the oppressor's relationships."[79] *Shakin' The Mess Outta Misery* dramatically endorses this strategy. Big Mama says to Daughter: "A story's like a map, you follow the lines and they'll take you somewhere."[80] The Big Mama's tales are meant to assist black women and their children in braving the psychological assaults bound up in dominant representations of blackness. They lead to a place where black women can feel safe enough to celebrate the diversity and dynamism of their own cultural practice.

When taken together, the plays discussed here give us a sense of how black mothering practices afford opportunities for cultural dissidence.

They also shed light on the way in which the relation between racialized femininity and motherhood in dominant discourse translates into a generalized pathology of black family life and how this impacts on the lives of black women and their families. The plays intervene in dominant narratives of mothering by contesting the representation of black mothers and their central role within black family units as deviant. They reveal that dominant efforts to "normalize" the black family are designed to deflect attention from the structural inequities of the heteropatriarchal capitalist order: the root cause of blacks' economic and educational underdevelopment. Finally, they have offered more evidence that, contrary to mainstream feminist thought on mothering, there is nothing in the nature of female-only parenting, either singular or collective parenting, which necessarily results in disturbed, unstable children or women. Rather, it is the result of white culture's exaggeration of the role of white fatherhood (particularly its emphasis on the father as breadwinner), with its concomitant image of a dependent wife–mother, which makes the experiences of women in alternative family structures with different political economies appear distorted. Although there are many problems facing the traditional nuclear family, society clings tenaciously to this ideal, and social policy is formulated so as to maintain this structure, with most government resources channeled to those who live in traditional family groupings. I would not deny that single motherhood poses difficult problems for many black communities, and, as we saw in chapter 1, for many lesbian communities. But it is essential that we recognize how economic deprivation creates most of the obstacles women and their children face and how the State acts to exacerbate them.[81]

# 3

# Friedan's Daughters: Representations of "Woman" at Work

Even when a writer seeks to evade all that is political, because it is thought politic to do so, that then becomes political.

*Alice Childress*[1]

## The Return of the Happy Housewife: Feminists Re-forming "Woman"

The earlier chapters have demonstrated how lesbian and black women's attitudes toward mothering and their maternal practices partly grow out of dominant constructions of "Woman" and "Mother." It has been suggested that the meanings of oppositional representations of "Woman" and "Mother," like their dominant counterparts, remain largely contained within the realm of family life.[2] What it means to be a mother in *Shakin' The Mess Outta Misery*, for example, is established clearly on the basis of a form of relations among women that is understood as familial, which indicates that the privileged terrain for the operation of ideologies of femininity and motherhood remains the family. From the inception of the second wave of the women's movement, mainstream feminists theorized the family as the principal site upon which the struggle for gender dominance is played out and through which male dominance is internalized. Hence, a principal aim of the movement has been to free white, middle-class, heterosexual women from the confines of their familial roles and establish conditions that would enable them to compete successfully in areas of work traditionally designated as male territory, in effect, to carry out Chodorow's prescription of broadening white women's participatory role in culture. Revealing the internal contradiction of the dominant form of family life was part of this project. By the 1980s, feminists had developed a strong case that the "ideal" family was threatened more by its own inherent contradictions than by any external instruments – including feminism.

And by the mid-1980s, this idea had become an integral part of the collective view of the family and those in power began to recognize its force.

This chapter explores the campaign to revive the nuclear family as the center of society. First I focus specifically on the strategies employed by the dominant in resurrecting the cult of domesticity. Some policies were overtly anti-feminist: for instance, the Reagan administration slashing federal funds to projects that benefited women; while in Britain a traditional avenue for the intervention of feminist activists in politics was closed when the Tories succeeded in breaking the strength of local councils. Others strategies, more subtle, were no less and perhaps even more effective. This included co-opting aspects of feminist discourse, largely by the dominant media outlets electing feminist "spokes-women." Those chosen were mainly women who, having achieved success in the system, were anxious to avoid rocking their own boat, and thus, were more likely to say what those in power wanted to hear. This chapter puts forward two texts as exemplary of this non-progressive stream of feminist thought: Betty Friedan's *The Second Stage* and Sylvia Hewlett's *A Lesser Life: The Myth of Women's Liberation*. Each text re-evaluates the social function of womanhood – post-feminism – and encourages women to re-think their positions at home and in society in light of the "failures and inadequacies" of feminism, with women encouraged to re-discover the "power" of being a "Woman." The ethno-centric perspective and racial/sexual hierarchies in mainstream feminist thought, unveiled in the two earlier chapters, become even clearer in chapter 3 as we examine not only how, but also why, the multiple contexts of women's identities are ignored by mainstream feminists.

Against the backdrop of Friedan and Hewlett's reform feminism, I consider the re-centering of "Woman" in the family in more detail through an analysis of how "Woman-as-Wife/Mother" is constructed in mainstream women's theatre, specifically the plays of Wendy Wasserstein. Among women playwrights, Wasserstein embodies the spirit of the backlash against feminism more than any other. She was quickly embraced by the theatre establishment as one of the new level-headed voices of feminism. Funded by the National Endowment for the Arts and the Guggenheim Foundation, hers are polished commercial productions for Broadway and London's West End which often attract top-name performers such as Meryl Streep, Glenn Close, and Maureen Lipman. *The Heidi Chronicles* received a Tony Award and a Pulitzer Prize, while *Uncommon Women and Others* was screened on the prestigious American Public Broadcasting Service. A graduate of Mount Holyoke and the Yale Drama School, Wasserstein personally possesses some of the most select establishment credentials. I would not deny that her plays are well-written, well-constructed dramatic pieces. However the same can be said for many plays by women; my point being that those with less palatable political world-views do not come in for many accolades. What came to be accepted by mainstream dramatic critics as the voice of American women's theatre was the voice of a very uncommon woman and the exclusive group of women who she epitomizes. The plays addressed here, *Uncommon Women and Others*, *The Heidi Chronicles* and *Isn't It Romantic*, encapsulate mainstream feminism's move back to a one-dimensional perspective on women's reality. Also covered here is Caryl Churchill's *Top Girls*, which, at first glance, seems worlds apart from Wasserstein's work. The play questions the morality of women taking on the competitive values of the marketplace, arguing that this damages both women and the larger society. The flaw comes as the play lapses into backing the artificial boundary between "feminine" caring values and "masculine" commercial values, which works to reaffirm traditional notions of sex/gender difference.

Next I look at another variety of post-feminist discourse – one which, counter to the pro-family kind, held that women's liberation was to be achieved by the movement embracing the prevailing values of the 1980s. "Power feminism," which resembles Friedan and Hewlett's version only by virtue of its post-feminist viewpoint, was most notably endorsed by Naomi Wolf in the much hyped *Fire with Fire: The New Female Power and How It Will Change the 21st Century*.[3] Analysis of this text focuses on its most interesting ingredient: the assertion that embracing the free-market philosophy is equally efficacious for white and black women; in fact, according to Wolf, black women were already successful power feminists, with a white-washed Anita Hill advanced as evidence. With reference to Cassandra Medley's play, *Ma Rose*, which features a protagonist modeled on Anita Hill, we shall explore the psychological distress and the social/familial problems that result when black women try to play power games according to white cultural rules.

One way of judging how well women have been getting on outside of the family, albeit a negative one, is to examine the ways in which the dominant responds to feminist representations of the career-woman by engaging with and working to undermine them. The ease and rapidity with which some women were moving out of the family and into previously male-dominated work zones in the 1980s meant that the dominant had to work overtime at maintaining ideological unity around the category "Woman." Some of the most strident attacks on feminism in the eighties were made not by declared anti-feminists, but by women, such as Betty Friedan, who were feminist-identified. Mainstream feminism's re-formation of "Woman" in the 1980s, though lamentable for its conservative character, in one sense testifies to the enormous and beneficial changes that the second wave of the women's movement has brought to many women's lives in the homeplace and in the sphere of work. By the 1980s, middle-class white and black women, at least, could expect easy access to higher education. Middle-class white women could reasonably hope to achieve a managerial or professional level job, to be self-supporting, and to maintain a single household. Perhaps most important, feminist representations of "Woman" enjoyed a wide enough cultural circulation so that many of these women no longer felt inferior in the workplace, but a substantial number could feel confident about competing in traditionally masculine economic spheres and deserving of the success they achieved there.

This is not to say that gaps in pay between men and women have disappeared or that general equality between the sexes has been achieved. And, of course, many different forces have shaped women's lives since the advent of the second wave of feminism. Post-war economic shifts have resulted in the feminization of whole sectors of the economy. These in turn have helped raise women's overall importance for national economic success. Nevertheless, on behalf of improving the material expectations of a substantial number of women, the movement can justifiably claim to be a success. Despite women's contribution to national productivity, the dominant continues to view the potential demise of or any serious deviation from the ideal nuclear family model as a threat to heteropatriarchal capitalist relations and to the psychic relations through which social relations are mapped onto subjectivity. The concept of the family needed to be rehabilitated in the 1980s, and a principal strategy adopted was an appeal to nostalgia. Traditionally, dominant definitions of the family appealed to the category of the Natural as a referent. When renegotiating the institution of the family, the dominant standard of validity shifted from a natural referent to that of time. In their study of nostalgic writing, Janice Doane and Devon Hodges refer to the nuclear family's new status as "Objective Given': a cultural product that accrues value over long periods of time.[4] The virtue of this category was its seeming transparency: it enabled the family to allude to the process of its own production, but, without having to concede the center ground by virtue of having been constructed in the archaic past. Beyond this new referent, however, not much else about the "ideal" family changed. The roles it offered to men and women were the same as in the past, with "Woman" as "Wife–Mother" still placed at the center of the family unit.

A revisionist appeal to nostalgia defines Betty Friedan's *The Second Stage*, one of the keystones of the pro-family backlash within feminism. Friedan, celebrated as the first woman to diagnose the problem that had no name for women in the 1960s until she christened it the "feminine mystique," resuscitated her career in the 1980s with an analysis of women's new malady – the "feminist mystique." The feminine mystique was the idea that the highest ambition for women should be the fulfillment of their own femininity through being subordinate to men economically and sexually, and through the expression of maternal love.[5] Similarly, the "feminist mystique" is a set of orthodoxies about family life and motherhood, but this time it is women who have locked themselves into a prescriptive politics which sets the standards for women's appearance, behavior, and sexuality.[6] Friedan blames misguided feminists, lesbians in particular, for repudiating "women's relation to men, children and the family."[7] The new "lavender menace" is comprised of those women who misunderstood what Friedan was saying in *The Feminine Mystique*; that is, those women who confused achieving equality and personal fulfillment with divorce, lesbianism, separatism, and the renunciation of children and family life.[8] In *The Second Stage*, Friedan aims to convince women that feminism is passé – a "dead end": all the enlightened people (and there are millions now in America it seems!) are already living on the new "frontier of the second stage." Here, they work "out the solutions to the new problems, personally and privately [apolitically she means], on a concrete, practical, seat-of-the-pants, no-time-to-think-about-it, day-to-day-basis" – but not unburdened by clichés. The great advantage of the new frontier is that it is uncorrupted by ideology – all you need to get there is plain common sense.

Sensible women know that they should stop wasting their time trying to find an alternative social system, grow up, start to revere life, and fight for the choice to have children. Once this right has been won, the unselfish woman might want to think about staying at home to rear her children; for the problem with child care is that it takes away the "real value, worth and function" for the parent.[9] These quotes reveal the extreme retrogressive character of Friedan's analysis. Society is characterized as a unified whole in which any problems encountered result from individual failings, or they are unfortunate side-effects which can be remedied *within* the present system without the need for any radical changes. This position obviates any social movement by women at all: for one cannot construct a social movement if the social system in place is recognized as legitimate, unless that movement is geared toward extremely limited ends. Friedan never seriously imagines much less desires deep structural change; on the contrary, this is portrayed as a frightening scenario. *The Second Stage* also demonstrates how closely the category "Woman" is being formulated in feminist discourse to the way that it has been traditionally formulated by the dominant; ironically,

Friedan writes "Woman" according to the same criteria that she criti-
cizes in *The Feminine Mystique.*

In the second stage of the second wave, a woman, whether or not she
is married or wants to be, has children, does or does not want to have
children, is being socially constructed in terms which make her responsible for doing both. *The Second Stage* illustrates that a central purpose
of a significant strand of mainstream feminism has become the preservation of the traditional family and of "Woman's" place therein. The
family has come full-circle. From a recognition of its role in feeding
sexism in the early stages of the movement, the family has been transformed into a symbol of the "last area" where women have any hope of
individual control over their destiny or of meeting their most basic
human needs.[10] By placing the family at the center of the movement and
men on its cutting edge, reform feminism provides scant space for
women's concerns. And given that human, in conservative discourse,
signifies white men, there hardly seems room in this feminist discourse
even for white middle-class women, much less space for lesbians or
black women. However, it must be said that Friedan has never made
any pretense of writing for any but those women who, by virtue of their
relation to the ruling male class, occupy a position close to the center of
power. Indeed, she sees this as the strength of her work "in a country
where all women (and men) – except for the Marxist daughters and sons
of the rich – would like to think of themselves as, at least, middle-class,
certainly not poor, (even if they are), and, if they are a minority, would
like at least the chance to enjoy what the majority take for granted."[11]
This kind of thinking proves quite convenient for mainstream feminism:
as long as women for whom the kind of choices offered by reform feminism are unavailable remain content only to dream of their chance at an
equitable share of social resources, feminists need not concern themselves with accommodating them.

Friedan's prescription for feminist movement arose as part of a larger
political and cultural shift to the Right in America. This general shift also
manifests itself in the work of Sylvia Hewlett. *A Lesser Life: The Myth of
Women's Liberation* is one of the most highly establishment-rated
critiques of women who have stepped outside the confines of the family
(it prompted a bidding war among mainstream publishers), as it revises
and depoliticizes many of the fundamental issues advanced by early
second-wave activists.[12] Here Hewlett regurgitates the specious argument that traditional marriage provided a practical division of labor
which women could rely upon to provide life-time security. Conversely,
feminist critiques of the family gave birth to the displaced homemaker
– the woman who has suffered as a result of feminism eroding the value
of marriage without providing conditions for women to improve their

earnings potential in the job market. Moreover by championing no-fault divorce, feminists removed the deterrent of alimony which had previously made men reluctant to leave their wives. Rather than the enlightened way to singleness, no-fault divorce meant that women could no longer derive financial security from their ex-husbands; thus, they were forced "to seek economic salvation in the labor market." Work, compared to marriage and motherhood, is never characterized as something that women might find fulfilling or at which they might excel, an ironic stance given that one of the first things Hewlett proudly relates is her stellar academic and professional CV.[13]

Just as feminism has destroyed the basis for women's financial security, Hewlett asserts, it has also damaged the basis of women's self-esteem: "Traditional women were and are deeply suspicious of the package we call the sexual revolution. They know that in the past women were valued for sex and reproduction and they believe that wives should cling to their monopoly on legitimate sex for the very simple reason that it enhances their "value.""[14] This version of feminism resembles Friedan's in its belief that the social system in place is legitimate and desirable. However, Hewlett goes even further in revaluing "Woman" according to the needs of a conservative masculinist culture, acting as a mouthpiece for those who find true challenges to sexist oppression in the work-place deeply threatening to the economic power of middle- and upper middle-class white men. Feminism had in fact helped create conditions whereby women could improve their economic status through participation in the job market. The real issue is that conservatives feared that as women advanced up the career ladder, especially as their earning power increased, they might seek to expand their influence within the corporate structure by modifying the conditions under which they and others earned their pay. The more women who rose through the ranks the greater the pressure that could be brought to bear upon the system. And "feminine" concerns about the family, health, education, and the environment were seen as incompatible with the masculinist values prevalent within the corporate milieu.

In reform feminism, equality becomes something women work to convince men they should be granted. Like Friedan, Hewlett has her list of equality-saboteurs, those few whose activities and speech ostensibly frustrate women's empowerment through their refusal to accept common-sense arguments. To the "Marxist daughters" and the "lavender menace," Hewlett adds "divorcees, widows, gays, and singles, many of whom bear grudges against the male sex," as well as the anti-family, anti-child abortion rights activists, whose creed denigrates the roles of wife and mother.[15] She also attempts to redeem an idealized past of fixed sexual difference. Her nostalgia for the ubiquitous good-old-days when life was uncomplicated because gays stayed in the closet, women stayed in abortive marriages, and those who remained single were social misfits is unabashed; although she attempts to soften her attack on feminism by couching her objections in the language of rights culture (a strategy which is most likely to be successful in an American context). She argues that feminism has failed to give women that to which they are entitled – husbands and babies. While she makes every effort to divorce herself from the likes of Anita Bryant, Phyllis Schafly and Marabel Morgan, whom she castigates for their half-truths and exaggerations, *A Lesser Life* embodies the same reactionary tone. The text is an odd mixture of conservative and liberal ideologies. And like much of backlash literature, her work is characterized by a confusing blend of well-researched fact and popular false assumptions. One thing it does make clear, however, is that in the 1980s women still lived with the specter of Doris Day.

## Resurrecting the Cult of Domesticity

Julia Penelope describes reform feminism as "a hand puppet mouthing the words its master supplies."[16] This puppet was also present on stage in the 1980s, and among women playwrights, no one had more strings attached than Wendy Wasserstein. Elaine Aston identifies Wasserstein's plays as part of the bourgeois-feminist dynamic in women's drama, the aim of which is to persuade the spectator that women's position in society may be improved "without any radical transformation of political, economic, or familial structures, etc."[17] Let us read the plays to see how Wasserstein's work perpetuates inequalities among women by virtue of their regressive reliance upon the concept of the isolated individual, who possesses abstract rights and choices.

*Uncommon Women and Others*, set in an elite east-coast women's college, is peopled with "quiet and tasteful" women who pose little danger to the established order.[18] The women in the play are obsessed with social rank, both their own and that of the men they hope to marry. For them, women's liberation means having a distinguished partner, 2.4 children, and a large house with a double garage in the exclusive suburbs of Connecticut, as well as having the desire for a prestigious high-paying job for themselves. Wasserstein's brand of feminism and her notion of what constitutes a feminist gesture is embodied in the figure of Rita. Rita's answer to male supremacy – "to this entire society [being] based on cocks" – is for women to feed off men like piranhas. She complains that philosophy, history, government and religion, everything that she can name, is male: "When I see things this way, it becomes obvious that it's very easy to feel alienated and alone . . . Therefore it is my duty to take advantage. Did I ever tell you about the time I left Johnny Cabot lying there after I'd had an orgasm and he hadn't?"[19] Wasserstein's satirization of feminist principles enjoys mainstream popularity because it embraces the residual notion that women *naturally* feel certain ways about men, marriage, and children. In the play, the traditional socio-familial role of "Woman" once again becomes the standard against which women judge themselves and are judged by others. "Woman-as-Wife/Mother" reasserts itself as the matrix of a variety of values, norms and definitions of reality for women – including those women who live out alternative roles. For those women who opt out of this system, feminism denotes little more than another lifestyle choice. Feminism appears as a means of justifying, but not always convincingly, their non-traditional choice of lifestyle to themselves as well as a means of reassuring themselves that a woman without a husband and children – those who represent "the uncommon bell curve" – is not a failure or a social misfit.

Wasserstein's best-known play, *The Heidi Chronicles*, records approximately 25 years in the life of Heidi Holland, a successful academic at Columbia University, who specializes in the history of women's art.[20] When we first meet her, she is a shy sixteen-year-old. The play follows her socially awkward progress through college, her coming to feminist consciousness in the 1970s, her loss of faith in feminism in the 1980s, and finally her decision to become a mother. On the surface, Heidi appears to be an excellent feminist role-model; however, as Aston notes, one way in which mainstream feminist drama reinforces masculinist values, while appearing to stage feminist concerns, is through taking a strong female character as its subject.[21] *The Heidi Chronicles* gives us a central figure who seems incapable of making decisions about her life on her own, that is, without recourse to the opinions of men. Although she is nominally the protagonist, ironically, Heidi, whose job is lecturing to others, has no voice of her own in the play. Helene Keyssar calls attention to how she is dominated dramatically and politically by the two men in her life – Peter and Scoop. Peter is the platonic, big-brother figure, who assists her in adopting a child, and Scoop her on-again, off-again, political opportunist lover who finally marries a traditional girl from "the best Jewish family in Memphis." As Keyssar says, Heidi doesn't act so much as react to the choices made by these men.

Only once does Heidi manage to find a voice of her own. However, its power is subverted by being framed in the context of a nervous breakdown. Keyssar's reading of this merits a full quote: "There is no place in the world of this drama for the voices of women and men who can speak the discourses of feminism; there is no room in this drama for the poor, the marginalized, the inarticulate, for those who are not successful in the terms of the eighties, for those who wish to transform and not react."[22] Like *Uncommon Women, The Heidi Chronicles* places us in the staid world of upper middle-class America. In an interview with Esther Cohen, Wasserstein explains why she chooses to write about these kind of women to the exclusion of others.

> *W*: And I think the thing is the women I write about are kind of middle class, upper middle class people, who have good jobs and they're good looking, and there's no problem . . . they're not sort of working class . . . there's nothing tragic there. And there's nothing romantic there. So I think that's why they're interesting to write about.
> *E*: Because you can relate to them.
> *W*: Because you can relate to them. It's like someone you knew in college.[23]

Wasserstein portrays white middle-class American culture as Culture with a capital "C." This slice of American culture is represented as a set of normative social practices which paradoxically do not comprise any particular cultural space. Drawing upon Bakhtin's "Discourse in the Novel," Keyssar refers to Wasserstein's approach to culture as a "refusal of 'decentering': *The Heidi Chronicles* reveals a national culture that remains 'sealed off,' 'authoritarian,' 'rigid' and unconscious of itself as only one among other cultures. And it does so to a dangerous degree."[24] Furthermore, it reveals an identity politics which denies that being a white middle to upper-middle class woman in fact constitutes any ethnic or racial identity at all and a feminist politics which denies the relationship between a subordinate group's ability to act and the economic, racial and sexual status of its members.

Sinfield alerts us to the ideological project behind the idea of a universal or normative culture: "an allegedly universal culture works to subordinate other cultures: it is defined as *not* special to a locality, gender, sexual orientation, race, nationality. It rises above such matters, and by just so much pushes them down."[25] Wasserstein attempts to justify using one cultural construction of "Woman" to stand for all women by declaring that middle-class/upper middle-class white people with good jobs, unlike the working classes, poor people or blacks, are not burdened by any particular class, racial or ethnic traits which might render them tragic or romantic. The notion of white middle-class culture as an unbounded cultural space also runs throughout her most ethnically inclined play *Isn't It Romantic*.[26] Despite its plethora of references to Jewish culture, its consciousness of Jewish identity seems not to extend beyond Jewish jokes and stereotypes of Jewish parents. The play follows the career paths and emotional lives of two twenty-something women, Janie Blumberg and Harriet Cornwall. Harriet, a Harvard MBA graduate, holds a high-powered marketing job, but is personally unfulfilled. Janie, also a Harvard graduate, is unhappy because she lacks a male partner and feels that she is under-employed as a freelance writer.

Both women are unsure of what they want in life. More important, they are unsure of what they *should* want, and this, Wasserstein suggests, is the postmodern "Woman's" malaise. Feminism is blamed for having helped to remove the moral and cultural certainties, which once made it easy for women to identify and take up their place in the social order. Feminism has left women dissatisfied: they are caught between resenting "having to pay the phone bill, be nice to the super, [and] find meaningful work" while having to reject the idea of marriage, now equated with dependency, as a solution.[27] Given its thematic resemblance to Friedan and Hewlett's texts, *Isn't It Romantic* is clearly grounded in recent social history. However, Wasserstein's method of casting doubt on feminist ideology is much more subtle and therefore potentially more damaging than the others' direct condemnation. Like the women in *Uncommon Women*, both Harriet and Janie would qualify as lifestyle feminists – Harriet being more solid in this respect. Janie and Harriet assume it is natural for women to pursue career success, live alone and pay their own rent, at least for a while. This reading of women's desires deviates only slightly from the desires of "Woman," which circulates in dominant culture and against which Janie and Harriet continue to measure themselves. Janie and Harriet function as counterpoints to each other. Janie is influenced by her family's traditional expectations for her. Her parents are so desperate to see her married, they bring a taxi-driver-film-producer from Moscow who barely speaks English to her apartment as a prospective bridegroom, offering to take him into the family business should Janie like him.[28] Understandably, Janie feels compelled to acquire a husband. Because she holds the same bourgeois value system as Wasserstein's other "uncommon women," she fixes on a surgeon, Marty Sterling, as a good catch.

Harriet, on the other hand, is the daughter of the "beautiful, successful, brilliant" Lillian. She grew up attending her mother's group sales meetings in Barbados and appearing as Lillian's date at candlelight dinners. Harriet's emotional block where men and relationships are concerned are contributed to her unconventional upbringing and the bad role-model of womanhood provided by her mother. Lillian, for example, substitutes nightly reruns of the Rockford Files for a sexual relationship with a man. Harriet carries on an office affair with an older, more senior executive who is married, because they "serve a perfect function blocking each other's lives." Tasha, Janie's mother, is likewise blamed for her daughter's imperfections. There is little emotional bonding between Lillian and her daughter. Lillian appears cold and calculating. The two communicate mostly via messages left with each other's secretaries. As a parent, Lillian is portrayed more as a paternal than maternal figure in that her principal contribution to Harriet's life has been through her financial support. Unlike the Blumbergs, she does not wish her daughter to marry, but wants to make her into a junior Lillian, someone who will emulate her career achievements. When Harriet mentions her partner to her mother, Lillian's only concern is his rank in the corporation; at forty she feels that he should be farther along in his career. The treatment of Lillian's character picks up a dominant theme in mainstream psychoanalytic theory, referred to in chapter 1, which posits that unfeminine women damage their children. Wasserstein also accepts the Freudian model, whereby mothers are the enemies of autonomy, which we earlier witnessed in Dinnerstein.

In the First Act, Harriet tells Janie that "no matter how lonely you get or how many birth announcements you receive, the trick is not to get frightened. There's nothing wrong with being alone." She claims to view marriage as a compromise of feminist principles, in some ways as an "antifeminist" and even "antihumanist" act.[29] In the Second Act, however, Harriet experiences a moment of enlightenment. Wasserstein effects a climactic reversal in Harriet's character, pairing her off with a man she has known for only two weeks. She is made to realize the source of her unhappiness: she has been living in an ideological straightjacket manufactured by feminist dogmatists. Freed of that constricting credo, now she understands the essential value of marriage and family life for women and can begin to enjoy a "normal" relationship with a man. Note again the similarity here between Wasserstein's vision of feminism as anti-male and anti-family and Friedan's/Hewlett's. *Isn't It Romantic* categorizes women as normal/abnormal based upon their choice of Wifedom/Motherhood versus career. Tasha, Janie's mother, straightforwardly tells her daughter that there is something wrong with her. Because she does not necessarily want marriage and children, there is something defective in the make-up of her femininity.

Although she still believes that women should learn to live alone and pay their own rent, at the end of the play Harriet learns the importance of women not becoming too good at it, as well as the negative consequences which accrue to those who miss this lesson. When Janie reminds her of her earlier views on the subject, she accuses her of immaturity: "you want us to stay girls together. I'm not a girl anymore. I'm almost thirty and I'm alone."[30] Feminism is depicted as a simplistic and naïve belief system embraced by childish and self-deluded women and one that will only leave then feeling emotionally barren. Wasserstein attributes Harriet's feminist beliefs to a state of delusion: "I lied to myself. It doesn't take any strength to be alone. It's much harder to be with someone else."[31] What matters is getting on with life and this means having children. By now, this should sound familiar. *Isn't It Romantic* represents women's autonomy as selfish, foolish, depressing, and dangerous. Janie feels betrayed by her friend because she decided not to marry Marty based on her advice and example. Nonetheless, she remains unsure whether Harriet's old or new viewpoint is the correct one. In one of the play's strongest post-feminist moments, she tells Harriet: "All the things you told me about learning to live alone, and women and friendship, that was so much social nonsense. I made choices based on an idea that *doesn't exist anymore*" (emphasis mine).[32]

Based on the final argument between Janie and Harriet, it seems that *Isn't It Romantic* explicitly aims to undermine a feminist representation of women as intelligent, strong and self-aware. Although she avoids having Janie humbled outright by Harriet's line of reasoning, Janie's final choice to remain a single woman and pursue a career, on the surface a progressive one, does not appear as a desirable alternative in relation to Harriet's intended lifestyle. Wasserstein creates Harriet as a more convincing figure than Janie – even allowing for the radical shift in the former's worldview. The play is made up of two counterplots, which more or less account for an equal amount of stage time and are examined in equal depth. Yet the counterplot involving Janie never mounts an effective challenge to that involving Harriet. That Harriet is to be seen as the more credible figure is established early on, with Janie always appearing as the more insecure and emotionally unstable of the two women. Janie vacillates about everything right until the end. Even after refusing to marry Marty, she retains a nagging fear of being alone and perhaps not meeting another man who will want her and confirm her as desirable. In contrast, Harriet is shown making firm decisions in relation to work, and it appears easy for her to end and recover from the dysfunctional relationship with her colleague. Most important, because Harriet's epiphanic moment is also the play's most powerful, her new vision appears as the more authentic one. And finally, it is Harriet who seems to get the happy ending.

The play ends with Janie vaguely dissatisfied with her life even though she is now more securely launched on a career path. She is still unsure of what she should want as a woman – as if there were a formula waiting to be discovered according to which women could live out satisfying lives, and of course, according to the dominant, there is one. Hence her last question to Harriet: "Do you really think anyone ever met someone throwing out the garbage?"[33] The play's final image of Janie tap-dancing as she listens to a phone-message from a woman friend who is desperately seeking a male lover is just as ambiguous. The dance could be read as dismissive of her friend's feelings, which suggests that Janie has come to believe whether one has or doesn't have a man in one's life isn't worth considering. Or it could represent an attempt by Janie to block out what she still deems a frightening scenario, living without a man. I think, overall, the evidence provided by the play supports the latter reading. Because the glimpse we are given is so brief, the image of Janie that will linger in the mind of the audience is that of a rather pathetic lonely woman soberly putting out a small, single-sized bag of rubbish.

*Isn't It Romantic* invites us to consider how theatre can be a site of social struggle. Along with the other two Wasserstein plays addressed here, this play embodies the struggle over what it means to be a "Woman" in society. The plays illuminate how the struggle is conducted through feminist discourse and that what is at stake is an authoritative voice within this discourse. The plays can be said to rest on a "faultline" in feminist discourse. The term faultline as used here is Sinfield's: "No text, literary or otherwise, can contain within its ideological project all of the potential significance that it must release in pursuance of that project. It is a condition of representation that such a project will incorporate the ground of its own ultimate failure."[34] Following Sinfield, regardless of authorial intent, ultimately the plays cannot entirely privilege an anti-feminist message. Wasserstein's plays work to subvert the progressive tendencies of feminism, yes; but she cannot attack feminism without, at the same time, giving voice to its core principles. The comparison/contrast format employed to highlight the credibility gap between Harriet and Janie's views also works to foreground the ideological gaps in the text as a whole; hence, Harriet's position, while it may be made to appear in a more favorable light, cannot be unequivocally advanced. *Isn't It Romantic*, the most explicitly anti- or post-feminist play to be discussed so far, is, at the same time, the most unstable and ideologically incoherent. As such, it is a good candidate for a bit of creative vandalism; given its many ideological contradictions and inconsistencies, feminist theatre practitioners could easily mount a politically sanitized production, an anti-version which could counter reform feminist ideas and promote a more progressive feminist politics.

## Who's On Top?: White Women, Work and the Family

Contradiction and inconsistency is a hallmark of dominant ideologies, not merely reform feminism. Sinfield identifies within dominant ideology "a looseness of structural fit between institutions and ideologies, and the very demands of maintaining the dominant order create conditions whereby contradictions in it may become apparent."[35] An especially interesting point of discoherence for our purpose is found in the market's need for women's labor as measured against dominant gender ideology and its insistence that women's natural role is to be found within the family. This discontinuity accounts for one of the principal contradictions in dominant gender ideology, the disparate valuation of women's domestic and paid labor. On the one hand, the economy can no longer provide those conditions, unique to the immediate post-war years in Britain and America, whereby families could survive on one wage. Women must also work if the present levels of consumption necessary to fuel the economy are to continue. Many industries now depend on a pool of part-time and poorly paid women workers. Finally, women can provide a convenient scapegoat when politicians need to account for unemployment: more people entering the workforce – meaning women, and not recession, Reagan claimed, was responsible for the dearth of jobs in the 1980s. On the other hand, career women pose a threat to the status quo arrangement of gender relations and the myth of a social structure secured by a nuclear family model. While this is now largely a defunct model of family life, it is nonetheless one that forms part of the cultural imaginary upholding capitalist heteropatriarchy. To cope with the contradiction between what the system would like women to be and what it requires women to do, dominant ideology must constantly revise the meaning of the institutions of motherhood, marriage and family. Andrew Hacker puts it this way: "the economy needs a breakdown of gender roles at the same time that it needs them to remain the same."[36]

This results in the persistent circulation of stereotypical representations of wives and mothers, whose attributes are often radically different from the characteristics of actual working wives and mothers. The divergence between representation and reality was particularly acute in the 1980s. Thatcherites were notoriously dismissive of women's rights, weakening or removing safeguards against discrimination and/or harassment in the workplace. Welfare provisions principally benefiting women and children were also cut.[37] Under Reagan/Bush, American women faced explicit anti-feminist administrations. Conservatives insisted on applying a 1950s definition of mothers and families to contemporary women, using it as the standard by which women would be treated and judged both in a legal and cultural sense. A Supreme Court dominated by conservatives reversed many of the gains made by the women's movement, particularly in the area of affirmative action and abortion rights. The official narrow and anachronistic version of "Woman" in use meant that it was increasingly difficult for women to reconcile the demands of childbirth, childrearing and domestic responsibilities, for which women in heterosexual relationships continue to shoulder a disproportionate burden, with the demands of the workplace. Their dilemma was compounded by the lack of publicly provided child-care (always seen as falling dangerously close to communism in America), adequate maternity leave, and the virtual non-existence of paternity leave – all of which remained a distant hope for most women in the 1980s and arguably in the 1990s as well.

Throughout the 1980s, women were bombarded with negative messages relating to careerism. Careers, singledom, and feminism were all touted as things which made women depressed, old before their time, and even as suggested in some cosmetic ads, ugly. Denunciations of the career woman were primarily directed against white middle-class women who took on non-traditional roles.[38] By the mid-eighties, these attacks had become so routine that feminists began to speak of a war against women in the media. Susan Faludi's *Backlash: The Undeclared War Against Women* is the most comprehensive feminist analysis of this phenomena to date.[39] Faludi documents how the mainstream media encouraged biased and frequently bogus social science research in an effort to reverse the achievements of the women's movement. First, a "man shortage" was declared. A shortage of marriageable men meant that women who pursued careers were likely to end up alone and it was assumed therefore, miserable. Women were supposed to be desperate for marriage, and ultimately, depression over their inability to find a partner would destroy their careers.[40] *Isn't It Romantic* feeds into the media hysteria, beginning and ending as this same message plays on Janie's answering machine. The Prologue has Cynthia Peterson calling to say that "Everything is awful. I'm getting divorced. . . . There are no men." Her final call tells us that she is alone on her thirty-fourth birthday, depressed because she didn't marry Mark Silverstein in College, and has read in the *New York Times* that there are 1,000 men for every 1,123 women in New York.[41] Faludi makes known the many surveys, neglected by the media, which gave different figures and showed that women's feelings about their sexual/romantic prospects in the 1980s were very different from those being reported. Fewer women than ever viewed marriage as a necessarily desirable state. And while more women were living alone, many of them, especially high-earners, did so by choice.[42]

Related to reports that men were in scarce supply was a concerted drive by the dominant to induce white middle-class women to reproduce. An "infertility epidemic," it was claimed, had hit career women. National newspapers were reporting that feminism and careerism had created a "sisterhood of the infertile."[43] Women were warned that if they waited to have a child, they were more likely to miscarry, have stillbirths, or give birth to sick, retarded or disabled babies. Abortion and even birth control were said to cause infertility. Again, none of these claims was backed up with reliable medical evidence. Rather they formed part of the general political and cultural trend aimed at reintroducing women to traditional womanhood.[44] Recall Friedan and Hewlett's argument about feminism being to blame for the paucity of choice available to women who want both career and family. If large numbers of women were choosing to forego marriage/maternity, Faludi's research demonstrates that it was the dominant's need to re-invest the category "Woman" with cultural worth, a project toward which reform feminism significantly contributed, that was forcing many women, especially working-class and single women, to choose between participating in family life and engaging in rewarding work outside the home.[45] The backlash phenomena, generated by the advances women were making in the workplace, meant that balancing work and family life in the 1980s was a profound dilemma for women. This was reflected in the fact that two of the major issues of the women's movement during this time were parental leave and childcare. Wasserstein's politics on women, work, and motherhood emerge from her class status. She occupies and, as the excerpt from her interview with Esther Cohen demonstrates, chooses to write from the centre-ground of American "Womanhood." Her politics reflect more traditional gender arrangements than most women were living-out in the 1980s. The playwright Caryl Churchill might be said to occupy a similar position to Wasserstein in British society: she is white, belongs to the middle-class, and she identifies as heterosexual. Unlike Wasserstein, however, Churchill elects to write from the Left, adopting a strong socialist-feminist voice. Janelle Reinelt places Churchill's work within the domain of British feminist theatre that critiques both the emphasis on individualism within bourgeois feminism and the essentialism of radical feminism, which would valorize and maintain an ahistorical female identity and culture discrete from that of the male.[46]

Churchill is a rare example of a feminist playwright whose work is admired equally by feminist and mainstream commentators. She has produced a substantial body of work, most of which is considered part of the canon of classic modern drama. Elin Diamond argues that the importance of Churchill's work to feminist theatre is due to the way it combines feminist theory and Brechtian techniques:

> If feminist theory sees the body as culturally mapped and gendered, Brechtian historicization insists that this body is not a fixed essence but a site of struggle and change. If feminist theory is concerned with the multiple and complex signs of a woman's life – her desires and politics, her class, ethnicity, or race – what I want to call her *historicity*, Brechtian theory gives us a way to put that historicity in view – in the theater.[47]

Diamond's seminal reading of Churchill's work maps the intertextuality of feminist and Brechtian theory in order to illustrate how the resulting feminist-Brechtian "gestus" – which entails "the synthesis of alienation, historicization, and the `not . . . but' – can make visible to the spectator the gender ideologies encoded in the playtext/performance." Diamond explains how the "gestic moment" opens a play to the discursive ideologies that inform its production. It enables a moment of insight into sex–gender complexities, not only within the world of the play, but more important, "in the culture which the play, at the moment of reception, is dialogically reflecting and shaping."[48]

Lizbeth Goodman explains why she considers Churchill's *Top Girls* in particular exemplary of good feminist theatre. The play encourages people to look at the "situation of the working mother and career woman, without suggesting that there are easy answers or that everyone should try to be a superwoman." Goodman's praise is partly based on the play's commercial success. Because "it reached massive audiences," it could focus public attention on the conflicts which women face in "juggling work and family responsibilities in the context of societies which do not yet provide adequate resources for working women."[49] Reinelt commends *Top Girls* for the way it demonstrates that progressive social movements such as feminism can be diluted or co-opted by capitalism: "the play shows the prices that women throughout history have had to pay for being unique and successful and suggests that contemporary women are also paying a price that may not be desirable." She goes on to suggest that "as an eloquent indictment of bourgeois feminism, the play's balance and structure guard against anyone mistaking its politics as antifeminist."[50]

These critical assessments of Churchill all refer in some way to the performance efficacy of her plays. I also propose to read Churchill's *Top Girls* as ideological transaction in order to determine its performance efficacy for a progressive feminist theatre and politics. However, going against the grain of most feminist interpretations of the play, I stress its ideological relativity. I do this not to call into question Churchill's place among progressive feminist playwrights, but in order to illustrate how deeply ingrained the formula "Woman" = Wife/Mother remains in our culture, and how difficult it is for women to elude the strictures on their thought and behavior which result from their relegation to this category. My argument is not that *Top Girls'* perspective on working-women is necessarily anti-feminist. However, I want to point out that its attack on bourgeois feminism may, depending on its performance context and the socio-political make-up of its audience, inadvertently endorse some of the ideas that underpin the backlash and reform feminism. *Top Girls* may be compared to *Isn't It Romantic* in that there is a sharp difference between what the play intends to say and what it may actually end up saying to different groups of women, not to mention what it could be made to say by those hostile to feminist principles. The feminist-Brechtian techniques highlighted by Diamond and Reinelt may guard against Churchill's critique of gender falling back into essentialist notions of the category "Woman." However, *to guard against* is not the same as *to obviate the possibility* that the play's representation of women, the way in which it balances feminist and socialist discourse, may produce contradictory effects and reinforce the values it aims to question or subvert.

In his study of radical theatre as cultural intervention, Baz Kershaw notes that a major factor in determining a text's susceptibility to ideological relativity is its inter-textuality: the ways in which a performance/text gains meaning for an audience/reader through its relationships to other texts, including non-theatrical cultural texts or events.[51] This agrees with Richard Schechner's performance theory, which posits that no item in the environment of performance can be discounted as irrelevant to its impact, performance being the "whole constellation of events . . . that take place in/among performers and audience from the time the first spectator enters the field of performance – the precinct where the theatre takes place – to the time the last spectator leaves."[52] Kershaw interprets the field or precinct of performance as indeterminate, which allows performance to include events and cultural practices quite remote from the place in which performing itself happens. Within this formulation, the field of performance for *Top Girls*, first presented at London's Royal Court in 1982, in addition to dominant gender ideologies, could be understood as including the specific material circumstances and attitudes informing the media backlash against women, the ideology of reform feminism, as well as Churchill's own socialist-feminist critique of gender relations.

It is open to question whether in the 1980s, or indeed the 1990s, white British middle-class career women in the main would interpret *Top Girls* in a Brechtian manner. Kershaw points out that the inter-textuality of a text/performance may serve as a foil to its contextuality by feeding contrasting ideologies within an audience. The ideological positioning of the audience (or reader) in relation to the performance (or text) crucially influences both the range of what can be "read" (via contextuality) and the types of "reading" that may be available within the range (via inter-textuality). Hence, the ideological relativity of performance is a function of the potential variability of value systems inscribed in all aspects of its conventions, and the synthesis of contextuality/inter-textuality can provoke wide variations in readings of the same text.[53] This would allow for some communities of women spectators to perceive *Top Girls'* theatrical signs as directly engaged with the ideology of their real extra-theatrical world and their individualized experiences within it, which at the time of the play's initial reception were being re-written according to a post-feminist paradigm. The Brechtian strategies explored by Churchill serve to foreground the gender ideologies encoded in the playtext/performance, but they cannot guarantee how the audience will bridge the theoretical gap between textual and social subject. Meanings are not fixed entities to be deployed at the control of a communicator, but, as Christine Gledhill argues, they are products of textual interactions shaped by a range of economic, aesthetic and ideological factors, which often operate unconsciously, and thus, they are unpredictable and difficult to control.[54]

*Top Girls* addresses many of the issues and viewpoints that propelled the backlash against women in the eighties, those attitudes which still force most women to choose between pursuing career objectives or the role of wife/mother and which add to the difficulties of those who try to juggle both.[55] The force of the play's critique is relevant beyond the eighties. The opening scene, which places Marlene in the company of a group of extraordinary mythical/fictional women, prevents her from appearing as just an eighties phenomenon. Churchill shows how a handful of women have always been allowed to defy conventional feminine roles and behaviour by buying into the systems of gender and class supremacy. As Janet Brown points out, it is important to recognize that these women do not comprise a community of women as much as a group of competitors – "egoists who interrupt one another continually."[56] Aston makes a similar observation and identifies the women's inability to communicate, "to listen to and share experiences with women," as indicative of intrasexual oppression at the same time as they verbally and physically enact a violent rejection of intersexual oppression.[57]

The play matches the indifferent and masculinist values of the marketplace against traditional "women's values" of concern for and nurturance of others. This competition is played out in the relationship between two sisters, Marlene and Joyce. Marlene, the managing director of the Top Girls employment agency, whose main criteria of human worth seems to be commercial success, is meant to symbolize the archetypal male oppressor.[58] Aston links Marlene's "male-identified subject positioning" to Churchill's critique of bourgeois feminism; Marlene, via her stable positioning, "functions as an oppressive 'block' to the desires and aspirations of other women."[59] In keeping with traditional gender roles, Churchill makes Marlene's success at work dependent upon her sister's labor inside the home. The fact that Joyce is raising Marlene's daughter suggests that the gender-based division of labor creates a divide between an ethos of altruism and one of rivalry and contention. Joyce represents the flip-side of Marlene and her colleagues; she is the play's voice of socialism. She believes that the dog-eat-dog ethic of Marlene's philosophy, with its emphasis on getting ahead and consumerism, is both amoral and dehumanizing. Whereas Marlene sees her success as a progressive example for other women, Joyce perceives her sister as a pawn of the system.[60]

Because Churchill has all but one performer play different roles, Lisa Merrill reads the economic rather than the psychological circumstances of *Top Girls'* characters as paramount in the play's structure and theme.[61] I approach *Top Girls* as a narrative of the contemporary situation of the career woman in which it is not the operations of capitalism, but rather the conflicts of femininity within the context of heteropatriarchal capitalism that principally structure the play. I suggest that the relationship between socialism and feminism in the play is an uneasy one. The play's ideological ambivalence rests largely on the way in which the audience/reader interprets the character and actions of Marlene both in relation to traditional constructions of "Woman" as well as to the general aims of the women's movement in relation to women and work. Bearing in mind how the constitution of different audiences might affect the ideological impact of the play in performance, the precarious structural balance between feminism and socialism could be read as endorsing overall a negative view of women who push against the gender barriers of the business world.[62] The main thrust of the play is to denounce the corrupt value system of the me-decade – the meanness and rampant greed of Thatcherism. However, in its effort to reveal the inequities of free market capitalism, it may be seen to veer toward reform-feminist opinions about how women should naturally be and what they should want. Michael Swanson sees the dilemma of eighties women in *Top Girls* crystallized in the form of the mother/daughter relationship.[63] This, I argue, leads Churchill to articulate the inherent injustice of heteropatriarchal capitalism by using maternity and the family, with their attendant concept of nurturance, to foreground what is positive about women's culture and following from this, what values would be good for society as a whole. This strategy allows for a reading of non-maternal women as suspect and thereby, it risks re-inscribing the meaning of "Woman" in a traditionally narrow familial context. Hence, it could result in the play's subversive critique of capitalist values playing into the hands of containment where the role of women in society is concerned.

In the eighties, working wives and mothers and childless-by-choice women were characterized as flawed in terms that would not have sounded out of place in the 1950s. The old idea that women who choose not to marry or have children are unnatural is resurrected in the play by Mrs. Kidd, the wife of the man over whom Marlene is promoted. Mrs. Kidd is the play's symbol of traditional womanhood. Her life represents the converse to Marlene and the other top girls. Her opinion of Marlene closely echoes the popular media summation of the pathetic career woman: "You're one of those ballbreakers, that's what you are. You'll end up miserable and lonely. You're not natural."[64] If Mrs. Kidd, the suburban housewife is the natural woman, then women like Marlene are, by default if nothing else, freaks.

*Top Girls* represents the successful career woman in masculinist terms. Aston notes that the "projection of a 1980s 'Superwoman' image as dramatized in the office scenes, demonstrates a need for adept role playing between high-powered lady and ball-breaking boss."[65] Even though Marlene retains the semblance of the feminine, effectively she passes as a man in the work place. She is able to escape her working-class roots and lifestyle for middle-class prosperity only by denying and denigrating those options open to her via her femaleness. And like her rapacious colleague Louise, she is forced to justify her existence every minute by proving that she can bring in as much money as a man. In contrast, women who hold onto traits deemed feminine (that which is soft and nurturing) are portrayed as unable to survive in the workplace, and those interested in traditional women's roles as unwelcome there. This is reinforced in the scene where Jeanine is interviewed for a place on the Top Girls' register: Marlene instructs her not to mention that she is married when applying for jobs and to consider her prospects in the business world as dim should she ever have children.

*Top Girls'* socialist theme alludes to how the established line separating femininity and occupational achievement now in place may be responsible for women adopting unethical, even immoral, standards of conduct. But in some instances its critique of bourgeois feminism stands in danger of sliding into the opinion that women who pursue careers are somehow deluded about what matters most in life. Especially in comparison to Mrs. Kidd, who fits Hewlett's description of the feminine victim of feminism, most of the play's career women are portrayed as disagreeable, shallow, and grasping. Consider that Marlene forgoes children and family life, be it marriage/children or extended family life, in favor of material advantages, handing her child over to her sister and maintaining only sporadic contact with Angie in the guise of an Aunt, as well as yielding care of her parents to Joyce. It would be unfair, however, to ignore the measure of self-awareness with which Churchill endows Marlene. Realizing the limitations of the lifestyle she has chosen, Marlene must work to rationalize its prescripts. Her choice of career over family is not presented as an easy or unconsidered one. Yet Marlene's remorse over her inability to mother and her two abortions, as well as her concern that she may now be infertile after years of taking oral contraceptives, functions to reveal her susceptibility to backlash propaganda more than to soften her character. In addition to appearing as the castrating career woman, Marlene also appears to be a member of the "sisterhood of the infertile," described by Faludi as those women who suffered from depression due to their failure at carrying out a "Woman's" role.

Marlene feels acutely that trying to pursue a top-flight career while balancing family life is an arduous, if not impossible, struggle. The play makes clear that Marlene rightly fears the limitations which maternity would impose upon her: Churchill leaves little doubt that caring for Angie has restricted her sister's choices in life. Only women in the highest income brackets are shown to be capable of occupying a comfortable middle ground between maternity and work. Marlene wistfully imagines herself in the position of a managing director who can afford to spend one hundred pounds a week on domestic help and thus, is able to keep her powerful position while rearing two children. For ordinary, even most middle-class women, with or without partners, such a scenario is fantastic. Marlene's maternal longings may be read in two ways. On the one hand, the play suggests that Marlene has been maneuvered into the position in which she finds herself by an inflexible and unequal evaluation of women's capabilities, one which defines women according to the economic needs of a male dominated capitalist society. On the other hand, this aspect of Marlene's characterization implies that "Woman's" traditional familial role and its attendant nurturing features is more a given and less an option for women. Whether or not a woman is married and has children – whether or not she might want to – the very fact of this possibility for a woman and the social construction of her responsibility for them can be made to appear inescapable. The manner in which a particular audience interprets *Top Girls'* critique of gender ideology, whether it is viewed within the terms of a Brechtian-feminist gestus or as subordinating feminism, bourgeois or otherwise, to socialism, will depend on a number of factors. For example, ideological theatrical subcodes, including but not limited to the social and economic influences on the theatrical transaction itself (e.g. prices, condition and location of the theatre), must be considered, as well as more encompassing cultural codes such as the political principles which sustain/oppose the dominant socio-economic order. Given the precarious balance between socialism and feminism in the play, what an audience of middle-class career women watching *Top Girls* within the confines of a comfortably middle-class theatrical space will make of it is likely to differ markedly from the reading of audiences who view it within a radically alternative theatrical milieu. The former are likely to read the play as feeding into reform feminist ideas of "Woman" while the latter may, or may not, read it as embarrassing them.

It should be the project of feminism to transform the category "Woman" so that it is able to accommodate productively non-traditional female behavior and allow space for ambitious, competitive, successful women; or women who choose non-familial roles are bound to be caught up within the popular myth of the career woman as castrating female or barren mother. Keyssar reads Churchill's overall strategy as bringing "together diverse discourses in such a way that they interanimate each other and avoid any overarching authorial point of view."[66] While this strategy can invigorate, at times, it can also confuse the issues. *Top Girls'* complex and ambiguous vision of "Woman" in the workplace defies easy and clear interpretations. I argue that the play's approach to the double bind faced by white middle-class women at work in the 1980s results in an ideologically double-edged construction of the category "Woman." Its criticism of the way that some women have used and perverted feminist principles may as easily reinforce dominant and regressive feminist ideologies, which criticize women for rejecting, in favor of work, the caring roles to which traditional femininity assigns them, as much as support oppositional ones. As Keir Elam argues, "however expert the spectator, however familiar with the frames of reference employed by dramatist and director [s/he] may be, there is never a perfect coincidence between the producers' codes and the audience's codes, *especially where the text is in any degree innovative*" [emphasis mine].[67] Consequently, for some audience members at the end of the play "Woman" as Wife-Mother may persist as a confining standard against which women's feelings and actions are measured.

## Power Feminism: The Genderquake

There is an abundance of feminist materials available that consider white women's experiences in the workplace, but there is little corresponding literature for black women. Due to the prevailing ethnocentrism of mainstream feminism, the experiences of black women who are in a position to enter the ranks of middle-class/professional occupations have largely been ignored altogether. Or, perhaps even more disturbing, when they do appear, usually it is as white-washed versions of black womanhood, co-opted in order to validate feminism's construction of universal "Woman." Nowhere is this more evident than in the work of those who adhere to the tenets of power-feminism, what I like to call me-feminism. Power-feminism was launched in the early nineties by Naomi Wolf, one of the most prominent media elected feminist spokeswomen, in her book *Fire with Fire: The New Female Power and How It Will Change the 21st Century*. I want to consider how this text works to re-validate a conservative Anglo-American movement and to re-fortify white women's hegemony in the movement. My reading will focus on Wolf's manipulation of Anita Hill's testimony during the Clarence Thomas hearings, the mis-representation of Hill herself, and the way that Wolf distorts the words of another prominent black woman, Audre Lorde.

Let me begin, as does Wolf, with her engagement with the feminist politics of Audre Lorde. "For the master's tools will never dismantle the master's house." Wolf takes Lorde's statement as a keynote to her book, countering it with the proverb – "fight fire with fire." She uses the concept of a "genderquake," sometimes called the "Anita Hill Effect," to validate her preferred adage and to substantiate her claim that all women now enjoy a powerful socio-political status due to their new found ability and determination to wield the master's tools. The "genderquake" refers to events on both sides of the Atlantic which are said to have followed from the 1991 Thomas–Hill hearings in Washington, for example, the election of 52 women to the US Congress and the British Labour Party's acceptance of women-only short lists. According to Wolf, the "genderquake" proves that only by adopting heteropatriarchal capitalist values, only by pursuing money and a high media profile, can women dismantle the master's house.[68] Wolf claims that Lorde would have women forgo these "advantages," the partial rewards that are available to women within the system. She tries to reduce Lorde's politics to a simple-minded separatism, implying that her agenda requires women to represent themselves as helpless victims, by taking her statement quoted above out of context.

There is nothing in the body of Lorde's work to support these charges. Lorde concedes that women's participation in dominant institutions has effected some positive changes for some women. What this strategy will never achieve is genuine structural change. "And this fact is only threatening to those women who still define the master's house as their only source of comfort."[69] Lorde stresses the importance of engaging with the system, but in ways that do not reinforce existing inequalities among people. bell hooks' reading of *Fire with Fire* notes that the distortion of Lorde's politics represents an attempt to deflect attention away from the need for all women, especially white women, "to interrogate [their] lust for power within the existing political structure [and their] investment in oppressive systems of domination," which is at the core of Lorde's work.[70]

Wolf's transformation of Anita Hill from female stoic to feminist champion is also marked by exaggerations and fabrications. She reasons that what made the Thomas–Hill hearings break the mould of standard rituals of female humiliation was that Hill knew how to play the same game as the old boys on the Senate sub-committee who were questioning her. A tenured law professor and graduate of Yale, she "sat facing her interlocutors, holding the master's own self-professed definition of authority and credibility in her hands."[71] By itself, Hill's testimony, however much publicity it generated, could hardly be expected to realize a great victory for feminism; for this to occur, Hill would have had to declare a purpose behind her willingness to testify that was in some way inspired by feminist considerations. However, this lack of motive, feminist or otherwise, does make it easier for her story to be rewritten from a conservative white feminist perspective. Wolf writes about Hill as if her educational attainment, professional skills, poise and verbal eloquence, in short, all those attributes which she views as contributing to her success, cannot be reconciled with her identity as a black woman. She implies that black culture is somehow synonymous with "lower-class" culture, that, in effect, a person's blackness disappears when that individual attains a certain class status.[72] Conceptually, Wolf erases Hill's blackness by drawing a clear line between it and her "womanness."

Hill is an unusual, not to mention an ironic choice for the matron-saint of a new feminist movement. hooks has commented that given Hill's misguided belief in the efficacy of the master's tools and the lack of success she met with in utilizing them she is much better suited to be a symbol of women's victimization; after all, her interlocutors finally judged her experience of sexual harassment to be neither authoritative nor credible, a point on which Wolf is noticeably silent.[73] I suppose these things don't matter when one's feminism amounts to a recipe for how to make yourself a comfortable middle-class lifestyle, with all the trappings. Wolf presents her brand of feminism in terms of a self-help program, one that will enable women to get in touch with our "will to power" [note the fascist connotations], the little girl in each of us, the unbridled megalomaniac, who wants to rule the world."[74] It's "fun," it's "lucrative," Wolf declares.[75] Statements like this tempt one to conclude that she has obtained her feminist consciousness from perusing back issues of *Cosmopolitan*.

## Working Across the Racial Divide: Imitating Anita

Thus far, we've examined some notable feminist texts that address a principal concern of white working women: how to balance comfortably work and family life and how to reconcile what are, in dominant terms, disparate identities – wife/mother/worker. We've seen that black women are either absent from feminist analyses of women and work or present as pseudo-white figures. This means that feminist discourse offers few, if any, coping mechanisms for black women who must juggle career and family, or who choose career instead of family, and who face racialized sexism in the workplace. Here, I want to consider the way in which mainstream feminist representations of the career woman, in tandem with dominant representations, impinge on black women's ability to comfortably integrate their recently available occupational roles with the familial and social roles which they have traditionally carried out in their communities, and further, how black representations of women at work replay some mainstream motifs in different forms, often reinforcing the barriers to black women's economic success and sense of psycho-social stability. Finally, I interrogate Wolf's assumption that black women who choose the route of assimilation can now expect the same rewards in the marketplace as their white counterparts. Also, I seek to answer a related question, posed by black cultural critic Glenn C. Loury: has it become necessary for black people, particularly black women, to choose between racial authenticity and personal success?[76] These questions are explored in relation to Cassandra Medley's play, *Ma Rose*, which addresses the tensions inherent within the gender, race, and class identities of a young upwardly mobile black woman.[77]

*Ma Rose*, first produced in 1988, features a middle-class black family living in the American Midwest. Its principal figures are Ma Rose, her daughter Vera Rose, and her grand-daughter Rosa. The events of the play are non-linear. It opens with Ma Rose in her nineties, but Rosa's reminiscences give us glimpses of the women at different life stages. The action is comprised of a series of interrelated conflicts. There are inti-mate struggles among individual family members such as the love–hate relationship between Vera and Ma Rose as well as between Vera and Rosa, which are further complicated by political conflicts over the value of family and the meaning of community. I will focus mainly on the conflict among Rosa, Vera and Ma Rose over what it means to be black, particularly a black woman, in the era of Reaganomics.

Chapter 2 mentioned how black women's work outside the home has traditionally been viewed within black communities; that is, black constructions of womanhood have incorporated black women's need to work outside of their own homes. However, there is a difference between black constructions of working women and that of the career woman. Medley suggests that black constructions of womanhood cannot so easily accommodate black women who work because they desire the personal freedom and satisfaction that may be gained from rewarding and well-paid employment, and not because it is necessary for economic survival. Black cultural reactions to black women climbing the corporate ladder in the US are not couched in terms of prescribed gender expectations, as exemplified in the backlash texts we've exam-ined (though these underlay some of the objections), but more in terms of racial disloyalty and to a lesser extent class disloyalty.[78] Vera's feel-ings regarding Rosa's chosen identity as a fashionable businesswoman are ambivalent. She holds to the tradition of race uplift; as such, she is proud of Rosa's success and speaks of her as a credit to her race. In the first scene, she looks at Rosa with awe and says: "Why I've never known a Negro face to face who made that kinda money in my life."[79] At the same time, however, she feels that Rosa has broken ranks with her family by leaving the Midwest for New York. Though herself middle-class, Vera often feels uncomfortable in the presence of her highly educated and accomplished daughter, and she suspects that Rosa now considers her relatives beneath her. "Just wish there was a way for folks to get educated and not stray from how they was raised  . . . ", she tells Rosa.[80] One senses a hierarchical distinction in Vera's (and Ma Rose's) estimation between the black and white middle-classes, the latter among whom Rosa now spends most of her time, which might account for Vera's feeling out-classed by her daughter. In an intimate essay on class and education, hooks writes of the fears which black parents commonly experience at their children's entry into a materially privi-leged white world: the fear that they might learn to be ashamed of their roots, or never want to return home, or return only to lord it over their families.[81]

The women's continuous arguments over class alliances pale in the face of those caused by Vera's disappointed expectations where Rosa's perceived gender obligations to her race are concerned. Within the context of her middle-class world, Vera sees her daughter as failing to fulfill her feminine raison d'être: to become a wife and mother. Vera wants to see Rosa carrying a diaper bag instead of a briefcase, of which she speaks scathingly: "Girl, that thing trails after you like an afterbirth – and I *wish* you'd cut the cord –!"[82] Clearly, the play constructs woman-hood and its attendant roles for middle-class black women along the lines of its white counterpart. However, Rosa's resistance to marriage is understood by Vera not just as a failure to behave like a woman: it is important to note the way in which she feels Rosa has failed as a *black woman*. Vera's relationship with Rosa's father illustrates her belief that an integral part of a black woman's role is supporting a black man. Brown-Guillory reminds us that the black family, while African in origin, is American in nurture.[83] Once again reflecting the dominant, middle-class blacks hold up the father–mother–children triad as the ideal backbone of community. Rosa's education, career success, and particularly her high income, separate her from a significant portion of the black male community.[84] In the 1980s, the decline in blue-collar jobs hit black men especially hard. The growth in white-collar jobs, occupa-tions which generally call for attitudes and aptitudes associated with white culture and on which count black women seem to satisfy employers more readily than black men, meant that black men lost more ground to black women in terms of status and income.[85] Rosa's situa-tion is quite different from the typical experience of a middle-class white woman, who would probably have a wide field of partners to choose from and who have the potential to earn at, and more often above, the same levels as themselves. Pay differentials increased the difficulty for black women seeking to balance career and family.

Vera recognizes that since desegregation the effect of black women's economic advancement on the community as a whole has also changed. It now has the potential to fragment the community by creating further class and cultural divisions between black men and women. In one of her more caustic remarks, she says to Rosa: "Girl, lookit them long and pretty fingernails!! Guess you go to saunas and stuff like that, huh? I guess the smalltown homeboys "round here and down at the plant – that kinda man – don't hold much interest for you – . . . " Rosa presents her objections to the "homeboys" in terms of a regrettable, but unavoid-able cause and effect of economic success. "Nothing *wrong* with the men "round here but when you advance in life you get expectations, Momma, that just comes with the territory . . . "[86] hooks offers an alter-native to Rosa's view: assimilation would be necessary only if the terms of success as defined by the standards of white supremacist capitalist patriarchy were the only standards that exist. "But they are not. Even in the face of powerful structures of domination, it remains possible for each of us, especially those of us who are members of oppressed and/or exploited groups as well as those radical visionaries who may have race, class and sex privilege, to define and determine alternative standards, to decide on the nature and extent of compromise."[87]

Rosa comes into conflict with her grandmother as well over the extent to which she has compromised her allegiance to the black community for entrance into the white corporate echelon. Unlike Vera, Ma Rose is not overly concerned about the fact that Rosa seeks personal fulfillment through work rather than marriage and children. Rather, it is the weakness of Rosa's identification with her own blackness that upsets her. Medley picks up the strain in black cultural discourse that theorizes blackness as a quality that can be lost or forfeited. Kim Dowell explains it this way: "Elite blacks do not have much personal contact with lower class blacks or middle class blacks. They may help the black masses from a distance, but they need to come and relate with black people of all classes. If not, they will lose their culture and heritage, *and even their blackness,* if they are not careful"(emphasis mine).[88] A parallel move is common in lesbian culture: in some circles, should a lesbian sleep with a man she risks losing her right to call herself and be recognized as lesbian.

Ma Rose distinguishes between Rosa's "real face" and her corporate face or "false-face Demon" as she calls it. Literally, Rosa has manufactured a new face for herself: she approximates as much as possible a middle-class white feminine appearance and manner. Her style of hair is but one instance. Her "fro" was "in my other life and former days" she tells Ma Rose. In her former days, Rosa was a Left activist. She fondly recalls the work she did in her early twenties, her proudest accomplishment being to secure a book-mobile for children in housing projects. This one simple step, she recalls, generated a neighborhood block party. This celebration of black community spirit leads the young Rosa to write to Ma Rose: "I feel so alive."[89] Rosa also proudly recollects accompanying Ma Rose on a Civil Rights march: "Oh, when we marched. When we marched. Finest day of my childhood, when we marched down the Square."[90]

Rosa's greatest sense of accomplishment in her thirties comes from having an office with windows on both sides of her walls four ways round – a sign of corporate success. Her current self-image is linked to the material things she possesses. Compared to a younger Rosa, the fashionable Rosa leads a rather soulless existence. In an article on double-consciousness, Kristin Hunter Lattany argues that "the loss of the soul, as well as of 'soul,' which means contact with the core self, is an inevitable consequence of identity change."[91] Rosa insists that things like hairstyle and clothes are merely peripheral to one's identity and continues to deny that she has rejected her black heritage: "... Okay, so I'm out in the 'big, wide world' but don't think I forget *where* I come from and what I was *taught* and what I got to be *proud* of!" She refutes the accusation that she lacks proper feeling toward her family: "*I'm so glad I came back this weekend.* . . . Cause family is just what my spirit needs – just what's gonna renew my strength, to keep on keeping on"[92] She cannot admit to herself that it is in fact her blackness that she has allowed to become incidental to her identity in exchange for success. Her blackness is not allowed to intrude anywhere in her life other than its appearance on her skin. Although she remains cognizant of white prejudice (she does mention tokenism), her race no longer occupies much space in her psychological make-up. Ruth. R. Frankenberg's definition of culture, as that which constructs "daily practices and worldviews in complex relations with material life," is useful for understanding how, despite her blackness, Rosa's material existence can be shaped by a set of normative cultural practices specific to white culture.[93]

In "Keeping Close to Home," hooks says that "maintaining connections with family and community across class boundaries demands more than just summary recall of where one's roots are, where one comes from. It requires knowing, naming, and being ever mindful of those aspects of one's past that have enabled and do enable one's self-development in the present, that sustain and support, that enrich."[94] Rosa's only regular contact with the black community occurs when she conducts seminars on Meeting the Challenge of Corporate Management as Chair of the New York Chapter of the National Coalition of Executive Minority Women. By the time she returns home, her identity appears so groundless and splintered that one must ask whether it would not be harder for Rosa to contrive being black than to continue acting white. Rosa's denial of her black identity is further evidenced in a speech she makes about success, some of which could just as easily have been spoken by *Top Girls* Marlene: "Do you know what's wonderful about my life? Winning is wonderful! There's a thrill when you win – when you plan to win and make your move and then find out that you have won – and figuring how to win more – winning my place in that wide and rough world out there – fighting my way in and winning and winning cause I deserve to."[95] This passage echoes the classic liberal American position that individuals are in control of their own destiny. Rosa wants to believe that she is in control of her fate and not particularly subject to any institutional forces such as racism or sexism. Lattany questions whether or not the black middle class believes that money, achievements, and possessions can make their color invisible.[96] Through

Rosa's estimation of her own circumstances, the play suggests that we should answer yes.

That Rosa relies on a cocktail of anti-depressants and anti-anxiety drugs to get through most days belies her triumphal voice. "You don't got no peaceful face on you," Ma Rose observes.[97] Strive as she might, Rosa never really feels secure in a white world. Ma Rose understands how uncomfortable for her it must be there: "all I can see is that crust of that false face is scratching you and scratching you – I can see you go through day after day of feeling like you ain't been inside your own flesh – . . . " Once Rosa comes close to admitting how much she has come to disregard being black. "I've had to accept that there are certain rules that have to be played by, followed. Okay, there is a way you have to be, took some, getting used to, but I've made my peace with it."[98] Whereas *Top Girls* showed women suppressing the signs of their femininity to succeed in the corporatist world, black women, Medley argues, must sacrifice their blackness, their cultural roots and identification, more than their femininity (which the dominant doesn't credit them with possessing in the first place) if they are to succeed in the white corporate world. Paradoxically, Rosa rationalizes this by thinking of her work as part of the struggle, alleging that her corporate role is distasteful to her and is one that she enacts more for the benefit of her race than for personal gain. "I'm on the front lines each and every day – Mommy, then that fright can come on me without warning – I start thinking I don't deserve this position and I can't hold it – but still I stand for my people, I stand for the family – everybody's got a stake in where I'm at . . . ."[99]

Rosa's gradual drive toward self-awareness comes to a halt when Ma Rose is placed in a nursing home by her children. This is also the point at which all the play's conflicts come to a head as the family argues over what should be done with Ma Rose now that her "mind ain't right." Rosa's solution to the conflict with her family is to attempt to buy her way back into their esteem. She offers to pay the majority of costs for Ma Rose to be cared for in her own home as Ma Rose would like. Contrary to her expectations, Rosa's efforts result in a complete break with her family.[100] Their ostracism of Rosa precipitates her nervous collapse. She hears demon voices mixed with the voice of Ma Rose. Indicating her own mind and body, she screams:

YES, I BLEED – BLEED BLOODY – I AIN'T NO WOOD THING,
. . . – YEAH YEAH THERE BE DEMONS DOWN IN HERE, OH
YES – OH YES – !! WHAT WILL I DO IF THEY CAST ME OUT – .
. . WHAT WILL I DO IF – IF I FAIL YOU – WHAT WILL I DO IF I FAIL
MYSELF – WHAT WILL I DO IF I FACE THE DEMON FACE . . .

HOW WILL I LIVE AND – WHAT WILL MY LIFE BE –
WHAT WILL I DO??!! WHICH OF MY FACES IS MY REAL FACE – ![101]

Throughout this encounter with her own demons, the spirit of Ma Rose continues her attempt to guide Rosa to a reunion with her "own soul's better half." We are not shown the end of Rosa's search for her real face, but given that she goes back to her job in New York and only returns home upon the death of her grandmother, one assumes that she is unable to find it. Ma Rose's death serves only to bring about an uneasy and frail truce between Rosa, her mother, and the rest of the family.

In *Ma Rose,* race loyalty and family loyalty is inextricable. Vera, her brother Wayman, and his wife Ethel's notion of family is strongly tradition-bound, whereas their children, the "new breed," have largely adopted the values of a modern highly mobile society.[102] As Ethel sees it, Rosa's generation has no sense of duty to family or, following from this, to the notion of black community. The decision to place Ma Rose in care is partly taken because her children cannot accommodate her on their own, and their children cannot be relied upon for assistance. The play posits an identity divide between the generations of blacks who came to adulthood before and after the victories of the civil rights movement. Lattany writes: "An entire generation – those who reached adulthood in the 1970s and 1980s – seems to have lost its biculturality and the dividing line between private and public selves, and, with it, the sense of race loyalty."[103]

She characterizes the black person in conflict with her/himself as "marginally functional" and, she argues, this is how she/he is viewed by other blacks: if half a person's loyalty lies elsewhere, his or her community cannot trust that person.[104] Hence, Rosa's noticeable and painful inner conflict, which one might reasonably expect to provoke a sympathetic response, serves only to widen the rupture with her family. The older generation sees Rosa's attachment to career and consumerism as indicative of her assimilation of white cultural values and as such, a betrayal of everything for which she and other blacks had marched. Vera comes to realize, even if Rosa does not, that her daughter now fights on the "front lines" largely for herself. By the end of the play, she can no longer be certain that the successes of individual black people will help advance the black community as a whole because the collective sense of responsibility held by her generation of middle-class blacks has been lost, just as the sense of obligation to one's extended family is gradually being forgotten.

*Ma Rose* names the end of American apartheid as the moment which marks the beginning of the segmentation of the black community, but it never identifies in detail just what it is that has changed in black culture as a result of desegregation. hooks gives us one possible reason for the shift; under segregation blacks of all classes shared more common experiences in relation to social institutions.[105] Frankenberg offers another possibility: as the US becomes increasingly stratified by race linked to class, blacks' racial and class identities can contradict each other. On a personal level, this means that individuals can live among either their economic or ethnic peers, but rarely are they able to live comfortably with both.[106] I would also suggest that the difference resides between one generation of middle-class blacks who passed in white culture and another later generation's greater opportunity and predilection for assimilation. Here, I use the term passing to indicate a kind of mimicry. There has always existed a core of middle-class blacks in America who propitiated the worst excesses of racism via their ability to emulate white cultural forms. In public, at least, this group spoke the language of white culture, but they retained a distinct private black voice. This double-voice allowed them to more comfortably straddle the black/white divide than those black people who lived in poverty and therefore, could not access this kind of cultural capital. In a new take on Du Bois' classic theory that blacks experience a "double-consciousness" (sometimes also referred to as a "two-ness" of identity), black neo-conservative Shelby Steele claims that today black people, that is, middle-class black people, suffer from a double bind, whereby the two parts of their identity threaten one another because the categories race and class are defined in antagonistic terms.[107] While I disagree with the essence of Steele's conservative apologia for racial inequity, his reading of the relation between the constructs of race and class in contemporary black culture is intriguing. It is a recurrent idea in *Ma Rose*. Rosa feels that she must suppress her black voice in favor of internalizing that of the dominant white culture. This denial of her blackness offers no effective means of negotiating between the two cultural spaces she inhabits as would a double consciousness; rather, as Lattany notes, it results in "a splitting of personality . . . that leads to inauthenticity [and] spiritual death."[108] Rosa's dilemma challenges us to examine our assumptions about the relation between being black and middle-class and about the role of the black elite in American society. It also raises important questions for black women about how best to negotiate the relation between their individual wants and their feelings of collective responsibility, as well as the space they inhabit within the race–gender-class systems.

*Ma Rose* proposes two kinds of middle-class people. One group works to materially improve their living conditions, but not at the expense of others, and there are those for whom the end justifies the means. Rosa comes closest to the latter and this, the play argues, is the reason why satisfying relationships with family or friends or lovers do not make up part of her life. Like *Top Girls* Marlene, Rosa justifies her competitiveness and acquisitiveness by claiming to work for the greater good of women/blacks as a class. Yet, both plays show that each woman's march up the career ladder does little to help anyone beyond the individual women themselves. Rather, each is motivated by the kind of individualist ethic we saw endorsed in the work of Friedan, Hewlett, Wasserstein, and Wolf. Thatcherism and Reaganomics and their feminist correlatives may have resulted in the individual success of one kind of woman, but they have done nothing to change the position of the majority of women. It is unlikely that we will ever see women like Marlene and Rosa offering a hand-up to their less materially fortunate sisters. Just as Marlene's hero, Margaret Thatcher, did little as Prime Minister to foster women's prospects, Marlene's position as top girl represents no great leap forward for her gender. In the same way, Rosa's success represents a muted victory for black women, and it indicates that the problems of inequality between genders, classes, and races defy individual solutions.

# 4

# *"Woman" as Object*

Feminism is not simply about rejecting power, but about transforming power structures – and in the process, transforming the very *concept* of power itself. To be "against" power is not to abolish it in a fine post-1968 liberation gesture, but to hand it over to somebody else.

*Toril Moi*[1]

## Universal "Woman:" The Trojan Horse of Feminism

Second-wave feminists based their definition of sexism on a model of racism developed during the American Civil Rights Movement.[2] Sexism and racism were both theorized as systems of exclusion built into the institutional fabric of society and sustained through stereotyping and prejudice. This definition suffices in purely academic terms. Problems arise, however, when this conceptual link is translated into a presumed experiential one. Mainstream feminism has constructed and forwarded various representations of "Woman" that rely on the dominant white culture's treatment of blacks as a marker to highlight white women's inferior status compared to white men, a fact crystallized in the movement phrase "woman is the nigger of the world." The assumption that the processes of exploitation and liberation will be the same for black and white women not only distorts power relations between them, but also embeds the exploitation of black women into the material conditions of white women's lives. In other words, white women participate in systems which construct representations of black women that are then used as a negative contrast to enhance their own reflections, in the same way that men use women as a class to reflect the images of themselves they want to see. Christine Delphy makes the case that white women benefit from this as a group, most notably, by amassing a disproportionate share of material resources. And without even mentioning these positive benefits, white women profit from a system that exploits black women by virtue of being themselves exempt from certain forms of oppression.[3]

A typical response by mainstream feminists to these charges has been that white women enjoy privilege rather than hold power. However, if we understand power as a network of material dimensions and discursive processes rather than a thing simply owned or wielded, then we accept that power is not held by anyone, a fact which does not necessarily entail an equal society. Ruth Frankenberg argues that whiteness as a normative space is constructed precisely by the way in which it positions others at its borders.[4] In which case, those women who fit the dominant criteria for inclusion within the category "Woman" possess the faculty for dominating women outside this preferred grouping; that is, in so far as white women participate in the maintenance of dominant cultural categories, they help maintain, along with white men, institutional forms of racism. One way that mainstream feminism has actively perpetuated the exclusion of black women from the movement, and the larger system of rewards which society reserves for "Woman," has been to resist taking differences among women seriously. The usual excuse offered is that concentrating on differences among women would threaten the unity and coherence of the movement (what unity and coherence?), or, a focus on difference would make analyses of women's oppression unwieldy if not impossible. As a result, mainstream feminists choose to write/speak "as-a-Woman." Elizabeth Spelman labels this construction the "Trojan Horse of Feminism." She maintains that even though many feminists now acknowledge in their writing that some women are black, white, rich, poor, etc., nevertheless, they continue to insist that they are all the same *as women*. This stance assumes that their differences reside in some "non-woman part of them." And if it is only the "woman" part – that part where differences cannot reside – of any woman that counts, then this is the same as saying that differences among women are irrelevant.[5] Typically, mainstream feminist analyses of white women have approached them as purely gendered subjects, while black women have been overwhelmingly designated as racialized subjects. Frankenberg, having analyzed the life narratives of a racially diverse group of women, concludes that it is difficult for the majority of white women to perceive "whiteness" in terms of race, despite the fact that their race evidently shapes their "experiences, practices and views of self and others."[6] She attributes their racial blindness to the fact that whiteness, when not signifying formlessness or void, is most often configured as norm. As such it stands as "an unmarked marker of others' differentness" as opposed to one's own.[7]

This evidence signals once again the necessity for feminists to analyze oppression based on the existence of a plurality of genders, and, as this chapter will argue, if constructions of gender and race are to be understood, they must be examined in terms of how they relate. The relation to be explored is not solely one within gender difference (i.e. between femininity and masculinity). As the troubled relations among black and white women active in the movement's second-wave demonstrate, the difference *between* gender(s) and race must be considered equally important as the difference *within*. These points will be mademore explicit through an examination of two plays, Elaine Jackson's *Paper Dolls* and Kathleen Collins' *The Brothers*, both of which challenge mainstream feminism's tendency to associate race and gender oppression while, at the same time, dissociating gender and race. Each play attempts to render the cultural mechanisms according to which black femininity is constructed, both in terms of dominant and black race/gender discourses, as transparent as possible. They represent, in part, attempts to work out how dominant constructions of femininity and masculinity are racialized, the extent to which those in power can effectively police normative gender categories, and the scope which black women possess for undermining dominant/mainstream feminist representations of racialized femininity. The plays will also return us to a topic of chapter 1 – the artificiality of gender itself. Recall (chapter 1) Judith Butler's definition of "intelligible genders," which basically refers to a conjectural "truth" of gender. Dominant or "intelligible" gender categories not only institute and maintain relations of coherence and continuity among sex, gender, desire and sexual practice (Butler's thesis), but to this catalogue must also be added race. When applied to race–gender identities in the plays, these categories illustrate how black constructions of femininity and masculinity, like their lesbian and gay analogues, recall the socially constructed status of the category of gender itself and its independence from one's sex and exposes the regulatory aims of the race–gender system.

## Colorizing Joan of Arc: Racialized Femininity and the Politics of Appearance

Elaine Jackson's *Paper Dolls*, first produced in 1982, maps out the interdependence of gender and race in the construction of black femininity and the engendered forms of racism black women experience.[8] These associated themes are presented through the life-histories of two former black beauty queens, Margaret-Elizabeth and Lizzie. Now in their sixties, they have returned to the pageant circuit after working as models and television/film actresses. As the play opens, they are on their way to judge the Miss International Sepia contest. Interspersed with this event are mini-scenes in which the women recreate episodes from their movies and their former roles as beauty contestants. The plot-time shifts from the 1980s to the 1930s, then forward through the 1940s, '50s and '60s, and finally back to the '80s. As the play moves through the decades, we come to see how standards of feminine beauty have remained unchanged for much of this century: as the women themselves say, the only thing that has changed are the titles and the bathing suits. Indeed, images of black women's looks and sexuality current today have formed part of the dominant cultural imaginary since the nineteenth century.[9]

*Paper Dolls* tackles the sensitive issue of black women's looks and foregrounds how appearance for black women is a political choice. In her introduction to the play, Margaret Wilkerson reads into it the warning that black women, by attempting to get the "right look" (read white look), render themselves and other black women easy objects of exploitation.[10] While Jackson objects to white America's use of western European standards of beauty to judge black women second-rate, she does not spare those black women who, out of a desire to enhance their social mobility, accede to white beauty-dogma and try to assimilate by down-playing their black features. Jackson emphasizes that black women who emulate white femininity do not wish to be white; rather, they desire what whiteness represents. The play acknowledges that at the material level the whiter a black woman's appearance is the better the standard of living she is likely to enjoy.[11] The whiteness of their looks allows Margaret-Elizabeth and Lizzie to rise into the middle-class, a move (and its accompanying relative affluence) which the two women view as contributing to the dismantling of racism. In reality, it merely allows them to blunt its edge in reference to their own lives. As in the case of Rosa in Medley's *Ma Rose*, the women's economic climb is accompanied by a transfer of class allegiance, from working-class black culture to middle-class white values and mores. I do not refer solely to their relatively privileged financial status, but more to their emulation of white womanhood; for "Woman" carries not only psychological and even moral encodings, but socio-economic ones as well. Although they finally come to understand the ways in which their behavior has fed their own and other black women's exploitation in terms of the race–gender system, Margaret and Lizzie fail to grasp how it has negatively impacted on the black community by engendering conflicting class interests.

As young women, Lizzie and Margaret imagine that adopting as much as possible the decorative signs of "Woman', many of the same features that white women perceive as degrading, is a means of liberation. In addition to liberating them from poverty and from the extremely limited horizons of a small segregated black township, they believe that it can liberate them from an existence, as reflected in the eyes of white culture, in which they are characterized as undesirable and expendable. This accounts for the great importance they give to what they call "class': certain behavioral characteristics generally associated with "Woman" such as "poise" and "charm" as well as genteel speech and etiquette. Because black women are not normally thought of as having dignity or value, Margaret and Lizzie mistake the traditional attributes of white femininity as being ennobling rather than objectifying and exploitative: charm, for instance, is one of those "empty" adjectives which are representative of dominant descriptions of "Woman."

Ironically, their attitude merely exacerbates the degree of sexual harassment they encounter. Margaret and Lizzie internalize the point of view of the dominant white culture out of a mistaken belief that this will confer upon them some authority of their own.[12] However, the implicit contrast between the different systems of signs which they attempt to combine (i.e. black and white, "Woman," female, and black) means that there is a significant difference between how their bodies are read within dominant ideology and what is signified to the women themselves by their performance of white femininity.

Patricia Hill Collins assesses race as the distinguishing feature in determining the type of objectification that a woman will encounter. She calls to mind that whiteness is symbolic of civilization and culture – two categories used to separate people from animals and both encoded as part of the domain "mind" within the western philosophical mind/body dichotomy. Within this dichotomy, white women "occupy an uncertain, interim position." As objects, white women are creations of culture and occupy the pre-eminent place in the binary. Black women, on the other hand, receive no redeeming dose of culture. They are represented as animals; their bodies signify an uncontrolled female sexuality; and they remain open to the types of exploitation visited on nature overall.[13] The bodies of black women carry a double cultural encoding: they carry the sign of blackness in a white racialized patriarchy and the sign of femaleness in a male supremacist society. Again, we see that they do not denote gender as it is understood within dominant logic: they do not signify "Woman." This is clearly apparent during Margaret's encounter with a Hollywood talent scout. As young women, neither she nor Lizzie see the grime behind the glitter of their chosen professions. They are unaware that for black women an acting career is more often than not a dead-end, particularly for those who aspire to portray positive images and qualities of black women. Margaret really believes Mr. Castle's promise to take her to Hollywood and to cast her as Joan of Arc because she sees herself to be an epitome of Joan, as the picture of innocence. The modesty of her typically white bourgeois style of dress is carefully designed to project a demure, girlish demeanor. When Castle asks her name (which he does several times as he cannot be bothered to remember it), at first she answers Gidget, then Tammy and Barbie – all extremely popular images of innocent white womanhood of the 1950s and '60s, and any one of which could be seen as the ultimate caricature of white femininity.

Gloria J. Joseph comments on the consequences of black women affecting male-defined feminine characteristics in the same way as white women. Black women can act "cute, dainty, etc," and these characteristics will be appreciated, reinforced, rewarded, and perpetuated in a typical western tradition within black communities. The conflict or psychological drama for the black woman occurs when she moves into the dominant society, and these same behaviors and characteristics are received and interpreted in a different manner because they hold a different interpretation for white society. The black female is either unnoticed or overnoticed and misinterpreted.[14] bell hooks contends that when measured against white cultural ideals, black features signify the "ugly, monstrous, and undesirable."[15] In the conventional sense, black women's bodies are unattractive because in order for beauty and sexuality to be considered desirable it must be idealized and unattainable: this is the kind of beauty incorporated into the definition of "Woman." In contrast, the black female body gains attention when it is synonymous with accessibility and availability or when it is sexually deviant.[16] This is evidenced in Castle's reading of Margaret-Elizabeth's appearance, which differs radically from her own. He perceives her as carnality personified, more as a sexually available Jezebel than a virginal Gidget; the first thing he asks her is to lift her dress so that he can see her legs.[17] He expects to find her eager to gratify the sexual needs of men, particularly white men of relative power and wealth such as himself. As one might expect, Margaret's hope of representing the purity and heroism of Joan of Arc on-screen prove futile. Foucault's concept of the "unthought" can be used to lend a better understanding as to why it is impossible for Margaret to play Joan."[18] Knowledge, being historical, is always created by the imposition of some limit. Stereotypical constructions of femininity and sexuality for black and white women are formed within a field of material, economic and social forces that incorporate rules of exclusion; these regulatory elements allow/limit one to being either a (white) woman or a (black) female – but not both. Thus, the sign black coupled to that of "Woman" would be relegated to the realm of the "unthought:" a theoretical space that defines the limits of socially acceptable thought.

Castle will only take Margaret to Hollywood if she will submit to him molding her into a racialized sex object for the pleasure and profitability of other white men (in addition to providing him with sex). Margaret insists that she would make a great Barbie, but Castle is just as insistent that she transform herself into Ebony, Raven, or Jetta. These names call to mind blackness, but Castle resists a straightforward presentation of black female beauty and undertakes to tone down Margaret's blackness by marketing her as a woman of mixed-race. He recommends that she bill herself as Jetta Johnson, an exotic combination of Polynesian, American Indian, Brazilian, Turkish, and "just for the fun of it, he tells her, we'll throw in a little Irish."[19] As further proof that black women's sexuality is regarded as deviant, the starring role that Castle has in mind for Jetta was written for a male transvestite. In dominant terms, transvestism is a perversion, and even within the world of the play, drag represents an insulting and degraded version of womanhood. In the same way that the dual presence of masculine and feminine signifiers in the person of a drag queen creates a tension that subverts normal cultural processes of signification, so too does the manifestation upon one body of black and white signifiers. Castle would represent the black female body as a play upon femininity just as he would present a male body playing at being feminine; for he realizes that the concomitant ambiguousness and strangeness of a white-authored black femininity renders it sexually titillating and therefore highly saleable.

Margaret eventually concludes that she and other black women must work toward forging a self-referential black femininity. Her resolution is only partly motivated by her own experiences. It also stems from observing the attitudes of her grandson's generation. The walls of her grandson's bedroom are plastered with posters of "beautiful" women – not one of whom is black. The absence of any images of black beauty, even stereotypically affected representations, leads her to realize that Arthur's generation, in the same way as her own, is growing up unable to positively perceive and value black womanhood. In the new space Margaret would carve out for black women, black would radically signify beautiful. *Paper Dolls* suggests that this transformation will come about only if and when black women and men confront their own internalized racism. Margaret and Lizzie seek to exorcise their self-loathing by rehearsing the humiliating ways in they have daily sought to obliterate their blackness: straightening their hair, bleaching their skin, tucking in their buttocks, and pinching their noses to make them appear straighter and their lips to make them look smaller.[20] As part of this exercise, they also replay the degrading images of black womanhood they represented on-screen. These mini-scenes amount to a procession of mammies in head-rag and flowered calico dresses, serving girls in awe of their white mistresses' beauty and polish, ignorant scrubwomen in tattered rags, and "native" girls in skimpy costumes who speak nonsense like "Bugga Wanna, Bugga Wanna Wanna Na."[21] At the end of the play, the women stage a minstrel show, intended to show up white stereotypes of black women. The show features well-known historical white representations of Black Topsy, Black Beulah, Black Mama, and Black Whore. Included also are several instances of Black Man, who trades racist jokes about the ugliness of black women. Addell Austin Anderson suggests that by satirically replaying their own past the women intervene in and seek to transform the racist "stereotypes created for and perpetuated by black women." She reads the minstrel show as another successful disruption of race–gender stereotypes: "having exorcised the images, the women finally emerge victorious over the traditional standards of beauty, which so long have haunted them."[22] According to Anderson, the minstrel show allows the women to exercise their ability to control their definition of womanhood, now defined in terms of its visual and physical distance from white womanhood.

Jackson's objective in *Paper Dolls* is quite ambitious and involves more than just the deconstruction of stereotypes. Through the play as a whole and specifically the character Margaret, Jackson seeks to fashion an oppositional discourse, one through which black women constitute active agents of change, agents who are able to speak and to be heard in new ways. Margaret tells Lizzie that "there are ever so many ways to tell a story . . . You can write people in or write 'em out . . . The most important thing is how it all ends."[23] (Her words recall Sinfield's theory of cultural production, discussed in chapter 2.) *Paper Dolls* is one of a number of feminist plays that place the power of shaping the signifier in the hands of black women, where, Austin notes, "it has rarely been and where the potential for radical signification is great".[24] The play attempts to transgress the territorial boundaries of "Woman," those boundaries which mean that at the end of the story black women are confined to serviceable roles which function to enhance and maintain an idealized version of white womanhood. Derrida writes that "there is no word, nor in general a sign, which is not constituted by the possibility of repeating itself."[25] Margaret and Lizzie challenge white conceptions of white beauty and black women's looks through critical parody of the sign "Woman." Before the minstrel show, they enact a mock beauty pageant in which the contestants are literally cardboard cutouts of Gidget, Tammy, Barbie, and Bridget Bardot. By having male actors carry some of the cutouts and assume the mannerisms of the representative "Woman," the play further destabilizes the category "Woman', and its satirization of ideal white femininity is magnified. If we accept Butler's thesis that displacement inheres in the repetition of gender categories and as they are reproduced they are simultaneously destabilized, then, through their repetition of the sign "Woman,"

Margaret and Lizzie may expand the field of potential race–gender configurations.[26]

What kind of space the women create for black femininity, however, is open to question. Anderson understands the mock pageant and minstrel show as establishing a positive representational space for black femininity. I believe that the play's mocking repetition of "Woman" subverts both its status as natural and ideal womanhood; I'm not convinced that disturbing the ideas of fixity surrounding this category necessarily leads to the creation of a black-defined space, one which would enable black women to articulate their own perspectives or their own stories. The space created could just as likely be negative in the sense that it might not go beyond reflecting black women's marginality within white gender discourse. Margaret and Lizzie speak of "the strange pictures we've been given," referring to how remote conventional representations of black womanhood are from the images they would like to present. Although in theory they repudiate white conceptions of white and black womanhood, their practical presentation of themselves continues to be shaped by dominant ways of knowing. At the end of the play, they are still affecting the appearance and behavior of white femininity. In the final analysis, they are unable to "bring those pictures up to date," that is, present a version of black womanhood which does not predicate itself on a white cultural ideal, which confounds their attempt to create, at best, anything other than a temporary cathartic space for black women.

*Paper Dolls* has served to illustrate how black women are encouraged to identity with a white cultural point of view as to what constitutes the ideal of feminine appearance and behavior. Black women are invited to regard white women's way of life as good and desirable and as superior to their own. Various social institutions operate to inculcate the idea that a racialized heteropatriarchal system of values – one of whose central principles is racism – is in fact normal and legitimate; the review of Wolf's *Fire with Fire* (chapter 3) highlighted the position occupied by mainstream feminism in this institutional apparatus. In exchange for non-resistance, the dominant offers the prospect of assimilation and its attendant, albeit meager, system of rewards. However, the ostensible validation granted by white culture to those blacks who assimilate can only ever represent a partial, and, in the material sense, a largely insignificant embrace: because, assimilating too many blacks or too much of black culture is seen as threatening to the status quo. At the same time that it seeks to assimilate blackness, paradoxically, white cultural discourse works to expel or marginalize blacks by representing them as alien. Kathleen Collins' play, *The Brothers,* treats these questions of assimilation and integration in relation to gender(s) and their constructions. The play offers a further exploration into the way that the dominant constructs black femininity and masculinity in terms of what white femininity and masculinity *are not.*[27] And it provides another perspective on black women's ability to approximate white femininity and how this impacts on relations between black women and men, as well as its effects upon black family life. The play shares the same theoretical perspective on gender as *Paper Dolls:* by replicating "Woman" with a difference, black women may open up within the terms of a white cultural matrix of intelligibility rival and subversive matrices of gender disorder. Yet, again, we see that black women's facility at putting on a version of white femininity does not necessarily enable them to gain social parity with white women.

*The Brothers*, which had its first production in 1982, focuses on the black middle-class Edwards family and the personal strategies its members adopt in order to come to terms with being black in a white supremacist society. The Edwards brothers are only nominally the hub of the play. No male characters actually appear on stage; rather, their presence is evoked in tales recounted by the Edwards women. The play spans a period of twenty years – 1948 to 1968: it begins with the announcement of Gandhi's assassination and ends with that of Martin Luther King, a period that witnessed a dramatic increase in black people's pride in their culture coupled with a demand to be treated as equals. The Edwards, however, appear indifferent and at times even oblivious to the momentous events occurring in the black community. In *The Brothers*, we have another play that draws a connection between apolitical tendencies and middle-class status, with its concomitant individualist ethic. The Edwards' financial resources allow them to sequester themselves as far as possible from the immediate and worst effects of white racism. They seem either unaware or unconcerned that the importance they place on economic prosperity and parity with whites as a means of ensuring blacks' welfare can profit only a small minority of the black community.

The Edwards' middle-class status also effects the family's gender relations, by enabling the women's roles to be firmly centered within a black version of the nuclear family structure. The secure financial footing of the brothers enables their wives to devote themselves to catering for the needs of their own husbands and children. In *Re/membering Aunt Jemima* and *Shakin' The Mess Outta Misery*, one noticed a tension between the women's desires to work for their own families within the home and the need to enter into domestic service within the white community. This tension is absent from *The Brothers*, suggesting that ample material means are necessary for black women to approach white dominant feminine roles. The domestic underpinnings of the women's roles also effects a change in the meaning of family for them, one very different from what we have seen family to mean for black women in *Re/membering Aunt Jemima* and *Shakin' The Mess Outta Misery*, but bearing some similarities to *Rose's Story* and *Ma Rose*. For the Big Mamas, family acted as a space where black women could develop a culture of resistance. *The Brothers* introduces a more complex construction of black family life, representing it as a contradictory site of oppression and resistance for black women. Foremost, the middle-class black family functions as a place of women's confinement. The potential of the brothers' wives for development is stifled by their domesticity, in a way not dissimilar to that of those white middle-class women upon whose lives Friedan based *The Feminine Mystique*.[28] Some of the women are desperately unhappy in their domestic roles. Nelson's wife, Danielle, is an alcoholic, who feels so smothered by Nelson's dependency that she literally smothers him in his bed. Caroline's self-esteem is destroyed by Lawrence's lack of sexual/emotional interest after several years of marriage. She tries to console herself for his infidelities in the time-honored white middle-class way by purchasing expensive jewelry and fur coats, while still desperately clinging to him for approval.

The Edwards acquiesce in white culture's version of "Man" and "Woman."[29] All the wives possess light skin and European features and thereby, to an extent, they conform to white standards of beauty. In so far as the brothers prize the women for their appearances, the wives fulfill the sex-object role generally accorded to white womanhood. The women's objectification is felt to enhance the image and value of the brothers' masculinity. There is a strong pathology of colorism active in the play's dialogue between black masculinity and femininity. The Edwards and the Goulds, relations by law, value themselves and others according to a hierarchy of skin color and bodily features, with those who most closely approximate whiteness ranked highest. For instance, Lillie Gould, Franklin Edwards' first wife, is bred as "white as any negro stock can be." She feels it necessary to preface the announcement of her engagement with a fearful apology to her mother because Franklin is "brown: not very, but a little browner than any of us."[30] Marietta Edwards, the sister who remains unmarried largely because she is too black in appearance, is reduced to playing the role of family servant. She is portrayed as an embittered and disagreeable spinster whose sole fulfillment in life comes from bullying her brothers' wives.

The family's similarity to whites in terms of looks and material advantages lends them prestige and power within the black community and to a lesser extent, induces a modicum of respect from some whites. But its force does not extend beyond this microcosmic range. Their lives remain severely restricted by structural forms of racism. Most of the play's action is a reaction to Nelson Edwards' pivotal decision at the age of 31 never to leave his bedroom because, he says, "negro life is a void." With his career as a track star over and with no other notable skills, he knows that his future prospects are dim in spite of his family's relative wealth. He sees no way to overcome the institutional forms of racism that contribute to his inability to support his wife through his own labor. Given the great importance the family places upon traditional WASP values, this increases Nelson's sense of failure as a "Man." The extent to which Nelson can exercise the socio-economic power accorded to masculinity is limited because, within dominant terms, his masculinity is counterfeit. Confirmation of his masculinity depends on a construction of black femininity, which is itself deemed a forgery by the dominant. The brothers always stand outside the category "Man" because inclusion therein depends in part on access to the real object "Woman." The only version of masculinity to which the brothers can reasonably aspire is a sexually defined masculinity constructed upon the domination of women physically, which hooks argues is the one avenue of manhood open to all black men, regardless of class.[31] The brothers are cognizant of their racialized emasculation, and this helps account for their intense need to bend their wives to their wills, as well as their obsession with ensuring that their wives embody a hyper-sexualized image. Franklin's greatest disappointment is that his second wife Letitia cannot be molded to the same standards as his first wife in terms of looks, style, or sophistication. For the greater degree those women subject to the brothers' control are able to embody a white feminine ideal, the more value accrues to these objects and thereby the more credit redounds on the brothers' masculinity.

The brothers are less successful than the wives at approximating white gender roles because masculinity carries far more significance than femininity within dominant race–gender discourse. Femininity's inferior status makes "Woman" more open to being replicated with a difference. Furthermore, black women's innocuous status relative to black men in white cultural discourse affords them greater scope for seeing the reality of whiteness. The importance of black women's "looking" becomes clear when one recalls the dominant culture's preference for rendering itself invisible, or, as Ruth Frankenberg describes it, "amorphous" and "indescribable." As a cultural category, whiteness is not understood as signifying a material discourse, and, as I mentioned earlier, those who inhabit this normative space and set of identities frequently cannot see or name them. Compare this to a range of other cultural identities, which are seen to be clearly marked by race, ethnicity, and class, and we can begin to see why white culture is often taken as meaning "no culture."[32] In order to perform white femininity, the Edwards women must be able to see it, that is, to see the processes of its production and reproduction that dominant race–gender discourse tries to mask. Unlike the women in *Paper Dolls*, whose distance from an idealized femininity means they can only mimic it, the Edwards women don't parody white femininity so much as inhabit it. The impressive slate of white feminine traits they possess, their closeness to the archetype, aids them in replicating an almost indistinguishable black twin to "Woman," one that stands both inside and outside of the dominant ideology of race and gender. Their ability to possess the reality of the white Other enables the audience to gain knowledge of whiteness. It undermines the position whereby these constructs are understood as normative, instead showing them to be produced and propagated through a dialogue among racialized gender discourses in conjunction with the material relations of racism. *The Brothers* allows the audience to become spectators of white culture's race–gender narrative, thereby foregrounding the materiality and artificiality of white race–gender constructs.

## The Pornography of Representation: Sex, Gender, Race, and Rape

Carol Lee Bacchi describes sexuality as feminism's "ideological minefield" because historically women have been defined through their sexuality.[33] Sexuality is also one of the most crucial and highly charged points of connection between black and white women. This is particularly evident in mainstream feminism's discourse on rape, which is marked both by gender and racial essentialism. My goal is to show that the way in which mainstream feminism represents black and white women in relation to rape directly and indirectly contributes to cultural assumptions about black sexuality that help to secure white identity and white culture's organizational status quo. In light of this aim, I examine the work of Andrea Dworkin and Catherine MacKinnon, the principal designers of mainstream feminist discourse on rape. Basically their ideas run along parallel lines. However, Dworkin's sensational rhetoric and the greater accessibility of her language (compared to MacKinnon's frequently convoluted style) has resulted in her work receiving much greater media attention and having more influence at street-level than MacKinnon's. Accordingly, I devote more attention to Dworkin.

In order to understand Dworkin and MacKinnon's work, it must be placed within the context of the mainstream feminist debate on pornography and violence against women. In the 1980s, rape, and particularly

the notion of pornography as rape, became a cause célèbre among mainstream feminists in the US and Britain. Material resources and a
significant share of activists' energies were spent on the sexuality
debates, a dialogue within feminism that revolved around the issue of
pornography. The question being debated was whether or not pornography leads to violence against women, in particular, to rape. A related
question concerned whether women who participated in the porn
industry did so out of free choice, or were they programmed by their
upbringing or a history of sexual abuse to engage in self-destructive
activities? Integral to both questions was the agency/victim dispute.

The position of the anti-porn campaigners was succinctly phrased by
Robin Morgan: "pornography is the theory, and rape the practice;"[34] this
was dubbed the Domino Theory of Sexuality by feminist sexual radi-
cals.[35] The subject of pornography and its arguable effects was the
impetus behind one of the worst splits in the US movement. The British
feminist movement, which lacked the corporatist structure of its US
counterpart, fared better, but not by much. Lynne Segal contends that
feminist polemic was responsible for discouraging new thoughts on
sexuality in feminist texts more than the male backlash. For a while, she
points out, "it was only a small group of defiant lesbians who felt confident enough to question the Utopianism and growing prescriptiveness
in feminist accounts of a distinctively 'womanly' desire for benign,
sensual, egalitarian relationships."[36] In many British feminist circles, the
anti-porn position became the only possible feminist position, and,
according to Avedon Carol, this included a significant number of
lesbian–feminist circles.[37] S/M lesbians, in particular, faced discrimination from feminists of all denominations; indeed, at times in the 1980s,
a black leather jacket was enough to get a woman barred from a lesbian
venue. It is not my intention to focus on the sexuality debates, but rather
to concentrate on mainstream feminist representations of rape, only
discussing the pornography question if and when it is directly applicable to how rape is theorized.

Dworkin and MacKinnon's standard argument is that male rape of
women is no more than the expression of "normal" male sexuality, an
idea that is in fact very close to nineteenth-century feminist opinion.[38]
Linda Gordon and Ellen Dubois have documented how the majority of
nineteenth-century feminists also accepted women's sexual powerlessness as inevitable, even as they sought to protect women from male
sexuality's worst excesses.[39] Dworkin writes in *Intercourse* that the sex
act itself is the basis of women's oppression, a statement indicative of
the general (and I would argue pathological) aversion to all aspects of
sexuality that appears throughout her writings on rape and pornography.[40] As Anna Coote and Beatrix Campbell have observed,

Dworkin's brand of feminism reduces "the whole structure of male supremacy to fucking."[41] In *Woman Hating*, Dworkin claims that "the nature of women's oppression is unique: women are oppressed as women, regardless of class or race."[42] And in *Our Blood: Prophecies and Discourses on Sexual Politics*, she asserts that "All forms of dominance and submission, whether it be men over women, white over black, boss over worker, rich over poor, are tied *irrevocably* to the sexual identities of men and are derived from the male sexual model. Once female slavery is established as the diseased groundwork of a society, racism and other hierarchical pathologies inevitably develop from it."[43]

MacKinnon puts forward a similar totalizing thesis that she calls "dominance theory."[44] Dominance theory posits sexuality as a social sphere of male power in which forced sex is paradigmatic. At the heart of MacKinnon's methodology is the belief that men are capable of consolidating everything under their power. Or, as Dworkin says, "being female in this world is having been robbed of the potential for human choice by men who love to hate us."[45] Dworkin and MacKinnon's representation of rape as a phenomenon that is essentially the same for all women follows from their thesis that sexism is the root of all other forms of oppression. The logic of their argument is circular, not to mention reductive: in sum, men rape women because they're men and women get raped because they're women or rather "Woman." Moreover, Carol Smart identifies in their argument an underlying traditional moralism with no nuance at all. Instead, sharp dichotomies of good and evil are established, with those anti-censorship feminists who willfully or mis-guidedly stand in the way of putting matters right characterized as the forces of evil.[46]

The notion that the patriarchy employs rape to mold all women into "Woman" leads Dworkin and MacKinnon to represent femininity in a way that is disturbingly similar to that constructed and imposed by hegemonic discourse. Femininity becomes an exclusivist category that can feed into conservative and even reactionary sexual politics. To advocate a prescriptive female sexuality, conspicuous for its absence of sex and instead characterized by a desire for closeness and affection, colludes in the regulation of women's sexuality. In America, some feminists went so far as to form alliances with the religio-political Right. Avedon Carol calls attention to Dworkin and MacKinnon's alliance with a group of right-wing legislators in Indianapolis when they lobbied for passage of the "Minneapolis Ordinance" as well as with "New Right" activists on the 1986 Meese Commission, a body which supported traditional ideas on censorship. This, despite the fact that these Reaganites had made it abundantly clear that they were hostile to the principles and aims of feminism. In this way, Carol argues, Dworkin and MacKinnon risked allowing the women's movement to be co-opted by some of the most virulently sexist men in the country.[47] Although the US Ordinance failed, Mandy Merck records that British anti-porn campaigners, most notably the Labour MP Clare Short, actually conferred with Dworkin about similar draft legislation modeled on the American Bill. Fortunately, the alliance broke down due to Dworkin's refusal to agree to the inclusion of a "public good" clause, which would have exempted sexually explicit works deemed to be art.[48]

Dworkin and MacKinnon's analysis of rape with its singularly gender-orientated scheme confirms the danger of failing to situate the meaning of rape historically. Their reading of rape, balanced as it is upon women occupying the domain of positive values, logically negates the possibility of gaining insight into the way that race and sexuality impinge on rape's cultural significations. It is no simple task to pin down Dworkin and MacKinnon's position on how gender, rape, and race intersect. Both women take a strong anti-racist stand and emphatically assert the limitations of feminist theory that purports to explain gender without reference to race. I do not mean to question their personal commitment to racial equity. Yet, a theory of gender abstracted from race is exactly what they put forward in their own analyses of rape. Dworkin appears most cognizant that race and racism do figure in the meaning of rape, as when she calls attention to the racism inherent in the construction of the "typical" (read black) rapist in American culture.[49] However, the general unarticulated assumption behind her theory remains that race is not a factor in understanding sexism because her definition of sexism does not hold up unless one presupposes race as a constant.

Judith Butler has commented on the racial bias inherent in the argument that sexual difference is the most fundamental form of difference: it amounts to saying that sexual difference equals white sexual difference.[50] This brings us back to Frankenberg's thesis that whiteness signifies no racial markings. If sexual difference denotes white sexual difference then white gender constructs appear as unracialized categories. Such a view of sexual difference asks black and lesbian women to make an impossible choice. In order to participate fully in feminist activity, a woman must elect to identify as female or black, black or lesbian, or, women must choose between giving their allegiance to a struggle for gender or racial justice. When sexism is treated as somehow distinct from other forms of oppression, feminist movement develops in such a way that it holds little attraction for women who do not see sexism as their main problem. Furthermore, by theorizing racism as derivative of sexism and as something that serves sexism by dividing black and white women, Dworkin and MacKinnon deny the positive aspect of black identities. Another consequence for feminist practice is that some women are precluded from admitting the ways in which they may benefit from the oppressive social and political structures endorsed by a particular male racial grouping at the same time as they are subordinated by a male supremacist society. The danger in promoting a discourse that supports the sameness/difference dichotomy, whether it be in relation to rape or other subjects, lies in the likelihood of room being made for some women in pre-existing cultural and economic structures, while other women are further marginalized.

MacKinnon also acknowledges differences among women while still, however, assuming the existence of an essential "Woman" underlying these differences. Angela P. Harris contends that MacKinnon's search for an essential womanness leads only to the rediscovery of white womanhood. Then, she re-introduces the experiences of "Woman" as "universal truth." Within the terms of MacKinnon's dominance theory, Harris detects black women being represented as white women – only more so. She argues that MacKinnon simultaneously recognizes and shelves racism. MacKinnon ends up paying only lip-service to differences among women because her theory of rape constructs black women as "Woman"-plus, or white women with an additional burden. Therefore, as Harris recognizes, her account of rape amounts to an account of what rape means to white women masquerading as a general account of rape.[51]

Neither MacKinnon nor Dworkin seriously take into account black feminist theories of rape. Dworkin's analysis never accounts for the fact that while all women may be subject to rape as an individual experience by virtue of their being female, rape as a political act has a more complex genesis and framework. To cite an example from Rich, the rape of a lesbian woman can be seen as a means of punishing a woman's rebellion against the system of compulsory heterosexuality.[52] There are many historical testimonies from women regarding the institutionalized use of sexual assault by the police to "teach lesbians a lesson."[53] Hazel V. Carby emphasizes how rape for black women is rooted as much in color as in gender: "rape itself should not be regarded as a transhistorical mechanism of women's oppression but as one that acquires specific political or economic meanings at different moments in history."[54] The point is that to understand what rape signifies to lesbian women or black women it must be analyzed in an historically and subculturally specific context. The ahistoricity of Dworkin and MacKinnon's stance leaves us with a radically incomplete picture of rape. Their omission of black women's experiences combined with their reliance upon a simple correlation between women and "Woman," men and "Man," suggests that the position of black women or lesbian women as victims of rape are *theoretically* insignificant. Moreover, by theorizing male power as omnipresent, their analysis overlooks the critical function that rape plays in the dominant's negotiation of the relation between gender, race, sexuality, and power. Dworkin and MacKinnon's work exemplifies the need for feminists to consider the diverse perspectives on rape that are attendant upon gender differences among black and white women; otherwise feminist representations of rape will continue to reflect and reinforce white women's hegemony within and without the feminist movement.

## Erotophobes

Rape and its presumed link to women's sexual objectification has figured prominently as a subject of plays by women. Eve Lewis' play, *Ficky Stingers*, takes many of its ideas about rape straight from Dworkin and MacKinnon's brief. The play, which was originally featured as part of the 1986 Royal Court's Young Writers' Festival, adopts feminism's standard definition of rape as a metaphor for the oppression of women. Its central idea is that rape is both an individual act and a social institution that underpins male supremacy.[55] Or, as Susan Brownmiller phrased it in her now classic study of rape, *Against Our Will: Men, Women and Rape*, rape is a "conscious process of systematic intimidation by which all men keep all women in a state of fear."[56] My reading of *Ficky Stingers'* construction of male and female sexuality is not intended as a further critique of Dworkin and MacKinnon, although it may fulfill this function as well, but to further highlight how a theory of rape built upon the belief that women's sexuality constitutes a vulnerability bears negative consequences for all women as well as the whole project of feminism.

The play comprises four characters. Although Lewis gives them individual names, for much of the play they are denominated by the generic terms "Man" and "Woman," with the three female characters distinguished from each other only by numbers. Their pseudonyms emphasize that Lewis is concerned with what she sees as gender archetypes. The play's action centers on the psychological and physical degradation of "Woman." In the course of the play, we witness "Woman's" verbal, emotional, and physical violation. In the physical rape scene, "Woman" is replaced by "Woman 1" who in turn alternates speaking lines with "Woman 2." The ease with which one woman can be substituted for another and then another in this scene is meant to suggest that what we are watching onstage is no different from what routinely happens to all women.

Lewis' project is to show how gender difference restricts women's freedom and ease of movement and how the physical spaces they may occupy are circumscribed by the patriarchy via the threat of rape. At the beginning of the play, "Woman" relates how as a child she and a friend went to play at the old pond, a place where adults warned they were never to go on their own. They are not there long before they hear a hissing noise which they believe to be a water snake (an obvious phallic image) and which they fear is "coming to get us and it's dangerous." In reality, the source of the hissing sound turns out to be a dead dog. Despite scrubbing her hands with bleach and steaming water, "Woman" believes that the smell of this dog never leaves her. This is the first allusion to an extended metaphor that the play draws between dogs and women.[57] What happens to "Woman" in the following scenes warns us that women who act in a free manner, without regard to what men tell them is acceptable behavior, can end up in the same condition as the dog in the pond – even if their actions are not intended as defiance: "It wasn't defiance. We just wanted to be there," "Woman" insists.

The most significant animal metaphor comes at the end of the play in the form of a joke, also a parable, about a dog and a dragon. In a new take on the myth of Little Red Riding Hood, a little dog is walking through the woods on its way to visit its grandmother. There it meets a drunken dragon that vomits all over its head. The little dog runs away in terror, while the dragon laughs and says, "Well fuck me! I don't remember eating that!"[58] If we take the dragon as representing "Man" with "Woman" again represented as the little dog, the message conveyed by this story is that "Man" exists to devour "Woman."[59] Other imagery which renders this a plausible interpretation is "Man's" description of women as tasty birds and as so juicy that one wants to lick them like one would an ice cream. These stories also serve to illustrate the way in which *Ficky Stingers* reduces the feminine to a physicality: "Woman" is represented as existing only as body, a body which men see as a serviceable, yet potentially dangerous thing. Her assumed danger would account for Man's seeming desire to consume "Woman" as illustrated in the parable.

The way that Lewis raises the issue of women's freedom of movement within a heteropatriarchal society, particularly the rhetoric of the parable, approximates closely the language of feminist sexual-conservatism. The story proposes that behind every tree there lurks a rapist, which risks undermining the self-confidence women need to exercise their right to freedom of movement. Avedon Carol adds that such rhetoric makes it sound as if a woman *should* expect to be raped whenever she leaves her home. This could lead, once again, to rape victims being asked: "What were you doing out there? What did you expect?"[60]

Women's general independence is inseparably tied up with their sexual freedom. Granted, sexual freedom is often mistakenly equated with liberation; nevertheless, the fight for the freedom to say yes as much as for the freedom to say no must be seen as an integral part of women's liberation. The chances of winning either fight will be slim should feminist discourse undermine women's autonomy by a campaign against rape based on a generalization of male sexuality as inherently rapacious.

Compared to many plays written by women about violence against women, *Ficky Stingers* is unusual in that it actually stages a rape. Charlotte Canning describes representing rape on stage as a "chancy proposition" in which it is easily possible to portray it as pornographically erotic.[61] Lewis recognizes this possibility; discussing the play's production, she refers to the danger of the scene appearing visually titillating.[62] Her concern stems from the risk, always present to some extent in the representation of female gender, that "Woman's" body will be constructed as an image for male consumption. Given that the play's text thematically assumes the "Woman-as-victim," "Man-as-agent" model of oppression, it is possible that in staging the rape "Woman's" body will retain its traditional meaning in representation, what Jill Dolan describes as "to-be-looked-at-ness."[63] Of course, the way in which "Woman's" body is read in performance will depend on the particular dramaturgical choices of the director/actors. If the fourth wall remains unbroken, then so will the seductive power of the text, and the female body will be displayed as object/victim, a position that disallows "Woman" the power of looking back.[64]

The play treats rape as an ordinary occurrence, something only to be expected within male–female sexual relations. "Woman 1" essentially blames "Woman," for her own rape, telling her she did a "dumbassed" thing by going to his room in the first place.[65] "Woman 2," who is also date-raped by "Man," reacts as if this kind of thing needs to be taken in stride. The rape of "Woman 2" is also brushed off as insignificant by another of "Man's" sexual partners, who tells "Woman 2" how "Man" used to stuff tissues in her mouth to stop her screaming. "But she got used to it after a while. The play seems to deny the possibility of consensual intercourse. It presents female sexuality as no more than male-induced masochism. Their is no link between sexuality and pleasure: how could there be any pleasure when one assumes male sexuality to be constituted by uncontrollable violence that might at any moment break out.[66] To "make women's pursuit of heterosexual pleasure incompatible with women's happiness" is, Lynne Segal remarks, a curious way to fight women's continuing victimization.[67] Because *Ficky Stingers* was written as a piece of young women's theatre, with one assumes some educational intent, it is also a questionable way of representing the nature of women's sexual experience to young British women.

Lewis' play is problematic and deeply disturbing because the way it portrays the women's responses to being raped and their lives after being raped seems to offer women no options except silence or passive acceptance (which the play equates with self-annihilation) or madness. The women's relationships with men appear as abstracted images of ugliness and disenfranchisement – as a prolonged metaphoric rape. Consequently, there is a wound at the center of femininity that is not an anomaly, but its defining element. It is through "Woman's" sexuality, the play argues, that she is silenced. The rape drives her to a mental breakdown. She can no longer do even ordinary things like shopping without running out in a panic. She can't ride a bus because she imagines that people are intentionally touching her: "Rubbing against me, Prodding against me." She believes that people avoid her and that she is marked in some way: "like the back of my skirt were bloodstained."[68] After the rape, every aspect of her existence is marred by her sexual object status so that by the end of the play she walks around in a daze, more zombie-like than human.

Accompanied by "Woman 1," "Woman" witnesses "Man" rape "Woman 2" in an alleyway. While her first instinct is to go to the woman's aid, her friend quickly convinces her that "you can't do anything. Go home," and she drives off, apparently accepting that resisting the exercise of masculine force is futile.[69] The final scene shows her sitting in a pub listening to a song about a man trying to convince a woman to stay the night with him. Becoming more and more agitated at the words, she gets up to leave when "Man" approaches. He says one word to her, "Watcha," and she immediately sits down: "I sit back down. Like I always do. Like we always do. Sit. Sit and take it. Sit back down." She then offers to buy him a drink. Our last glimpse is of "Woman" silently wiping off the beer "Man" has spilled on her, too timid even to mention this.[70]

*Ficky Stingers* amplifies one of the fundamental weaknesses of the anti-rape/anti-porn movement: its identification of men *in toto* as the enemy and of women as the powerless prey of rabid misogynists. It demonstrates that a manichean view of gender only serves to distort the debate on women's objectification and sexual exploitation. The idea of "woman-always-already-victim" arrests the possibility for women to explore without guilt their own sexuality, whether it be in the context of straight or lesbian sex. Segal argues that "straight women, like gay men and lesbians, have everything to gain from asserting [their] desire to fuck if (and only if), when, how and as we choose."[71] Ine Vanwesenbeeck adds that "if we define the sexualization of women as objectification per se, and thereby as degrading and disempowering, we lose touch with an image of strong female (hetero) sexuality, we forget what female sexual (heterosexual) power looks and feels like, and we create difficulties for women about how to promote themselves as heterosexual beings."[72] Mainstream feminism's discourse on rape contributes little to the movement for women's liberation; for it cooperates with the dominant by using women's own sexual repression as a method of control. In this way, it contributes to the problem of women's victimization, while leaving the heteropatriarchy largely intact.

## Black Women and the Sexual Politics of Rape

The position "Woman" occupies in the Dworkin–MacKinnon model of rape, mirrored in *Ficky Stingers*, has clear racialized overtones. Judith Butler explains the problems inherent in a theory that differentiates or excludes the feminine from the masculine, namely that it reinforces "hierarchies and binarisms through a transvaluation of values by which women come to inhabit the domain of positive values."[73] I am concerned here with the way that theorizing "Woman" as the center of positive values disables an account of race bias within feminist discourse as regards the representation of rape. Through an analysis of Robbie McCauley's play, *Sally's Rape*, we shall investigate the way in which logically negating white women's participation in a racialized heteropatriarchy hampers any effort to conceptualize the inseparability of racialized sexism and rape. *Sally's Rape* identifies two of feminism's most pressing strategic problems pertaining to black/white female sexuality: (1) the different way in which black and white women are constructed and positioned in relation to rape; and (2) the connection which white women have to the socio-political ideology which has deployed rape as a tool for controlling "uppity" black women and men.[74] The play interrogates mainstream feminism's representation of rape as a specific tool of male sexual violence and an inherent part of the heteropatriarchal system that is somehow untouched by racism. This is carried out through an examination of the way that relations among black and white women are affected by their commonalities and differences in relation to rape and its representations.

*Sally's Rape* is a moderately experimental piece, coming closer to performance art than any play so far discussed. In addition to substantial sections of improvisational dialogue, it incorporates biography and music. It has an atypical structure divided into parts rather than acts or scenes, with each of the eight parts highlighting a distinct, but related subject. First presented as a work-in-progress in New York City in 1989, the published version has been largely constructed in performance. The play is also a relatively short piece and has only three characters. Robbie, a black woman originally portrayed by the author, is introduced as "the one who plays the people in her and who tells all she wants to tell," and Jeannie, a white woman, is described as the one "who plays the roles she's given." The audience, "those who witness and talk back," comprise the third character. The way in which the audience engages with the piece is central to its meaning, hence its experimental quality. The title figure actually represents two historical women: Thomas Jefferson's slave–mistress Sally and Robbie's great-great-grandmother Sally. Robbie extemporizes the character of her ancestor who was brutally assaulted by her owners and Jeannie that of Thomas' Sally, whose alleged seduction by Jefferson is portrayed as rape sugar-coated with romance. But the primary focus is on Robbie's great-great-grand-mother and how she and her female descendants have perceived and coped with her rape.

The play addresses what were once taboo subjects and which are still uncomfortable ones for some people, such as black and white women's common ancestry. Robbie confesses what has often been treated by black families as a shameful secret, a part of black women's history that had to be kept hidden: "Almost everybody in my mother's family was half white. But that wasn't nothing but some rape."[75] The casual way in which this is said epitomizes how rape was not an exceptional occurrence, but part of a larger dynamic of dominance and submission that governed all aspects of black women's lives.[76] Although blacks might conceal their descent from white men, this history could not be forgotten by black women. White women, however, have been more successful at disregarding it. Robbie tells a story about a work colleague, a white woman Ivy-league history graduate, who is incredulous at the idea that "white men did anything with colored women on plantations." The historical connection that white women, including many first- and second-wave feminists, bear to the sexual terrorism practiced by white men against black men and women has been largely overlooked by mainstream feminists.[77] According to Nellie V. McKay, these "cultural assumptions continue to reinforce majority public perceptions of rape as the violation of white women and/or white womanhood to the exclusion of black women and other women of color."[78] This is true even though black women are especially vulnerable to sexual violence because they are also targets of racial violence, which often involves sexual harassment and abuse.

Alternatively, white women have reacted to this history by adopting the mantel of liberal guilt. Jeannie suffers a kind of paralytic guilt that prevents her from addressing the past and present differences between the lived reality of one who is gendered as a black female as opposed to a white "Woman." Jeannie's strategy typifies the way that mainstream feminists have chosen to deal with racism in society-at-large and within the women's movement. Minnie Bruce Pratt designates it "cultural impersonation." She explains this as the tendency among white women to respond with guilt and self-denial to the knowledge of racism, which leads to a usurpation of the identity of the Other in order to avoid a sense of guilt or self-hatred.[79] Robbie dismisses as naïve and fruitless Jeannie's guilt and the humanist philosophy that she uses both to assuage it and to justify her belief in an essential womanness. Expressing guilt over the past is not the same as recognizing its truth, nor can guilt lend anything of value to what should be the project of a progressive feminism, that is, to heal the breach caused by past and present differences in treatment. Rather than directly addressing black women's particular forms of oppression, cultural impersonation, like metaphorization, indicates that black women are only present in the movement in the absence of their particular reality as black women. For genuine dialogue between black and white women about the sexual politics of rape to happen, feminists have to begin by acknowledging white men's historical license to rape.

Many prominent studies of rape, in addition to Dworkin and MacKinnon's, by accepting with scant criticism dominant images of sexuality, unintentionally perpetuate race-biased imagery, particularly the notion of the black-man-as-rapist. Lynne Segal notes that in dominant terms the beast of male sexuality is also the beast of darkness – *the black beast*.[80] Angela Davis points out how this representation of sexuality props up the belief that black men harbor animal-like, irresistible sexual urges, and, once this is accepted, all black people become invested with bestiality. This, in turn, intensifies the sexual objectification/exploitation of black women.[81] Focusing on some of mainstream feminism's earliest and best-known commentaries on sexuality and rape, Davis identifies the ways in which feminists have insinuated that black men are motivated in especially powerful ways to commit sexual violence against women, especially against white women, and she cites a plethora of cases where provocative and questionable statistics are used by mainstream feminist writers to suggest that the majority of rapists are black.[82] Davis targets Brownmiller's *Against Our Will* as setting the stage for the reintroduction of the myth of the black rapist into second-wave feminist discourse. As an example of the subtle racism pervading this text, she cites Brownmiller's reinterpretation of the Emmett Till case. Till, a fourteen year-old boy, was lynched for whistling at a white woman. In Brownmiller's interpretation, Till emerges as a guilty sexist intent on displaying his right to possess a woman – not a young boy responding to a dare from his friends. As we saw in the work of Dworkin and MacKinnon, *Against Our Will*, which purports to be about women's experiences of rape, actually reflects the position and perspective of only one racial group of women. Despite its wealth of research, if black women's experiences exist in Brownmiller's book, they do so only as an absence.[83]

Rape is a difficult subject for any woman to write about, and I don't mean to underestimate how tough it is for white and black women to speak across race on this topic. The dialogue on rape that takes place between Robbie and Jeannie reveals how uncomfortable and confused black and white feminist women can feel in each other's company when the subject of rape arises. Jill Lewis attributes this to the fact that the reference points of black and white women are in separate and opposed, yet for racist sexism, intrinsically complementary cultures. They are based upon different angles of the same historical process within which the sexual sense of self and of others for black and white women has evolved in contrasting ways.[84] For instance, Jeannie is of the opinion that she suffers the same commodification of her body and sexuality as Robbie – by virtue of being a woman. Whereas Robbie wants Jeannie to recognize how, in fact, she doesn't and to also admit how white society has profited and profits from the exploitation of black women's sexuality.

*Sally's Rape* examines how rape involves more than enforced sexual relations. McCauley shows how institutions can also violate women. History as a controlling institution, for example, is delineated as an arena in which the balance of power between black women and white women and men is constructed: it is depicted as perpetuating sexual violence against black women by virtue of its silences concerning their sexual exploitation.[85] Accordingly, the play equates black women speaking with history speaking so that empowering black women's speech becomes fundamental to ending their oppression. For this reason, Robbie assumes her ancestor's place on the auction block and in the cabin and the fields where she is raped and translates Sally's emotional response to these assaults for the audience: "I wanted to do this – stand naked on the auction block. I thought somehow it could help free us from this."[86] "This" refers to her body and the history of oppression written on it. Placing Robbie on the auction block, however, even in a context directed toward anti-racism, is a risky gesture, and I remain unsure whether the play succeeds in displacing the dominant culture's view of a black woman's body as sexual commodity. While I would grant that this kind of exercise, perhaps even exorcism is appropriate here, may provide a catharsis for black women, freeing any body from its history cannot be this simple or straightforward, if it is possible at all.

However, I do think that it can help to bridge historical distance. In the play, all time becomes present as Robbie psychically replays black women's collective history, thereby helping to bridge the historical space between herself and her ancestor. It is important to note that Robbie considers Sally's story to be *the* black woman's story. The play suggests that black women share a collective consciousness of sexual victimization. As Robbie speaks Sally's history, we are also meant to hear her own. This is emphasized by the degree of physical and psychological pain she experiences while she recounts the events of Sally's life. Through recitation, the rapes become so real for her that one day she finds herself screaming randomly at white men on the street: "YOU RAPED ME! GODDAMN MOTHER-FUCK! YOU RAPED ME!"[87] Robbie must find a way to limit the degree to which she interiorizes Sally's history while at the same time gaining insight from it. She does not resolve this dilemma within the course of the play, although she remains determined to discover a strategy both for self-definition and self-perpetuation in the face of past and present sexual and racial prejudice.

That the struggle is ongoing is demonstrated by the way that McCauley ends the play. She has Robbie and Jeannie walk off the stage after giving the audience instructions to furnish the final dialogue themselves. Jeannie explains: "our idea was that you were going to turn to somebody else and find out something."[88] Canning notes that plays falling within these categories frequently assume that audience members form part of the larger political community and allow the work to be affected and/or completed by the presence of the spectators.[89] Provided that the audience is composed mainly of feminist-identified women, allowing the audience to write the outcome makes the play into a potential feminist event.[90]

The play is concerned with women's speech both on a micro- and a macro-level. Talking is presented as the way that Robbie and Jeannie can transcend their differences. It is also presented as a means whereby those in the audience can effectively imagine themselves in the place of the Other or at least come to understand the Other's point of reference.[91] The play has an educational thrust aimed at realizing new relationships between black and white women. However, at several key points, McCauley gives the overall impression that ignorance is the basis of racist views, and herein lies the play's weakness. For instance, Robbie quotes her grandmother's explanation of segregation: "my grandmother taught us that white people were . . . just dumb, and when they learned something, they would be smarter about us . . . and we could get together and change the world.[92] Besides being simplistic, this explanation is also misleading; for it implies that the problem between the races is one of cultural bias, which is not the same as racism. Deborah K. Chappel comments that "Knowledge isn't enough. It only creates this façade so that the racism goes underground, becomes submerged and more subtle." For change to occur, increased awareness must be coupled to social activism.[93]

*Sally's Rape* seeks to create a new feminist knowledge out of highlighting black and white women's different and at times contesting ways of reading history, culture, gender and race, both within a theatrical and extra-theatrical frame. It recognizes that the power and violence of race domination come together in the black mind around white male rape of black women and white male lynching of black men. Nellie V. McKay writes, "With this concept deeply engraved on their psyches and the realization that white women's words remain empowered to unleash such violence, it is extremely difficult for black women to separate themselves from the history of race and to link their oppression by rape to that of white women."[94] Yet, by inviting the audience to complete the play, it ends on an optimistic note because this demonstrates a trust in the possibility of change, no easy feat given the distressing nature of its subject.

We've been trying to see the dangers to feminist movement posed by the element of biological determinism contained in mainstream feminist discourse on rape and how this element threatens black and white women in different ways. We've suggested that this position enables white women to deny their roles in the maintenance of a racialized hierarchy. Mainstream feminism's assumption that sexual difference is more fundamental than racial difference, which simply equates sexual difference with white sexual difference, has been identified as instrumental in maintaining the authority of white women's speech over the lives of black women and men. We've also suggested that mainstream feminist's inattention to the historical lineage that makes black women's experience of and relation to rape different from white women's has created an anti-rape movement which is largely irrelevant to black women's special concerns about rape and violence. *Sally's Rape* makes a strong case for concluding this to be one of the principal reasons why black women have resisted aligning themselves with mainstream feminist campaigns against violence and rape. As long as feminists continue to focus on men as the only source of harm, a strategy that simply inverts the male supremacy doctrine, then the legacy of division between black and white women will not be surmounted. Progressive feminists must work to foster an environment of trust and security, where both sides may feel safe in voicing their experiences and taking the first steps toward overcoming this legacy of division.

# 5

# *"Woman" as Subject:*
# *Negotiating Multiple Identities*

Oh where Oh where has my feminism gone
Don't you know it's chasing after
my blackness
Somewhere in the white sea
Oh where Oh where has my blacknes gone
Don't you know it's chasing after Ms. feminism
Somewhere in the white sea.[1]

## A Movement Out of Step With Itself

Cheryl L. West's poem "I Ain't the Right Kind of Feminist" articulates the dilemma that black women face when they attempt to participate in the mainstream women's movement. West experiences difficulty defining herself as both a black woman and a feminist. Her blackness appears to preclude her adoption of the title Ms. Thus, if she is to proclaim her feminism, it must be at the price of downplaying her blackness. The poem renders the term black feminist an oxymoron by placing it within the context of a white sea – a metaphor for the mainstream women's movement. West finds herself having to choose between her blackness and her feminist identity because, as the preceding chapters have sought to illustrate, the accommodation of difference within feminist discourse as it is currently structured, be it racial, class, or sexual difference, is highly problematic. Chapters 3 and 4 discussed how a black feminist identity and a middle-class identity can function as mutually incompatible constructs, both from a dominant perspective and within a black worldview. In relation to this, the idea of pure blackness which circulates in black cultural thought was mentioned; that is, blackness as an essential construct from which middle-class black feminist women may be excluded. Chapter 5 aims to further problematize the theory of a pure racial identity, black or white, or a pure gender identity.

Robert Young's *Colonial Desire: Hybridity in Theory, Culture and Race* provides a useful summary of the discourse of hybridity and its relationship to black cultural politics.[2] Young traces the emergence of hybridity as a critical term for a politics of opposition from its Bakhtinian origins through its transformation in the work of contemporary black cultural critics. Bakhtin defines the novelistic hybrid as an artistically organized system for bringing different languages in contact with one another and having as its goal the illumination of one language by another. He identifies the political import of hybridization in the moment where, within a single discourse, one voice is able to unmask the other. This is the point at which authoritative discourse may be undone.[3] Homi K. Bhabha also suggests that hybridity entails a moment of oppositional critique and the potential for resistance. In "Signs Taken For Wonders," Bhabha writes that an important change of perspective takes place when colonial power is understood to produce hybridization rather than colonial authority or the silent repression of native traditions: "It reveals the ambivalence at the source of traditional discourses on authority and enables a form of subversion, founded on that uncertainty, that turns the discursive conditions of dominance into the grounds of intervention."[4] Stuart Hall discusses hybridity in terms of its potential to call into question the integrity and universality of the sign and to open a space for contesting dominant representations of subordinate groups.

Hall's work on new ethnicities is especially relevant for my argument in this chapter because it puts forward a concept of black cultural identity in which black signifies *by virtue of* and *not despite* its hybridity. His theorization of black cultural politics interprets black experience as a "diaspora experience." He argues that locating black identity in this way carries consequences "for the process of unsettling, recombination, hybridization, . . . – in short, the process of cultural diaspora-ization . . . "[5] Young calls attention to the dialogic construction of difference in Hall's reading of black cultural politics, which he explains in Baktinian terms. Hall's theorization of blackness involves processes of merging and dialogization of ethnic and cultural differences set critically against each other, and he notes that this doubleness is necessary both theoretically and politically if hybridization is not to be mistakenly read as assuming the existence of prior, pure racial categories. Rather, it comprises active, disjunctive moments or movements of homogenization and diasporization.[6]

The importance of Hall's construction of black experience to the politics of representation lies in the value it accords to heterogeneity, in particular its force to put an end to the notion of the essential black subject. This, in turn, allows for the recognition of the "extraordinary diversity of subjective positions, social experiences and cultural identities which compose the category 'black'; that is, the recognition that 'black' is essentially a politically and culturally *constructed* category." This brings into play the recognition of the diversity and differentiation of the historical and cultural experience of black people, which inevitably entails a weakening of the notion that "race" or some composite notion of race around the term black will either guarantee the effectivity of any cultural practice or determine in any final sense its aesthetic value.[7] The general theme of this chapter is femininity and subjectivity. Following Hall and Bhabha, this chapter assumes that a subject position, conscious or unconscious, is not a unified entity. Rather, one's subjectivity is composed of multiple identities that often compete and conflict with one another. By subject position(s), I mean to convey a place from which one may speak and be heard. The subject position should be understood as a material cultural space. As such, I focus more on the conscious aspects of identity as opposed to the unconscious, and the way in which I employ the concepts subject position(s) and subjectivity is only slightly inflected by postmodern/psychoanalytic models.[8] By the use of subject position(s), I also mean to connote a political standpoint from which one may articulate and live out certain political convictions as well as define and interpret the meaning of one's own experience.[9] It is from a position as subjects in culture, I argue, that women may derive the power of self-representation; that is, the power to tell their own stories and to ensure that their stories are heard over rival and often harmful versions.[10]

I offer a reading of two plays that interrogate the notion of pure race and gender categories. *Combination Skin,* by Lisa Jones, a black American writer, examines the position of mixed-race women within the dominant racial hierarchy and explores how these women negotiate between their dominant and subcultural identities. *Chiaroscuro* by Jackie Kay, a black British writer, duplicates this theme, but with the added element of sexuality. Each play explores the connection between identity and politics, and each questions the extent to which one's identity or subject position(s) determines and/or should determine one's politics. In other words, they explore the causal and teleological connections between identity and politics.[11]

Jayne O. Ifekwunigwe describes the negotiation of a mixed-race or "metisse" identity as a form of "psychosocial struggles between subjectivity and alterity."[12] The dominant does not afford space in which a person may be a combination of black and white. Anyone not possessing the protypic phenotypic features of whiteness is seen as black even though they may have been raised in a primarily white cultural milieu. Thus, people of mixed-race are often forced to choose between rendering their white heritage invisible or, if they are able, some may choose to negate their blackness and pass literally and/or socio-culturally as white. The readings of *The Brothers, Paper Dolls,* and *Ma Rose* addressed the pressures black women face to assimilate and called attention to the fact that black people will be considered alien no matter how much of white cultural practices they take on. Rather than leading to acceptance, these plays demonstrated that assimilation enables the dominant to dilute the threat that a strong black community could pose to the status quo.

By means of its attempt to orchestrate racial identity and to maintain its position in the superior/inferior racial dichotomy, the dominant white culture apparently provides a door through which some black people, those of mixed-race, can tentatively enter into a white space. Tentative is the operative word because the measure of acceptance granted is relative and is always legislated by white power, which sets the criteria according to which one may gain entrance. Therefore not everyone will be granted honorary "white" status, nor can one be sure for how long one's provisional place is assured. In general, those who most resemble or effect to resemble a white racial and cultural proto-type get in, and the door is firmly closed on those deemed to possess too many black traits. One of the participants in Ifekwunigwe's study of mixed-race identity, Akousa, provides an example of how the dominant distinguishes between acceptable and unacceptable levels of blackness. She relates how white people assume that she will naturally desire to minimize her blackness, and she reports the frequency with which she is encouraged by them to change herself in order "to look White," for instance by covering her "black" hair with a wig. Those whose black-ness is seen as capable of being ignored, masked or contained like Akousa's are deemed acceptable. In this process of white-washing people of mixed-race, white is posited not only as the pre-eminent race, but also as the only race in so far as white cultural practices are treated as the only ones that signify.

In contrast to Akousa's experience, those people of mixed-race who cannot easily be assimilated are often encouraged to name themselves black: Ifekwunigwe calls this phenomena "black-washing." This approach is sometimes masked as a benevolent gesture, what Ifekwunigwe describes as the argument for "protective coloration." The idea is that black people are better off associating with their own kind because there is safety in numbers. Group solidarity certainly helps provide safeguards against racism. Nevertheless, there is a substantial psychological risk for an individual who represses either the black (or white) part of her/his identity as opposed to working toward psycho-logically integrating them. Both black-washing and white-washing could lead to self-hatred and identity confusion. As Ifekwunigwe points

out, more often than not an individual's home background is predominantly white or black, and thus, one's "choice" of blackness (or
whiteness) as an identity may result in a substantial part of one's
psychosocial foundation being eroded.[13]

Running parallel to the dominant white culture's desire for its practices to stand as a goal toward which all races will strive, Ruth
Frankenberg identifies a cultural and legislative history that constructs
whiteness as a biologically pure category. Chapter 4 referred to
Frankenberg's interpretation of whiteness as a position of racial
neutrality.[14] The construction of whiteness as a racially unmarked category logically leads to its designation as a pure racial and cultural
category. A desire to maintain this purity explains why dominant
culture assigns the majority of mixed-race people to the black race.
Another way in which the dominant maintains the purity of whiteness
as a category is by postulating blackness as a permeable and therefore,
a contaminated category. When people of mixed-race who do not
measure up to the caucasian yardstick are classified as black, blackness
is made to function as a catch-all category, a kind of racialized waste-
bin.

Trinh T. Minh-Ha notes how the status of minority cultures as náme-
able goes alongside their marginalization from the dominant.[15] Among
Ifekwunigwe's collection of ethnographic narratives, Akousa's again
stands out as particularly attuned to this kind of dominant strategic
move: "I think at the end of the day, White society has never accepted
me. They've seen me as a contamination to their stock. Diseased person,
and even worst than havin' two Black parents . . . "[16] This narrative
suggests the way that racism may work to coerce rather than encourage
some into identifying with their black cultural heritage as opposed to
their white racial and cultural roots. Using the word "coerced" does not
mean to suggest that people would not otherwise value their blackness
and wish to identify as black. However, as the preceding chapters have
demonstrated, whether one is a black woman, a lesbian woman, or a
white woman can signify dramatic differences in one's life chances.
Because in dominant terms blackness is seen as an inferior racial designation, a person thus categorized faces the social and economic
disadvantages which society imposes upon people of color.[17]

## Women on the Borders of "Womanhood": Negotiating Race, Sex, and Gender(s)

Lisa Jones' *Combination Skin* demonstrates how these two contradictory
strands of dominant racial ideology – the desire to hang-out the carrot

of assimilation and the desire to maintain the fiction of race as a biological category – are in constant play.[18] It provides ample evidence of the zeal with which the dominant protects the borders of "Womanhood" from the threat of racial contamination. Jones' award-winning play, first produced in 1986 in New York City and again in 1991 and 1992, belongs to the genre of "passing literature." She borrows the genre to "interrogate America's contemporary constructions of race." She describes her play as "an exploration of the tragic mulatto archetype . . . It's also a send-up of assimilation and the sugar plums of "crossover" success offered to black artists in the eighties."[19] The setting is a television game show – "The $100,000 Tragic Mulatto." The time is the late 1990s. The game show functions along the lines of a beauty pageant, with the women competing for a one-year modeling contract for Crossover Dreams Fade Cream. In addition to fitting the appearance of the mulatto stereotype, the winner is determined by who can tell the "most ghoulish . . . most muckraking mulatto tragedy."[20] In this way, Jones locates the real drama of the play in the language, through which, she says, a "war of representation" is being fought. The contestants are referred to as Specimens One, Two and Three. They are caricatures of the tragic mulatto archetype, and they are meant to be symbolic figures of different kinds of black womanhood rather than individual black women. Physically, they are distinguishable only by a difference in skin tone. Politically they are more clearly differentiated. Each Specimen/black-woman has come to terms with her blackness in a different way, and each has a distinctive way of reconciling her black and white identities.

*Sally's Rape* chronicles the history of black women's institutionalized rape under slavery, as a result of which many black women gave birth to and raised the children of white men. It draws attention to the fact that the existence of mixed-race children was often treated as a shameful secret within black communities. Bi-racial children were also denied outright by white communities who feared interracial mixing as a threat to the power structure in which race, class and gender are inextricably linked. *Combination Skin* draws attention to a new openness in mixed-race discourse within black and white cultures, but one that is not necessarily a good thing. Now the bi-racial woman, like the bi-sexual woman, has become quite fashionable: "she's a hot item these days. From the slave quarters to the big house, from Convent Avenue to Hollywood, she's on everyone's lips. She used to be a family skeleton, a dark secret. But now she's a box-office thorough-bred."[21] However, this frequently exploitative emergent discourse must still compete with the residual notion of bi-raciality as an ignominious identity. Frankenberg writes about the terrain of whiteness as a subjective location; she states that "the white subject and the white imaginary . . . by no means confine themselves to the present in their construction, but rather draw consciously and unconsciously, on moments in the racial order long past in material terms."[22] *Combination Skin* posits the same as true for blackness as a subjective location and in the space occupied by women of mixed-race. To emphasize this point, Jones opens the play with a series of historical and contemporary images of racial mixing, which are flashed across an electronic billboard as the show's theme music – a medley of blues, doo-wop, spirituals, and black pop – plays in the background. The images juxtapose a black and white cultural view of mixed-race identity, ranging from a black Christ, images of mulattos from family photographs, magazines, movie posters, and book sleeves, to advertisements for skin-lightening products. The final image is a headline from *Ebony Magazine* which reads "HOW BLACK IS BLACK?"[23]

The play's three journeys into the black unconscious, via the Specimen's personal histories, reveal how each Specimen/black-woman must confront both the black and white mulatto historical legacies in order to craft what is felt to be an agreeable and authentic subjective narrative. Specimen Three, represents the ultimate passing artist. She works to completely separate herself from what she sees as the boundaries of a black racial and cultural inheritance. Her mulatto story, like all the stories, is framed within the context of the black uncon-scious (which Jones uses as a check and/or balance against the Specimens' conscious subject-position). It illustrates the degree to which she acts under the control of the white male gaze. Ashamed of her black-ness, Specimen Three seeks to annihilate it through union with a "white-collar hubby" or a "white knight in his white castle." Only a white man can "fulfill my great white hopes with his big white whip-ping stick," she says, meaning that only the white man's gaze can affirm her as desirable."[24] Her sense of self and the social position she pursues closely resembles that of the classic mulatto girl in the film *Imitation of Life*, only Specimen Three would forego the tragic rejection by the white male. She knows too well the story where the mulatto woman is used sexually and then discarded. Hence, she aims to follow the white man not only into the bedroom, but also into the networks of power – the White House and Whitehall – by becoming Mrs. White. For this, she will watch as the white man "at his white-walled office down on White Street in White Plains, white America, whites out what's left of black America"; that is, she would negate even the possibility of representing blackness.[25] Specimen Three enacts Foucault's theory of the instru-mental gaze, which is both the looking of authority and an identificatory gaze whereby the gaze of authority is internalized. That Jones makes her the game's clear winner illustrates that the box-office thoroughbred referred to earlier is the whiter-than-white black woman – the figure who confirms rather than interrogates the white male sexual gaze.

Specimen One represents those women who make capital from their honorary white status by appropriating and commodifying aspects of black cultural life which they have never shared. Unlike Specimen Three, who grew up poor in an urban housing project, Specimen One has always enjoyed class privilege; she "hails from Old Boy, Connecticut, where she spent her formative years in a split-level colonial-style home in a predominantly Caucasian neighborhood, where the daddies head for power street in the morning . . . "[26] Her advantageous position in the social hierarchy enables her to profit from her dual identity by sublimating her blackness in literary representations. Through her work, she sells a set of values, attitudes, and ideas about black selfhood that perpetuate racial, sexual and economic inequalities – one of her principal black male characters is named King Kong. She lacks the frame of reference and the experience to accurately represent black people because she has no black friends. Her sole contact with black figures comes through the characters she creates in her novels. And these characters are based on a knowledge of black culture she has gleaned from research conducted while visiting "black" parts of the world. She writes "black" novels for commercial reasons: "some little birdie told me it was important to write about *The* black experience or I wouldn't get published . . . "[27] Thus, she speaks for blacks rather than as a member of a black community, or rather, she speaks to blacks from a position of patronage, not social equality. This is evidenced by the way in which she supports the black arts. Just as she figuratively colonizes black history and culture for monetary gain, she literally procures it in commodity form. Her hobbies are travelling the world collecting "primitive artifices to decorate her Manhattan pied-a-terre," also described as "coon art."[28]

Specimen One prefers to consider herself "strictly a member of the human race." She lays claim to practically every ethnicity except black, describing her background as: "my mother's French, German, and Caribbean, and my father's Venezuelan from the coast. Actually, you know, I don't think I have much American Negro in me at all."[29] She is indignant when the game-show hostess persists in querying her on race. She prefers to speak the polite middle-class discourse of race, characterized by color-blindness. Frankenberg describes color-blindness or color-evasiveness, the strongest element in current American public race discourse, as a mode of thinking organized around an effort not to see race differences.[30] The game-show hostess summarizes it as "color is a state of mind."[31] The idea that noticing a person's color is not a good thing to do, even an offensive thing to do, suggests that color, which here means non-whiteness, is bad in and of itself.

The example of Specimens Three and One may give the impression that *Combination Skin* argues for the existence of a black feminine experience that is both unified and knowable. In fact, Jones represents black feminine subjectivity as far too complex, uneven, and unstable to be reduced to any unitary structure. This comes through most clearly in Specimen Two's story, the play's most significant narrative. This narrative denies that experience can be compartmentalized and argues that it is impossible to distinguish which parts of one's identity stem from one's black or white heritage. Despite a physical appearance that would easily allow her to pass as white, Specimen Two adopts a strong black political identity and professes a willingness to accept the social disadvantages that go along with it. She models herself on powerful black female images, such as Sojourner Truth, and uses the game-show as a platform from which to argue her case for dismissing entirely the "blood question': "I only came on this show to let you know that some honkie capitalist media running dogs are in the next room cashing in on this bogus mulatto stuff."[32] But likening her experience to that of Sojourner Truth, Rosa Parks and Queen Mother Moore rings a false note. Whether or not she decides to pass as white, the point is that she, unlike the women she emulates, is better able to determine her experience in the race–gender system by virtue of having the choice to pass. Her white racial/cultural ties bring with them certain privileges, and these privileges affect the degree to which Specimen Two can empathize with the kind of discrimination and oppression that black women who cannot pass daily face.

No doubt, the vociferous manner in which she argues for sisterhood and her support for an African Rainbow coalition stems from her belief that, as a woman of mixed-race, she must justify her membership in the black community. From this insecurity grows the mistaken and contradictory opinion that in espousing a black subject position she must and can purge herself of all elements of her white heritage. In spite of her professed allegiance to a rainbow of black identities, Specimen Two aspires to construct her subjectivity upon a foundation based on "blood," speaking of the black race as the "chosen people." Her black father, whom she meets in her trek through the unconscious and whom she imagines as a famous jazz musician living in exile, points out the contradictions in her account of her own identity. Rather than negotiating a subjective space in which she can live out both sides of her self, she searches for blackness within the space of a physical relationship (descent from a black father) and a geographical setting (Africa). She performs a similar move by naming Nigeria as her birthplace, when in fact she was born in Palo Alto, California. In her father's words, she seeks blackness in the "seed," which, he points out, has been literally his only contribution to her make-up: "that wicked witch of the west, your mother, claimed you years ago."[33] The critical consciousness out of which she must fashion her subjective identity has been predominantly shaped by her white mother's western European worldview.[34]

Specimen Two attempts both to forge and erase the boundary lines demarcating a racialized physical or geographical space and a psychological or subjective space. However, because the geography of race and its psychology intersect and are in flux, the relation between these two spaces cannot be separated out, nor can one be submerged beneath the other. Judith Butler puts it this way: in the construction of identity, a constitutive or relative outside is composed of a set of exclusions that are nevertheless *internal* to that system as its own nonthematizable necessity.[35] Any counter-representation of identity Specimen Two might construct will be invalid if it is constructed without reference to her initial socialization into white culture. And her father's reaction to her makes clear that no amount of devotion to black solidarity could gain her the acceptance and approval she seeks from the black community were blackness determined by blood. In his mind, her blood is "too thin." You'll never be black," he tells her. And you'll never know what it's like."[36] We can trace in the play how racial essentialism leads to cultural racism. Specimen Two's view of community merely replicates the dominant belief that openness to racial and cultural differences signifies racial contamination and cultural corruption.

What comes through most clearly in Specimen Two's narrative of identity is the sense of cultural rootlessness or homelessness that may result when one's subject position straddles two diverse cultural spaces. Despite her declarations of black nationalist pride, her story betrays the self-conscious manner of her attempt to live as part of a black community. She is the play's saddest character, the one who is the most psychologically and politically unsettled from her appearance on the show. She never realizes that the artificial boundary that she draws between her black and white identities, positing one as the insider and one as the outsider, necessarily contains the possibility of acquiring knowledge or understanding of self. Her inability to cross-over the racialized boundaries of womanhood, to subjectively synthesize her blackness and whiteness, results in a split self, a woman who ends up feeling nowhere at home.

Jones declares one of her goals to be creating a comfortable place in Capitalism for women of mixed-race in the post-millennial world. That she seeks to create a multi-race subjective space first by destabilizing and undermining the "purity" of whiteness is understandable.

However, simply deconstructing the category of whiteness is not the same as theorizing a convincing alternative model of mixed-race identity. While the play aims to help women negotiate between a self-defined standpoint and image of self and the larger white and black cultural narratives of subjectivity for "mulattos," it never moves far enough beyond deconstructing white cultural representations of the mulatto and toward providing positive self-definitions of mixed-race identities. The play is more successful at showing how black femininity depends on white femininity for its meaning than showing how white women's subjectivity is produced as an effect of the dominant's construction of a black female Other. Thus, Jones' Specimens largely remain objects rather than subjects of representation, and as such, they cannot serve as foundation models for the construction of a mixed-race feminist epistemology; nor can they point the way toward a primary and constitutive new race–gender order.

## Difference: What Makes a House a Home

Genevieve Fabre describes how black theatre has often endowed cultural identity with the attributes of a protagonist, one alternately threatened or scorned, defended or sought after . . . This kind of theatre represents cultural identity as a "difficult conquest, not as something granted."[37] Jackie Kay's *Chiaroscuro*, written for The Theatre of Black Women in 1985, falls into this genre of black drama: cultural identity is not only its subject matter, but also its main character. It resembles *Combination Skin* in that it is shaped by the politics of negotiating multiple identities and self-representation, only it extends the factors involved to include lesbianism as well as bi-raciality.[38] The play works against a notion of hybridity as a cultural description that always carries, according to Young, an implicit politics of heterosexuality.[39] Kay recalls that through all the drafts of the play she was obsessed with naming, with the question of "what . . . we call ourselves as lesbians and black women." Because if we are to change our condition, "we have to examine who we say we are and how much of that has been imposed."[40] The following reading of *Chiaroscuro* focuses upon those textual elements that are informed by and which may, in turn, inform the debate surrounding the politics of definition and identity.

*Chiaroscuro* has been characterized as a "coming out play."[41] The play does depict women coming to terms with their sexuality, most notably Aisha's should I/shouldn't I be a lesbian internal dialogue. However, unlike Jill Posener's *Any Woman Can* and Catherine Kilcoyne's *Julie*, both early liberation plays which imply that conditions will change for the

better once women openly declare their lesbianism, *Chiaroscuro* demonstrates that coming out – and living out one's lesbianism – is less
straightforward within a multiple framework of identities. Echoing
West's poem, Anna Lee, a lesbian-identified black women, attests: "to
acclaim all of who I am . . . puts me in conflict with each of the groups
from which I could reasonably expect support and nurturance"[42] The
women in *Chiaroscuro* struggle to recognize and accept their same-sex
feelings while combating the disadvantages of being women, black, and
lesbian in a sexist, racist, and homophobic society. To speak of it simply
as a coming out play does not do justice to the complexity of the issues
that it addresses.

The play opens with each of its four characters – Aisha, Beth, Opal,
and Yomi – recounting the origin of her name as a means of reassessing
her identity. Beth is the child of an Afro-Caribbean father and a white
English mother. She is a middle-class university graduate, and she is
lesbian. Opal, her partner, never knew her parents. She is also of mixed-
race, and Beth is her first woman lover. Yomi, second-generation
Anglo-Nigerian, is a single mother, who is both naïve and biased in her
opinion of lesbians. Aisha, a black woman from a working-class background, secretly flirts with the idea of a lesbian affair with Beth; it is she
who works to hold the group of women together, even though Beth is
the one who sees best the connection between the devaluation of differences and racial, sexual and other forms of oppression.

The play is highly ritualistic with music and dance skillfully woven
into the narrative. Music in particular, Fabre writes, has always been
connected with various activities in the everyday life of blacks, and this
ensures its functionality. It is the mark of black art that seeks a social
role.[43] The ritual has two functions: to distance the play from white
dramatic traditions and to make the world of the play resemble a place
of sisterhood and communion, such as black women have traditionally
found within the black church. The narrative itself takes its form from
the black oral tradition. Kay allows each character to tell her own story.
They are stories that the women have told before and will tell again: time
and space are not specific to the action. Sandra Freeman reads it as a
"symbolic reconstruction of the lived-through experience of black
lesbians." All four characters have "invented themselves"; what they
perform for the audience is the story of their invention, arrived at
through a recognition, an acceptance of their racial, sexual heritage.[44]

For Aisha, the stories mark the start of a journey toward a shared
homeplace, a way that the women can move on from their originary
homespaces and reinvent themselves. Homeplace is a concept similar
to family and community. And like the black definition of family, that
of homeplace is pliant. Also like family, homeplace does not entail

necessarily blood-bonds or a male presence; for example, Yomi and her daughter are not seen as a broken family unit. On the contrary, Yomi says, "we are a whole family, . . . me and her."[45] Homeplace is where the women can anchor their identity and learn to love themselves, knowing that they will be accepted in all their differences. Although this sense of community is not achieved at the end of the play, the audience is left with a strong feeling that the women are on the right path toward discovering that they "are different from one another but that we still have something to share."[46]

Beth's story begins with her recalling that she was named after a grandmother who was "taken from Africa to America and raped often": "My Daddy told me he called me Beth because my grandmother's African name was whipped out of her. This was the name the white people gave her with welts in her black skin. He said *that* history had to be remembered too."[47] Beth's search for a new name involves a negotiation with her black familial and cultural history. Her story illustrates why it is important for blacks to remember "that history': because it foregrounds the extent to which their identity has been constructed within the parameters of white cultural institutions. She further recalls that despite the pain and violence that informed her grandmother's existence, she was a strong woman, "a woman who made change, who was change herself."[48] On the one hand, Beth's cultural inheritance is one of overt oppression; on the other hand, it is marked by resistance in the face of oppression. Through an engagement with the history and traditions of black people, the possibility of reshaping her subject position begins to seem feasible to Beth. Thus, she represents a woman in transition, one who, paradoxically, is drawing the strength to move toward the liberation of self-definition from a history of brutality and degradation.

Beth can draw upon her grandmother's history to affirm her sense of identity as a black woman. However, her lesbianism threatens to invalidate her assumption of black as a political identity. Jeffrey Weeks reminds us that sexual identities are in part self creations, but that "they are creations on ground not freely chosen but laid out by history."[49] *Chiaroscuro* theatrically plays out Weeks' assertion: its theme treats the way that one's gender and race, as well as class, delimit one's choice of sexual identity and the extent to which one can comfortably live out that identity. James T. Sears explains that black lesbians and gays often experience their racial and sexual identities as incompatible. Their efforts to define themselves are complicated by the fact that the "twoness of identity" reflected in being black and gay, even more so than the fact of being black and middle class, is not easily sustainable in either the black or gay communities.[50] The tendency within the black community to postulate homosexuality as a "white thing" is reflected in Yomi's reaction when she encounters some black lesbians on a women's retreat; shocked, she comments: "I didn't think we produced them."[51] Yomi would prefer to believe that Opal is simply going through an experimental phase. This is made easier as she assumes that there is such a thing as a "REAL LESBIAN," that is, "a tall angular looking woman white with men's things on."[52] Here, blackness and lesbianism are posited as mutually exclusive categories. Yomi provides a powerful example of the exclusions and repressions that can at times constitute the notion of black women's homeplace.

Jewelle Gomez and Barbara Smith speak of the unique problems faced by black lesbians. First, homophobia in the black community prevents them from representing themselves as uplifters of the race, particularly if they are childless, and, as we have seen in *Re/membering Aunt Jemima* and *Shakin' The Mess Outta Misery*, this image forms an important element of black women's identity. Second, in contrast to many white women, especially feminist-identified women, black lesbians are nevertheless likely to feel a need to uphold the black family given the close connection between extended families and the concept of black community, a situation which can lead to much personal anguish.[53] For a Black woman (or man) to make an unconventional sexual choice is to risk being branded a counterfeit black, or as Beth puts it a "sham." Often, to be *out in* the black community still means to be *out of* the black community. Yomi and Aisha rehearse the black community's standard homophobic reaction: "Wanted for murder! For killing off the race," which alludes to the belief that the dominant encourages homosexuality among blacks in order to limit black reproduction. This intolerance produces detrimental effects both at the level of the personal and the political. Individually, one perceives one's identity as bifurcated because the price for feeling at home in the black community is the denial of one's sexual difference. And this division makes activist coalitions among sub-cultural groups more difficult to achieve. As did *Combination Skin*, *Chiaroscuro* illustrates how inhabiting two contexts critically may lead to a sense of totally lacking roots or any space where one can feel at home.

Aisha's dinner party demonstrates the way in which Beth has had to forego asserting her sexual identity and, in the same way as Specimen Two, feels the need to distance herself from her white heritage so that others may feel at ease in her presence. The product of a bi-racial union, Beth must struggle toward self-definition against the ideological baggage that the term "half-caste" carries among blacks and whites. Rejected as "Other" by the white community because she is only "half-White," Beth has met with an equally demeaning view of herself among Blacks. To escape a sense of psychological fragmentation, she makes a futile gesture to suppress the signs of her whiteness, trading Dostoyevsky for James Baldwin and Dire Straits in favor of blues, funk, and jazz. This can be compared to Specimen Two's rewrite of her birth-place and genealogy.[54] As a result of her bi-racial background, Yomi treats Beth as a suspect character, while condescendingly voicing pity for what she calls Beth's "dilemma." She even resents it when Beth wears a shawl from Nairobi, believing her to be impersonating black-ness. What Yomi fails to perceive, however, is her own collusion, albeit passive, in the perpetuation of Beth's struggle. She complains because women like Beth are always angry, always on the defensive. Beth asks her: "have you ever thought about who puts me there?"[55]

In her autobiographical essay entitled "Identity: Skin Blood Heart," Minnie Bruce Pratt writes that it is our fear of the "losses" that makes us resistant to welcoming difference into those places that we call home. She discloses how her membership in the "unknowing majority" (read white, middle-class, and Christian) has constructed barriers in the way of communicating with women of different cultures, races, and classes. She admits to fear as that which has hampered her destruction of those barriers: "As I try to strip away the layers of deceit that I have been taught, it is hard not to be afraid that these are like wrappings of a shroud and that what I will ultimately come to in myself is a disinte-grating, rotting nothing. And my feeling is based in the reality that the group identity of my culture has been defined, often, not by positive qualities, but by negative characteristics, by the absence of."[56] However, it is not only the dominant that is capable of constructing itself in terms of what it is not: those who constitute the "absence of" in the dominant also build communal identities based upon what their communities will not allow inside. The discrimination and repression experienced by people within subordinated groups can lend them a greater sense of identity as contingent, that is, a fragile construct. The fear of difference, which, in part at least, powers the dominant, may permeate the subor-dinate in such a way that it generates an extreme fear of difference. This helps explain Yomi's antagonistic attitude toward Beth when she reveals her bi-racial background and toward Beth and Opal because of their lesbianism.

Because she was abandoned as a child, Opal feels the most acute need for a homeplace. For this reason, unlike Beth, she is more willing to make her homeplace in a closet. She is the only character who cannot give the lineage of her name, other than to say she thinks that she was named after an old nurse at the home who wore opal earrings all the time. Estranged from her subjective history, she seeks the security of an unconditional love, more parental than romantic, from her relationship

133

with Beth. Opal cannot find the comfort of feeling at home in all her racial and sexual differences among her closest friends. For this reason, she wants Beth to promise they are "forever" because, she tells her, "You're the only family I have, Beth, the only one I can call home."[57] As a result of growing up in an institutional setting, Opal has always felt unwanted. Her desire to belong makes her act the chameleon: at times, she will say, do or be whatever she feels will ensure acceptance. She fears to live openly as a lesbian: "even though I have no family, I still turn my insides out, when I imagine what they would say, the old school friends, the old home friends, the nurses and doctors and all the anonymous, who should mean Nothing . . . "[58]

The story Kay writes for Opal may be understood in terms of Bhabha's category of the "unhomely," which he argues, resonates in fictions that negotiate the powers of cultural difference in a range of transhistorical sites. "Unhomeliness" is that condition of extra-territorial and cross-cultural initiations, in which the "domestic space becomes sites for history's most intricate invasions." And, Bhabha goes on to say, "uncannily, the private and the public become part of each other, forcing upon us a vision that is as divided as it is disorienting."[59] We can see clearly how for Opal the borders between home and world become blurred and confused.

Growing up within the confines of a white institutional space has also implanted in Opal the idea that to be black is to be inferior and unacceptable. As a child, she fantasized that she was white:

> My face was a shock to itself. The brain in my head thought my skin white and my nose straight. It imagined my hair was this curly from twiddling it. Every so often I saw me: milky coffee skin, searching eyes, flat nose. Some voice from that mirror would whisper: nobody wants you, no wonder. You think you're white till you look in me. I surprised you, didn't I. I'd stop and will the glass to change me.[60]

Opal shares the same dream as *Combination Skin's* Specimen Three: an idyllic white middle-class suburban existence. "When I was a kid I used to have these fantasies of me and my lively middle class white husband and our children. I even had names for my children: pauline, graham and amanda."[61] At the beginning of Act Two, the audience acts as a mirror for Opal's image of herself: the same "inferior" image she relates above stares back at her. This reflects how the idea of blackness as second-rate comes from and is perpetuated by society at large, but also, given that this moment occurs within a feminist theatrical space, it suggests that some feminist women invalidate racial difference by acting in alliance with color hierarchies.

Kay contends that one of her main interests in writing the play was to "show how difficult communication is in a racist and homophobic society." She asks, "Can these four women communicate or not?"[62] My answer is, for much of the play, no. And I would attribute the reason for this to the conception of difference as profoundly disturbing that predominates in their world. This is also one of the reasons why the women in *Combination Skin* cannot connect. Each of the women, in denial about her own difference, has cut herself off from a significant part of her identity, and in an effort to assert their right of place in the dominant order, Specimens One and Two feel the need to absent themselves from any noticeably black cultural space. In *Chiaroscuro*, Kay argues that feminists must build "new places" where women may communicate in all their difference and that the meaning of being different must be transformed within the context of these new spaces. The play encourages women to ask themselves what image they throw back at women of mixed-race, at black or lesbian women, or any women who are in some way different from themselves and others in their group. Do we, like Yomi, tell these women that they are "unnatural" or "something terrible?"

## Learning to Dance as Sisters

The idea of difference as a negative component, one that can only disrupt the progress of feminism, which is current within mainstream feminist discourse, has proven a formidable obstacle to women's struggle for social equality. Generally, mainstream feminism addresses women's differences in two ways: they are overlooked or the voices of difference are used as a metaphor for the oppression of "Woman." By erasing or suppressing difference, mainstream feminism seeks to inscribe women of subordinate groups in a narrative of subjectivity that affords them no space for expressing their own concerns or strengthening their sense of identity. The motive underlying the silencing of difference is the desire to maintain existing power relations among those inside and outside the category "Woman." When women who fall outside this category attempt to tell their stories of oppression, they are accused of jeopardizing the struggle for gender equality by breaking ranks.

West ends her poem with an invitation:

> Come dance with me sister feminist
> Let us dance in the movement
> Let my blackness catch your feminism
> Let your oppression peek at mine.

The kind of "dance" envisioned by West, a women's movement that offers a significant space to all kinds of feminists, necessitates the recognition of difference as a positive dynamic. Mainstream feminism characterizes asymmetry as negative and divisive in an exclusionary move that replicates heteropatriarchal values. In this way, mainstream feminists have created a Dance which, if black lesbians or any women who are not "Woman" wish to join, requires them to follow in the footsteps of a largely white, heterosexual, middle-class agenda. Audre Lorde submits that women of subordinate groups must define themselves, or they will continue to be defined by others, for others' use and consequently, to their own detriment.[63] Feminist discourse must empower women to write the self and give them the means to inhabit comfortably the in-between spaces of hybrid identities if we are to forge a progressive women's movement, one in which all women can achieve the status of full participants.

# 6

## Infiltrating "Woman": Butch/Fem Lesbian Subjectivity

I like to think that we can play the part and comment on it at the same time. That we can put on femmeness in a way that signals the fact that we know we are being femme. There is a space between the photographic image and the real thing. It's in that misfit or crack that I like to think you can see the resistance.

*Lois Weaver*[1]

### Woman as Discursive Subject

Chapter 5 broached the issue of lesbian subjectivity in relation to negotiating gender, race, and sexual identities. Chapter 6 moves the lesbian subject center stage, specifically the subjectivities of butch and fem. Butch/fem, of all the models of lesbianism current today, best demonstrates how lesbian references may be subversively encoded in dominant discourse, despite meaning being organized and regulated according to a heterosexual paradigm. It has been argued that progressive feminists must reverse the trend whereby difference is posited as disruptive and/or threatening to feminist movement and theorize difference as a positive dynamic. This chapter aims to do this in relation to lesbian sexuality and desire by exploring the potential for subverting the category "Woman" which inheres within the constructions of butch and fem sexuality. Through an analysis of the work of the celebrated American theatre group Split Britches, a theoretical elaboration of how gender and sexuality are constructed specifically within the lesbian discourse of butch/fem is offered and the promise these constructions may harbor for establishing an alternative subject position for women is addressed.[2] Butch/fem subjectivities afford feminists an opening through which they may establish a reconfigured feminist subject space for women.[3] In order to better discern how these roles reconfigure dominant representations of masculinity and femininity, they are theorized separately, showing how each occupies a distinct relation to the poles of sexual difference.[4] It is their firm alliance with the poles of sexual difference that lends them their subversive potential.

If we are to understand how the discourse of butch/fem may appertain to the creation of a feminist subject, or indeed, to the acceleration of its inception, we must be able to negotiate between that vision of butch/fem held by theorists, who would utilize these roles for more purely conceptual concerns, and the view of those who live out these roles. In addition to Split Britches' *Beauty and the Beast, Upwardly Mobile Home*, and *Belle Reprieve*, personal and historical accounts of butch/fem are employed in conjunction with literary ones. It is important to know who created butch/fem roles, what historical factors have shaped their construction, and how they have been perceived by those women who identify with them if theoretical formulations are to be grounded satisfactorily in practice.[5] Conceptions of butch/fem as expressed in lesbian personal narratives are treated as both historical and political texts, as being encompassed within the larger body of contemporary lesbian feminist works. The perspective here derives from a conviction – shared by Judith Roof – that configurations of lesbian sexuality are dispersed and reflected through discourses that range from theory to "street language" and not in any vastly different form.[6]

## The Butch/Fem Debate

Because butch/fem roles are a hotly contested subject within lesbian–feminism, before addressing the plays it is necessary to set out the terms of the debate as well as my own position within it. The current revalidation of butch/fem which began in the 1980s represents a dangerous political development to some, while for others it symbolizes a liberatory practice. Whereas the former hold that women's culture and values, especially in regard to sex, are different from and better than men's, the latter argue that women's sexual feelings have been repressed by the heteropatriarchy, and therefore women must adopt those practices which historically have been male prerogatives and adapt them to their own needs.

Sheila Jeffreys, a leading critic of butch/fem, treats the roles as anachronisms, as the practices of women in the 1950s and '60s who simply did not know any better. She attributes its continued practice to those who are unfortunate enough to live in "less trendy areas, geographically and politically," those areas less affected by the women's movement and Gay Liberation. Alternatively, she assigns responsibility for its survival to recalcitrant women on the sexual fringe, women who have been corrupted by the pseudo-liberatory practices of gay men. She concludes that the only theoretical support that exists for these roles springs from a male sexual-freedom agenda that is based on "internalized homophobia, gender fetishism, power imbalance, and sexual objectification."[7] Jeffreys ranks among those who oppose butch/fem because they perceive it as an expression of "excessive sexuality," which, as we saw in the work of Dworkin and MacKinnon, is something conservative feminists deem a male trait.

Butch/fem supporters point out that these identities do arise from a sexual definition of lesbianism, but argue that therein lies their value.[8] In the discussion of lesbian motherhood in chapter 1, a link was drawn between the fear of female sexuality and disapproval of lesbian motherhood. And in chapter 3, attention was drawn to the way in which some campaigners against pornography and violence against women dwelt upon the dangers of sex and women's supposed sexual powerlessness. Part of what we see in objections to butch/fem, particularly Jeffreys', is a similar feminist conceptualization of sexual danger, one which is informed by the dominant disapproval and fear of women's sexuality. Lesbian–feminism in the 1970s and '80s comprised a conservative strain which, while purporting to offer women the pattern for a solely feminine sexual practice, in fact, advanced lesbianism as a sexless practice. Lesbian–feminist orthodoxy suggested that women might sleep together – *so long as nothing got wet*. This version of the conservative conception of women as sexless in nature rendered lesbianism a metaphor. Jeanne Cordova, a butch, attests that "feminism had saved me and shoved me back into the closet. Feminism rescued women but subverted lesbianism."[9] One of butch/fem's most valuable features for lesbian sub-culture is the way in which it overturns the taboos surrounding women's sexuality and provides the means for developing a liberated female sexual discourse.

Complaints against butch/fem also arise from its presumed resemblance to traditional heterosexual relationships in which the female partner is positioned as subordinate to the male. The argument is that the male/female polarity, around which sexual difference is constructed, proves one of dominance and submission. Any erotic communication conducted within the terms of this polarity must necessarily be damaging for women as it is based on the eroticizing of power difference. According to Jeffreys, this is the reason why difference cannot be treated as benign.[10] However, it is difficult to sustain an objection to butch/fem on the grounds that it superficially duplicates a heterosexual model. Foucault's assertion that ideology is neither straightforwardly imposed by those in power nor straightforwardly internalized by subordinate groups and that all relations of power necessarily afford the possibility of resistance should be borne in mind, and it is not conceivable that one might construct new sexual categories ex nihilo. To reiterate a point raised in chapter 1, the identities one may take on are "always already" extant in some form in society. If new categories of identity are to be constructed, they must emerge from a process whereby existent ones are manipulated.

If we accept gender and sexuality as culturally constructed, it follows that they are constructed within existing power relations. In spite of operating within this power matrix, the discourse of butch/fem is not sentenced to replicating unchallenged relations of domination. Within the discourse of butch/fem, context is everything, and feminists must be careful not to conflate the power relations of heterosexuality with those of the sex act itself. Power is experienced in very different ways in butch/fem relationships as opposed to relationships between straight men and women. Therefore, alternative meanings should be possible. Furthermore, cultural symbols can be used for either radical or conservative objectives. Whether or not women's use of masculine and feminine codes is regressive or progressive depends on the context in which they are deployed and the effect toward which their use is geared. For example, most women who identify as butch describe their use of masculine imagery as a way of signaling the manner in which they like to arouse their partners.[11] Similarly, many fems assert that their feminine appearance signifies a particular way in which they want to be aroused; as one fem attests: "My femme eroticism [is] not passivity but receptivity."[12]

In chapter 4, Foucault's theory of the "unthought" (a space which cannot be defined within the limits of acceptable thought) was used to describe the place black femininity occupies within dominant discourse. I would place butch and fem roles within this same theoretical space. The discourse of butch/fem pushes against the terms of heterosexual logic, breaching the exclusivity of gender discourse and causing the meaning of this discourse to overflow its authorized forms of signification. Its force may also be conceptualized in Derridean terms: its force is a certain "infinite equivocality which gives signified meaning no respite, no rest, but engages in its own economy so that it always signifies again and differs."[13] That the "unintelligible" genders of butch and fem nevertheless persist and proliferate within a structure where, presumably, they cannot be located results in the opposition between true and false, between the real and the unreal, within the system of heterosexual logic breaking down.

In "The Order of Discourse," Foucault defines discourse as a juncture, a conceptual terrain in which knowledge and power are formed and produced.[14] Discourse assures the reproduction of the social system through procedures of selection and exclusion. Accordingly, discursive rules are linked to the exercise of power. The discursive rules of selection and exclusion which are exercised by and upon discourse lie veiled beneath the myth of a founding subject: this subject stands as the origin of truth. Thus, the opposition between true and false can be identified as one of the systems by which things are designated as either acceptable or unacceptable within the socio-discursive field. Butch/fem's repetition of gender categories as a kind of drag performance can be compared to a linguistic performance that "refuses even to attempt to 'say what it means,' to speak from a privileged and serious position of unambiguous truth."[15] Butch/fem's distance from a position of "truth" renders it valuable to the project of creating a feminist subject position because it makes butch and fem identities non-reducible to the traditional "Subject," by virtue of their firmly denying the subject its customary status as origin of truth. Hence, the subjects of butch/fem may be theorized as discursive subjects who, declining to speak the dominant language of masculinity and femininity, are equipped to generate a new space for themselves within the field of discursive and social forces. By deploying codes of masculinity and femininity on an all-female terrain, I contend that the discourse of butch/fem reconfigures the heterosexual zones of "Man" and "Woman."

## Signs of Seduction

In her introduction to the work of Split Britches, Sue-Ellen Case states that more than any other group they have set the stage of lesbian and feminist performance in the US: "their work has defined the issues and terms of academic writing on lesbian theatre, butch-femme role-playing, feminist mimesis, and the spectacle of desire."[16] Their work has also received considerable exposure in the UK: Lois Weaver has served as co-Artistic Director of Gay Sweatshop.

Split Britches' representations of lesbianism embody lesbian subjectivity par excellence and not only for an academic audience. Their representations of butch and fem have played a major part in the construction of contemporary lesbian identities and have contributed to lesbians understanding of their sexuality. In their work, the accent is always on woman-as-sign, and through the deconstruction of "Woman" they separate out lesbian experience from dominant gender ideology. Lizbeth Goodman points out that Split Britches' work is so heavily influenced by performance art/theatre techniques that critics find it difficult to address the work purely as plays, without qualifying them as post-modern/poststructuralist performances.[17] I shall try to redress this difficulty by approaching the texts from an eclectic array of theoretical perspectives.

As with most of Split Britches' texts, *Beauty and The Beast*, originally produced in 1982 in New York, is comprised of multiple narratives with each actor performing several roles.[18] In this play a "real" butch/fem couple, Peggy Shaw and Lois Weaver, are cast respectively as an elderly butch vaudevillian performer called Gussie Umberger and a fem Salvation Army Sergeant called Joy Ratledge, who in turn, perform the roles of the butch Beast and the fem Beauty in an adaptation of the fairy tale.[19] There is a pause in the action of the play-within-a-play that allows Weaver and Shaw to comment on their personal experience of butch/fem, where Shaw recalls her fantasy of being James Dean and Weaver relates that she used to cast herself in the role of Katherine Hepburn to a butch Spencer Tracy. The text notes that for simplicity the characters are referred to by their fairy-tale names but that all three of the character levels should be apparent throughout the piece.

In *Beauty and the Beast*, Shaw and Weaver embrace a relaxed, playful attitude to butch/fem roles. Throughout the play, their role-playing functions as a sexual language among the women, which enhances the erotic aspects of their relationship as well as their enjoyment of it. The dominant language of heterosexuality – Jeffreys' eroticization of power difference – is not spoken here. The intransigent attitude toward roles which Jeffreys locates in butch/fem practice collapse as Weaver and Shaw swap control of the action as well as comic banter. They play out butch/fem sexuality, in the words of Joan Nestle, as "mistresses of discrepancy."[20] As butch/fem sexuality is normally understood, the butch actively desires and pursues the passive fem, and the fem is active only in the sense of desiring to be desired. However, neither Beauty nor the Beast ever restrains her desire to act or dreads being passive. Power may be eroticized, but it is also shared, with Beauty and the Beast continually swapping the active/passive roles.

A good example is the marriage proposal scene. The Beast takes the traditionally masculine lead by proposing marriage to Beauty. But it is also the Beast who later exits crying when Beauty refuses her consent. Beauty clearly has the power to withhold herself emotionally and sexually from the Beast. Another example is when the Beast performs the traditionally feminine function of providing for the physical needs of Beauty (e.g. preparing the meals). In fact, most of the Beast's functions are physical and sensual in nature. She offers to take Beauty on a honeymoon to Olympus, "and feed you mint and honey with my hands," both a sexualized and a fostering image.[21] And finally, the Beast holds out the opportunity for Beauty to play at being butch too: "I'll be James Dean to your . . . Montgomery Cliff," she tells her.[22] These scenes reveal the arbitrary relationship between butch desire and fem receptivity; in the play, lesbian sexuality is shown to bear an indeterminate relationship to power and to the masculine/feminine and active/passive binaries.

In her article "Toward a Butch-Femme Aesthetic," Case submits that butch/fem seduction is always located in semiosis. The point of lesbian semiotics, she says, is not to "conflict reality with another reality, but to abandon the notion of reality through roles and their seductive atmosphere. . . In other words a strategy of appearances replaces a claim to truth."[23] *Beauty and The Beast*'s most theatrical discourse, a rejoinder to Juliet's "What's in a name" speech, foregrounds how language is used to construct models of reality and how lesbian semiotics can undermine the dominant's version of truth. Shakespeare has Juliet say "That which we call a rose / by any other name would smell as sweet."[24] Whereas Beauty tells her father:

> In a rose I see what's in a name. A name is a name is a name, but Father, in a rose is everything. One single, beautiful red rose.[25]

Within dominant systems of logic, a rose is a rose because of a "real" or essential presence within that object; just as some females are "Woman" by virtue of possessing the quality of woman-ness, and a male is a "Man" because he embodies masculinity. Beauty queries the certainty with which we can identify material and social phenomena. A rose by any other name, she argues, would not be a rose anymore because meaning is determined by and contained within the name. That which is in a rose is a process of signification which, in the same way as constructions of "Woman" and "Man," butch and fem, contains only the traces of its own mode of production.

The semiotic thickness of the sign "rose" in Beauty's statement extends to a metaphor for beauty in general, "Woman," femininity, and fem. These categories carry certain dominant assertions that reflect in their pattern of usage the difference between sex–gender roles and sexual practice among other things. Those groups in society that control the bulk of material resources also dominate the operation of naming: a proper name also refers to claims of ownership. What something means is to a degree determined by what those in power say it means, and the play suggests that nothing, not even a single red rose, stands outside of this power dynamic. This is not to say that those in positions of power can close down meaning. Through social usage, new and alternative meanings can be initiated. While language may be an index of heteropatriarchal attitudes and relations, subcultural groups may use language in such a way that the play of meaning is opened up and, perhaps, the normative patterns suggested therein are disrupted. The play suggests that opportunities exist for subcultural groups to challenge the heteropatriarchy as the locus of cultural meaning in the relation between language and sex–gender categories.

Recall from chapter 1 Dollimore's contention that binaries hold in place more than they actually designate so that their displacement effects the moral and political norms which are both independent from it and in part constitute it. By alienating sex from gender and gender from desire and sexual practice, *Beauty and The Beast* demonstrates how butch/fem interrupts the principle of coherence and continuity through which heterosexuality represents itself as the norm of truth and displaces its foundational pattern. By undercutting the category of the natural upon which the binary relations constituting heterosexuality are predicated, butch/fem as practised by Weaver and Shaw reveals how "Woman" and "Man" are spaces that any sexed subject can fill. In this way, the play reveals how the discourse of butch/fem, instead of consigning women to rigid sex–gender roles, as its opponents would argue, can afford the possibility of new social and sexual practices for women. This is not to say that we can always predict the effects of performing gender. Sinfield warns that "the strategies available to lesbian and gay people, and other subordinated groups, are always double-edged. We have to invoke dominant structures to oppose them, and our dissidence, therefore, can always be discovered reinscribing that which it aspires to critique."[26] Dollimore puts forward a compelling theory of repetition in the form of a repetition that corresponds to a reinscription, one which remains sensitive to the fact that the discourse of butch/fem is produced by and sustained within the frames of dominant gender ideology. He explains the concept of Transgressive Reinscription as: "a mode of transgression which seeks not an escape from existing structures but rather a subversive reinscription within them, and in the process their dislocation and displacement."[27] Transgressive Reinscription signifies "a turning back upon something and a perverting of it typically if not exclusively through inversion and displacement."[28] The "something" to which in repetition butch/fem returns represents the poles of sexual difference and their related binaries. By transgressively reinscribing the sex–gender system's regulatory fiction (sex = gender = desire), butch/fem disrupts the principle of consistency among sex–gender binaries and generates a proliferation of new, alternative meanings. This view differs from that of Sue-Ellen Case, who advances butch/fem as occupying together a single subject position: "the two roles never appear as . . . discrete . . . These are not split subjects, suffering the torments of dominant ideology. They are coupled ones that do not impale themselves on the poles of sexual difference or metaphysical values . . . "[29] If butch/fem takes on the appearance of a collective subject position, particularly in the work of Split Britches, it may be attributed to the group's postmodern perspective, which in general works to subvert bipartite structures through the layering of roles, rather than to an indissoluble coupling of butch/fem categories.

The relative merit of promoting a discourse of sexual difference versus sexual indifference is both a controversial and critical issue in feminist practice. Implicit within Case's reasoning is the assumption that the feminist subject will be engendered through the negation of sexual marks. Granted, as Wendy Holloway recognizes, "because traditional discourses concerning sexuality are gender-differentiated, taking up subject or object positions is not equally available to men and women."[30] Whether or not neutralizing sexual difference will in fact provide greater access to a subject position for women, however, is disputable. Jane Gallup voices suspicion of a discourse of sexual indifference on the grounds that it might be but another mode of denying women.[31] In the same vein, Naomi Schor asks: What is to say that the discourse of sexual indifference is not the latest ruse of phallocentrism? While sexual indifference may lead to the achievement of integration, she fears that this integration might be "crowned with the fatal irony of disappearance through absorption."[32] Once again, when judging the value of sexual difference/indifference, one needs to keep in mind that gender and sexual identities are constructed within existing power dynamics. As indicated in the work of Judith Butler, any gender construct postulated as outside or beyond power is a cultural impossibility, "one that postpones the concrete task of rethinking subversive possibilities . . . within the terms of power itself." In so far as the power regime of phallocentrism augments itself through a constant repetition of its logic and metaphysic, repetition is bound to persist as the mechanism of the cultural reproduction of identities.[33] Therefore, feminist analyses should be less concerned with generating a strategy to inaugurate a neutral field for the feminist subject and more with calculating what kind of subversive repetition might upset the dominant regulatory practice of identity.

I contend that butch/fem does not (and does not need to) surmount the binarism of sexual difference; for as Derrida posits:

> the movements of deconstruction do not destroy structures from the outside. They are not possible and effective, nor can they take accurate aim, except by inhabiting those structures. Inhabiting them in *a certain way*, because one always inhabits, and all the more when one does not suspect it.

The enterprise of deconstruction operates from the inside by borrowing all the strategic and economic resources of subversion from the old structure . . . [34] Hence, if the discourse of butch/fem seduces the sign system, this seduction arises *by virtue of these roles alliance with* the poles of sexual difference. Amplifying Derrida's statement, Dollimore identifies how containment, although it does not necessarily presuppose subversion, in principle, is susceptible to it. He offers the example of binarism as confirming the way in which contradictions are manifested in and through representation: "binarism . . . produces internal instabilities in and through the very categories it deploys *in order* to clarify, divide, and stabilize the world." In this way, it "affords the opportunity for transgression *in and of its own terms*; transgression is in part enabled by the very logic which would prevent it."[35] Whereas Case deems the context of hetero/sexual difference as the subject's prison-house, following from the remarks of Derrida and Dollimore, I would argue that it is butch/fem's existence within the nexus of heterosexual values which makes it a fertile ground for de(re)constructing the female subject. Shaw's butch Beast and Weaver's fem Beauty play *on* the heterosexual economy in the sense that these roles emerge from within it and are sustained by the repetition of its terms. However, they also play *to* it, using its terms as building blocks in the process of differing from it. While the representation of gender, which is its construction, aims to reproduce specific formations, butch/fem simultaneously approaches and defers the transaction of these formations and in so doing, contests the validity of their logic and consistency.

The play recognizes that the order of the real intersects with that of the symbolic. According to Case, Weaver and Shaw's "real life roles [obliterate] any kind of essentialist ontology behind the play." The roles are played in signs themselves rather than ontologies so that the structures of realism become "sex toys" for the butch–fem couple. She also notes that work on the female subject usually places her firmly within a heterosexual context. As long as the female subject remains within this context, she will remain entrapped within dominant representations. Only when placed solely within the context of other women can the female subject become the feminist subject, that is, one capable of ideological change.[36] *Beauty and the Beast's* material representations of lesbianism and the discursive knowledge about lesbianism it generates exist in a contiguous relationship. By maintaining the connection between the actor's private and theatrical selves, the play works to subvert the dominant and ostensibly authentic social context for gender categories by foregrounding the acting of gender and sexuality. The best example of this is the scene in which Weaver and Shaw refer to their own butch/fem history and recount their early Hepburn/Tracy fantasies.[37] Weaver and Shaw deploy dominant cultural terms of masculinity and femininity only as a frame around which to construct desire between their characters. There is no correlation between biological characteristics and gender-roles, just as there is no strict division of role behavior. For instance the stereotypical correlation of strength with masculinity and weakness with femininity is not sustained. Further, they subvert the masculine/feminine binary by alternately placing both Beauty and the Beast in the sexual exchange as the desiring and desired partner. The play makes it clear that the butch Beast desires to give sexual pleasure to the fem Beauty. Thus, in the sexual exchange the active/passive binary is inverted: Beauty who occupies the nominal space of woman is here positioned as the receiver rather than the giver of pleasure. By refusing to tame the beast of butch desire, *Beauty and the Beast* portrays role-playing as a positive and exciting lesbian sexual practice. At the end of the play, the beast rises, takes Beauty in her arms and kisses her. Their kiss is unremarked by the Father, meaning that in the context of the play the butch getting the fem is not censured, but rather is seen as a happy, proper ending.

## Butch, Fem, and the Mask of Womanliness

Madeline Davis claims that a butch's masculine appearance makes her seem more normal.[38] To whom does she appear more normal: to straight society, to other lesbians? And why does she appear more normal? Certainly, the stereotypical image of lesbians held by many heterosexuals remains the "mannish" woman or the diesel dyke. However, the idea that fems may not be "real" lesbians is shared by lesbian subculture. That the fem's identity has always seemed a more ambiguous construction, even to lesbians, can be traced back to Freudian conceptions of female sexuality as well as to the work of the early sexologists. Within the Freudian system, lesbian sexuality is defined as a derivative of male sexuality. In "The Psychogenesis of a Case of Female Homosexuality in a Woman," Freud attributes his patient's female object choice to a masculinity complex: "A spirited girl, always ready for romping and fighting, she was not at all prepared to be second to her slightly older brother; after inspecting her genital organs, she had developed a pronounced envy for the penis . . ."[39] Freud is unable to conceive of lesbian sexuality outside of masculine desire: he can only envision it as organized under the control of the phallus. There is no space for female desire, for desire between women, in Freudian thought.[40] Hence, he must masculinize the "romping," "fighting" girl. At the outset, he notes that the woman exhibited "no obvious devolution" from the feminine type, that she was a "beautiful and well-made" girl. Nevertheless, he focuses much attention on seemingly insignificant physical details such as her "tall figure" and her "sharp" rather than "soft and girlish" facial features, taking these as indicative of masculinity. However, this calculated masculinization reveals a point of contradiction in Freud's text. His initial observation that his patient was well-made according to the feminine type precludes an easy equation of lesbianism and masculinity.[41] Therefore, his subsequent attempt to ascribe to the woman masculine tendencies represents the text's self-deconstructive moment, the point at which his attempt to fit the woman to the theory misfires.

Sexologists also questioned whether or not the feminine type could be considered a "true invert." Havelock Ellis described the "feminine" partner in lesbian couples as "the pick of the women whom the average man would pass by."[42] George Chauncey cites another as saying that "one could imagine her remaining involved with inverts only until she came under the influence of a man."[43] According to this synopsis, although lesbianism is itself an anomalous condition, there is, paradoxically, such a thing as a "normal" lesbian; this is the "masculine" lesbian. Lesbians who are feminine in appearance are considered to be straight women really, in other words they are "pretend" lesbians and thus they might easily revert to heterosexual practices. As pointed out in the discussion of *Beauty and The Beast,* it is the idea of a normal lesbian that underpins many lesbian feminist objections to butch/fem roles. Again, the notion of a female sexual discourse is conspicuously absent from this hypothesis of lesbianism, so much so that the question of a "feminine" lesbian cannot be broached. However, as Weaver's Beauty illustrates, fem does not equal feminine. The role of the fem defies any attempt to pigeon-hole it.

Amber Hollibaugh and Cherie Moraga draw attention to the many images available to butches within dominant culture: "they could always look at movies and see the boy kissing the girl, and they were the boy. Well, you know, it occurs to me that the reason it is so hard to figure out why you are a femme is that there are really no images in the other direction. I don't have any images of femmes."[44] As Hollibaugh's testimony bears out, the butch appears more normal due to the fact that our cultural discourses offer us no way to perceive traits traditionally associated with femininity as being lesbian. Consequently, in lesbian sub-culture there has also been a scarcity of positive role-models for the "feminine" lesbian. Literary representations such as Radclyffe Hall's, which portrays the feminine lesbian as a latent heterosexual, fed into the distrust and discomfort with which some lesbians have regarded and still regard fems. They have encouraged the notion that fems are somehow not quite as queer as butches. Often, even the name *fem* provokes uneasiness in the lesbian community. Within lesbian sub-culture, fems are sometimes labeled female impersonators or transvestite butches, labels which represent an attempt to work through feelings of anxiety regarding the possible ambivalence of fem sexuality, and it represents another attempt to fit the fem role into received defin-itions of lesbianism.

By promoting the androgynous lesbian as the politically correct model, lesbian–feminism internalized this opposition. In fact, the androgynous, slightly boyish type still predominates in lesbian sub-culture. Thus, fems continue to be judged either against a heterosexual standard of femininity or the "standard" version of the lesbian, which is closer to the butch model. Measuring fems against these standards obviates the possibility of revaluing those attributes designated as femi-nine for a specifically lesbian discourse. One fem notes that "even if she is beautiful by male standards, a femme dyke may do something to disrupt the image, intentionally break the rules. And she breaks the cardinal rule: her audience is female not male."[45] The Butch threatens dominant gender ideology by parading her brand of masculinity and thereby, works to de-center phallic privilege. The fem, in contrast, can appear as the epitome of "Woman." Notwithstanding, her subtle play on gender does more to alter the relations of dominant cultural config-urations of sexuality. The fem quietly inserts lesbian desire into a phallic economy of the same through playing at being "Woman" while actively desiring another woman.

Weaver's portrayal of Tammy Whynot, a hyper-feminine fem, in Split Britches' *Upwardly Mobile Home*, illustrates how the fem role works to sever the ties that bind "Woman" to the imperative of male desire.[46] Produced in 1984 in New York at the WOW Cafe, the play tells the story of three women – Tammy, Mom, and Levine – who scratch out a living through odd jobs while attempting to break into showbusiness. The women live in a van, but hope soon to move up to a mobile home.[47] Their hopes are pinned on a woman friend's winning a radio contest (who can last longest on top of a billboard), which offers a mobile home as a prize. Against this backdrop, Weaver plays Tammy in the style of Marilyn Monroe. On one level, she is the stereotypical dumb blonde of whom Levine remarks: "She's always half asleep."[48] Sandra Lee Bartky argues that to stage the body according to conventional standards of feminine display constitutes an incoherent act from a feminist perspective.[49] Weaver's representation of Tammy, however, demonstrates the space available for a lesbian fem to parodically re-enact the role of woman-as-object. Elin Diamond contends that through subtle exaggeration, Weaver defuses the obvious fetishization inherent in that role . . . Weaver foregrounds Tammy's exploitation "without" (as

Irigaray puts it) allowing herself to be simply reduced to it."[50]

In the play, Tammy appears as a "normal" woman. The stage directions read: Tammy enters in a yellow dress and sweater with a slept-in look; her hair is in curlers and she carries a cosmetic case.[51] The play stages femininity as the way that the body is dressed. The audience is privileged to watch Tammy literally putting on her femininity, which she extracts from the cosmetic case. When Tammy has finished making herself up, her gender appears to coincide with her sex; yet, Tammy's flirtation with Mom informs the audience that her (fem)ininity does not signify a "proper" desire. It is interesting from the perspective of lesbian practice that Weaver is able to play Tammy as recognizably lesbian fem without a strong butch counterpart. While Shaw does enact a lesbian role, one might say *the* lesbian part (a good lesbian mother with nice legs), hers is not a particularly butch role. Tammy's ability to enact fem without an easily identifiable butch supports the argument that butch and fem roles need not be theorized in tandem.

Weaver exploits the contradictions of femininity from within the discourse of femininity. Her subtle exaggeration of femininity makes her a model of the fem as "subversive infiltrator." Jewelle L. Gomez considers the great value of the fem role to be her ability to sneak "into the heterosexual world unobtrusively and again [give] the lie to what heterosexuals say lesbians are."[52] Case locates the discourse of butch/fem within Joan Riviere's theory of womanliness as a masquerade.[53] Butch/fem partakes of a game in which women play at either possessing the phallus or being the phallus. The butch openly displays the possession of the penis, while the fem adopts the compensatory masquerade of womanliness:

> The femme … foregrounds her masquerade by playing to a butch, another woman in a role; likewise, the butch exhibits her penis to a woman who is playing the role of compensatory castration. This raises the question of 'penis, penis, who's got the penis; the fictions of penis and castration become ironized and 'camped up.' Both women alter this masquerading subjects function by positioning it between women and thus foregrounding the myths of penis and castration in the Freudian economy.[54]

Riviere drew no line between womanliness and its masquerade: "whether radical or superficial, they are the same thing," suggesting that "Woman" is the effect of her representation.[55] This is comparable to Butler's theory that femininity has meaning only in performance and to Lacan's supposition that woman's sexuality is produced by and inseparable from its representation, making it, too, a kind of masquerade. Riviere characterizes the heterosexual woman's masquerade of femininity as a performance directed toward men. Stephen Heath correctly recognizes that "the masquerade is the woman's thing, hers, but is also exactly *for* the man, a male presentation, as he would have her . . . " The problem raised by Riviere's theory, he suggests, is not whether woman-liness is a mask; that women assume this mask is taken for granted. What proves intriguing about this mask is its "fit or misfit," with the latter disclosing it as a mask.[56] The mask of womanliness plainly does not fit the fem. The dynamic of butch and fem engenders a new space in which women may enact a masquerade of gender. One can discern this most clearly in the construction of the fem's role. According to Heath, by giving the masquerade in excess, holding and flaunting the male gaze, a woman proffers not a "defense against," but a "derision" of masculinity.[57] In the play, Tammy daily peddles her "stuff" on the street, while presenting an excessive show of femininity. In a moment of sexual jealousy, Mom comments on her highly eroticized appearance, particularly her revealing outfits: "Your outfits couldn't hide much. Are you going out like that?[58] Mom warns her to be careful that she doesn't get picked up by the police. Tammy responds that "its not me they pick up its my stuff," meaning a suitcase full of feminine accoutrements – hats, handbags, and sequined jackets.[59] When we consider that Tammy's persona equals the sum of her "stuff," we see that Mom's warning is really pointed at Tammy herself.

Tammy's dream of a butch Christ is another example of how she flaunts the male gaze by explicitly playing her femininity to another woman's gaze. She also fantasizes about becoming a famous country-western singer in the style of Dolly Parton, another image of femininity that represents a hyper-masquerade of womanliness: "I'd feel the red and blue lights bounce off my platinum wig and I'd see little specks of light like diamonds reflectin' all over the auditorium from my sequin outfit."[60] Weaver playing Tammy playing Dolly comprises a self-reflexive mechanism, one which doubles back on itself and produces friction within the space where femininity is performed. This friction furnishes the potential for a reconstructed feminine space. In the play, Mom says: "Life imitates art." Tammy demonstrates how in the construction of the category fem, life imitates art imitates life imitates art and so on.

## Performing Gender(s)

The discourse of butch/fem is often performed by Split Britches in tandem with the discourse of camp. Esther Newton's definition of camp, although an early one, remains useful for interpreting Shaw and Weaver's performance of gender(s). Camp does not represent any single position or thing in Newton's interpretation; instead, what it signifies is "a *relationship between* things, people, and activities or qualities, and homosexuality."[61] The relationship between things, et. al., and homosexuality which may be judged as camp, derives not from any essence unique to homosexuality, but from its relation to the dominant culture – that is, to homosexuality's consistently subordinate position within dominant culture.[62] In one sense, Newton elides camp taste with homosexual taste in so far as camp represents a cultural economy that seeks to invert legitimate definitions of taste, especially in regard to sexuality.

Case traces the origin of lesbian camp to the "hothouse atmosphere" of lesbian bar-culture in the 1940s and '50s. She submits that historically butch/fem roles have been lived-out among women as a conscious parody of heterosexual role models; even in the '40s and '50s, these roles were not perceived as "biological birthrights" or "any other essentialist poses': "the bars were often abuzz with the discussion of who was or who was not a butch or femme, *and how good they were at the role*" (emphasis mine).[63] My interpretation of lesbian subculture and its relation to camp differs from that of Case. I would argue that prior to the women's and Gay liberation movements, there was no cultural economy in place that might afford a majority of lesbian women the chance to perceive their butch/fem roles in terms of camp. Moreover, Case's reading relegates butch and fem roles to the position of static structures and, thereby, robs them of the dynamic potential they need if they are to function as the transformative categories she requires for her own thesis. To conceive of butch/fem as a monolithic structure is to render it useless as the basis of a liberatory practice.

Elizabeth Lapovsky Kennedy and Madeline Davis, in their study of lesbian communities in the 1940s and '50s, find no parallel to gay male camp culture "despite the fact that butch identity was constructed around being masculine, but not male, and was therefore based on artifice."[64] The basis of gay male camp rests on the incongruous juxtaposition of femininity and maleness as well as on the reordering of socially received power relationships between men and women, masculinity, and femininity. Although individual women might have been able to objectify a man, in the proto-political '40s and '50s women as a group, having no solid organization, did not have the social power to objectify men in general. Kennedy and Davis also state that "after listening to hours of butch life stories, we realized that butches rarely used camp humor as a way of presenting their vision of the world; rather they surrounded themselves with an aura of solemnity."[65] Shaw's portrayal of the butch Della in the play *Split Britches* is a good example of the solemnity with which butches were likely to treat their performance of masculinity.[66]

During the first half of the twentieth-century women possessed no cultural concept of ungendered sexual relationships. Bear in mind also that in the 1940s and '50s lesbian bars were frequented primarily by working-class women and women of color. While many white, middle-class women could see the advantages of a marriage between equals, the cultural milieu of working-class and non-white women extended to them few, if any, such examples. The pattern they had witnessed before choosing a lesbian lifestyle was one based on a strict division of sex–gender roles; hence, "a functioning couple for them meant dichotomous individuals, if not male and female, then butch and femme . . . "[67] The extent to which these roles were taken seriously is evidenced by the adamant rejection of those women who refused to choose a role. The rigid formulation of butch and fem roles can be regarded as an attempt by lesbian sub-culture to create legitimacy for itself through the establishment of its own traditions and rules. Women who were neither butch nor fem were referred to as "ki-ki" or "bluffs." The term "bluffs" indicates that these women were not regarded as full members of the lesbian community because they did not embrace the codes through which lesbianism was signified within the community. They were viewed with a certain amount of distrust by butches and fems because they were considered to be confused about their sexual identities.

There was a strong essentialist strain to the conception of butch/fem in the 1940s and '50s, which continued through the mid-sixties. Jeffrey Weeks indicates that prior to gay liberation, popular opinion on homosexuality was shaped by the work of early sociologists. This work attempted to fit homosexuality into heterosexual concepts of sexuality and social organization, both of which relied upon biological referents; this led many people to assume that, as a matter of course, homosexual relations should follow existing patterns.[68] Arlene Stein explains that there was a great deal of permanence and consistency implicit within the old notions of roles: "One's identity as butch or femme was an essential part of one's being. Once a femme always a femme. The same for butches."[69] In fact, some lesbians (particularly working-class women and lesbian essentialists) still hold the idea that their butch or fem identities may be attributed to "gender destiny."[70]

What is being extolled as neo-butch/fem differs in several important ways from earlier role formations. Many neo-butches and fems choose their roles in order to make a statement, one directed both toward straight society and moralistic members of the lesbian–feminist community. Neo-butch/fems perceive themselves as sexual heretics and often choose to be butch or fem out of a sense of adventure. Gay liberation and the women's movement have afforded lesbians greater freedom to embark on sexual adventures and a greater capacity for radically transmuting cultural symbols. For example, the idea of a "butch bottom" or a "fem top" could not have been accommodated within the earlier definition of butch/fem. Whereas, in contemporary lesbian communities, more often than not, butch/fem allows an interchange between and a variation within roles. These roles no longer represent a system of masculine and feminine extremes; instead, there now exists within this discourse a whole spectrum of positions which lesbians may occupy: stone butch, butchy femme, femmy butch and so on.[71]

Those who oppose butch/fem because they perceive these roles as oppressive fail to recognize that today's role-playing is not a repetition of role-playing as it was practised among women in the 1940 and '50s. Lillian Faderman convincingly argues that contemporary role-playing among lesbians derives from a conscious attempt to break with the limiting orthodoxies of lesbian cultural-feminism in order to create sexual polarities that will enhance erotic relationships between women.[72] Whereas it was once a matter of necessity, now adopting a role can be a matter of play. Although some women continue to identify with one role more strongly that the other, now there is a greater possibility of choice. Stein contends that in the 1980s butch–fem became a self-conscious aesthetic that plays with style and power, rather than an embracing of one's true nature against the constraints of straight society."[73] Moreover, there is no longer a clear one-to-one correspondence between butch/fem appearance and identity. One former fem relates how she experienced her fem identity as an imposition, something imposed on her simply because of her appearance: "If you had long hair you were a femme, it didn't matter what you wore."[74] Now clothes too have become interchangeable. "You can dress as a femme one day and a butch the next. You can wear a crew cut along with a skirt. Wearing high heels during the day does not mean you're a femme at night, passive in bed . . ."[75] While this mix-and-match attitude to lesbian genders may seem frivolous to some, the fact that women can now blend aspects of butch and fem identities illustrates the flexibility of these categories. It reflects lesbians' success at transforming the either/or mechanism comprised within earlier butch/fem role formations, and in addition to reflecting the diverse ways in which lesbians may perform their gender and sexuality, it contributes to their continued freedom to re-invent these categories. Most important, the new lesbian dress sense represents a style of gender that is undoubtedly directed toward the gaze of other lesbians.

*Belle Reprieve,* Split Britches' most camp production to date, is their first collaborative effort with the gay male theatrical duo Bloolips.[76] The play explicitly asserts that "realism works against us," meaning that realist modes of representation only serve to reflect lesbians and gays' subordinate position in society and specifically denies the subjectivity of lesbians. Goodman recognizes that the play questions not only "the nature of desire, but also the nature of a society which allows us to assume that we [can] know the sex and gender of those around us," or that we can be absolutely sure of our own sexualities.[77] Hence the play's accent is on artificiality. *Belle Reprieve*, which premiered in London in 1991, presents a woman playing a woman (Stella), a butch lesbian playing a man (Stanley), and a queer man playing a man (Mitch). The discourse of butch/fem, combined with that of camp, functions to free sex–gender roles from the confines of interiority and plays up the fact that masculinity and femininity can be read only by means of their exterior deployment. In her introduction to a collection of Split Britches' work, Case compares this play to their earlier productions: "The tender coming out stories in *Beauty and The Beast* and the flashes of flirtation in *Split Britches* and *Upwardly Mobile Home* seem timid and exploratory compared to the full-out passionate affair between Stanley and Stella."[78] *Belle Reprieve* places lesbian sexuality and desire center stage. "Peg and I took on the physical/carnal kind of sex usually attributed to gay male sex," while the men went for romantic friendship which is supposed to be the lesbian model, Weaver relates.[79]

Although its characters originate with Tennessee Williams' *A Streetcar Named Desire*, Shaw and Weaver's version of Stanley and Stella draw their meaning more from the film version than from Williams' play. Their portrayal is based on the iconic standing which Stanley and Blanche in particular have acquired in gay subculture. The variety of sources for these roles along with the way that the roles are distributed doubles the complexity of the masculine/feminine divide. The role of Blanche is particularly complex. On one level, Blanche is a man in drag. And s/he overtly acknowledges her/his role as camp. S/he tells Stella: "One day I'll probably just dissolve in the bath. . . Drag Queen Dissolves in Bathtub, that'll be the headline."[80] Alternatively, the play also allows for an interpretation of Blanche's role as a man playing a woman playing "Woman." In a sense, Blanche can be considered as much of a fem as Stella. In fact, Stella admits that she has learned to play "Woman" by watching Blanche:

> I used to follow her into the bathroom. I loved the way she touched her cheek with the back of her hand. How she let her hand come to rest just slightly between her breasts as she took one last look in the mirror. I used to study the way she adjusted her hips and twisted her things . . . Then she would fling open the bathroom door and sail down the staircase into the front room to receive her gentlemen callers.[81]

The value of butch/fem and camp as they are combined in the play do not reside only in their revelation of the equivocal link between "inside" and "outside." Butch/fem, as genders-in-drag, also serves to undo the very notion of an "inside." *Belle Reprieve*, particularly through its representation of Blanche, annuls the idea of a "natural" referent to which the expression of gender might be tied.

Drag, closely associated with the discourse of camp, emphasizes style over content. Its exaggeratedly theatrical style can shift the focus from what a thing is to what it appears to be. According to Newton, at the heart of drag's theatricality lies role deviation and manipulation; drag says that sex-role characteristics and behavior are appearances: they are "outside" and therefore susceptible to manipulation.[82] In this way, drag calls into question the "naturalness" of the sex–gender system. Many feminists, however, object to drag when it is enacted by men, gay men included. Their objections are based on the idea that in parodying femininity male drag mocks and degrades women. While I recognize that in our culture images of femininity are overwhelmingly connected with women, I believe that for women themselves to insist on too strong a bond here risks reinscribing women as the necessary owners of femininity.

Other feminist critics, such as Kate Davy, dismiss gay male drag as nothing more than an assumption of the dominant culture's polarized sex–gender roles; whereas female drag is assumed to foreground and undermine these roles.[83] Again, I would disagree. Leo Bersani's account of gay male drag is most convincing. He recognizes that a gay male parody of femininity *may* signify hostility toward women; nevertheless, "paradoxically, this practice may also help to deconstruct the image of femininity for women."[84] Butch/fem role-playing may be interpreted in terms of a drag performance in so far as it is suffused with the perception of being as playing a role. Butch/fem as drag eradicates the power of heterosexist realist modes by replacing a notion of the real with a "strategy of appearances." It should be noted that in many cases of male drag there is an attempt to hide the individual's sex. In connecting butch/fem and drag, I do not mean to suggest that the butch's role represents an attempt to hide the lesbian's sex. Butch lesbians should be distinguished from lesbians who are attempting to pass as men.

In terms of their theatricality, Case illustrates how butch/fem roles take on the quality of a character construction. Following from this she asserts that butch/fem lends agency and self-determination to the historically passive female subject by providing her with alternative options for gender identification.[85] Sinfield, on the other hand, approaches the idea of mimicry as a subversive strategy for gays and lesbians with greater caution. He alerts us to how easily the dominant can cope with mimicry: "Lesbians and gay men have long been perceived as disturbing conventional categories – masculine souls in feminine bodies and so on – and [in political terms] it hasn't got us very far." The level of disconcertion possible in the performance of butch/fem depends on the nature of the audience, and one should not expect a single stylistic maneuver always to have the same effect. Theories about camp and drag, Sinfield argues, must be addressed as social practices and not in the abstract.[86] The meaning of lesbian performance and its potential for constructing an oppositional sexual politics must be seen as inextricably tied to the nature of the audience and performance space. Split Britches' plays were written for a lesbian audience and for performance in lesbian-friendly theatre spaces such as the WOW Cafe in New York. As Davy notes, outside of a lesbian space, butch/fem can be read as male/female, and meanings can shift radically when a site-specific work is taken out of its intended production space.[87] Although the idea of a lesbian spectator is important for its potential to undermine the heterosexual model, founded upon the universal male spectator, we must be careful not to generalize *A Lesbian Spectator*. There are many different kinds of lesbian communities. And as Sinfield points out, we must consider whose knowledge, experience, beliefs, and feelings are appealed to or taken for granted in the context of lesbian drama. Only by considering a performance's constituency, Sinfield contends, can we judge the efficacy of any stylistic maneuver.[88] Comments below on the effects of performing butch/fem as drag in *Belle Reprieve* are based upon the assumption of a predominantly lesbian-identified/lesbian-friendly audience who might view the performance of butch/fem in a lesbian or alternative theatre space.

*Belle Reprieve* opens with Mitch wheeling three large trunks onstage, two of which contain Stanley and Blanche. In the trunk from which Blanche emerges are contained all of the conventional signs of femininity: "pink things and fur things, dainty things, delicate and wistful things" is how Blanche describes them.[89] Stanley, in the guise of a customs agent, brings one of the trunks center stage and demands that Blanche prove her identity before he will let her pass. "Pass" should he understood in the sense of allowing Blanche to literally pass the barrier that he has erected, but more important is the sense that by allowing her to pass Stanley will be assenting to Blanche's performance of femininity as satisfactory. Stanley finds that she looks nothing like the picture in the passport that she produces as evidence and accuses her of lying. That is one way of looking at it Blanche admits. However, s/he prefers to consider her/himself an improved version of nature and the information contained in the passport as merely "a convention." Stanley insists on carrying out an "intimate search" in order to discover her "true" identity. He doesn't propose searching her body, but her luggage to make sure that Blanche isn't smuggling something personal in the trunk. And the play is adamant that there is no personal discovery here. The trunk contains no more than Blanche's "necessaries": those things necessary for her to effect femininity. By searching her baggage, Stanley discovers what little girls are made of: diamond tiaras, high-heeled shoes, and feather boas. After discovering that this collection is the only ground or "motive" for Blanche's identity, Stanley mimics Blanche's mimicry of femininity: "I put my whole body in, I take my whole body out. I grab myself a frilly thing and shake it all about. I pin it on my shoulders and I sashay up and down, that's what it's all about."[90]

Taken as a kind of drag performance, Stanley's re-presentation of Blanche's gender-identity may be viewed as a performance that, by virtue of imitating "corporeal theatrics," produces the illusion of inner depth. Stanley's performance of femininity illustrates Diana Fuss' point that "gender produces on the skin – through gesture, move, and gait – the illusion of an inner male or female essence."[91] The play constructs masculinity in a similar manner – remember that Stanley emerges from a trunk just like Blanche. And Blanche soon detects that Stanley's masculinity is also a pose: "I don't believe he's a man." In the scene where she tries to seduce Stella, Blanche again questions Stanley's sexual identity: "There's . . . something about the way he has to prove his manhood all the time, that makes me suspicious."[92] S/he bases her suspicions on "shape," rather than "content," that is, upon the total effect that Stanley produces rather than an assumption of anything contained or not contained within, and she reads this effect as evidence of "planned behavior": "The noises he makes, the way he walks like Mae West, the sensual way he wears his clothes, this is no garage-mechanic working-class-boy, this is planned behavior. This is calculated sexuality, developed over years of picking up signals not necessarily genetic is what I'm trying to say." Rather than detecting the butch lesbian beneath the masculine pose, however, Blanche mistakes Stanley for a gay man: "I think he's a fag."[93]

Stella does not need Blanche to tell her that Stanley's masculinity is symbolic. Stella tells him: "You're not real." But she also finds him "cute," if a bit too obvious. However, it is Stanley's ostentatious performance of masculinity that allows Stella to catch a glance of the butch behind the performance. When she tells Stanley, "I want to see what you're really made of. I want to see what it is that makes me want you," she already knows what she will find beneath the masculine garb.[94] In this scene, the site of Stella's desire is not conventional masculinity, but instead the lesbian phallus, the site of an alternative erotic imaginary. The significance of speaking of the lesbian phallus is that it promotes an alternative, specifically lesbian, sexual imaginary as opposed to a hegemonic one. Barbara Smith helps illustrate the particular way in which Stanley's role may prove disruptive to the phallocentric organization of gender and sexuality:

> A dildo is not a penis, but it is a mask. I can wear my cock and admire it in the mirror, like the satyr and the mirror of revelation. I can fuck my lover with my cock mask, I can take it off and fuck myself with it, or she can fuck me with it. Or I can put it away and forget about it. Tell me, how many men can castrate themselves, bugger themselves with their own cocks, fellate their own cocks attached to someone else's body, take their cocks off, put them in a drawer and forget about them – all that and not bleed to death? I can do anything that a "man" can.[95]

Smith's statement reflects the different ways in which the construction of the butch role complicates "Woman's" function within the phallic economy. Despite being located within the terms of phallic relations of power, the butch subverts male desire as the cause and meaning of sexuality by appropriating the dynamic of desire and loosening its bonds to male subjectivity.[96]

Smith's quote echoes Gayle Rubin's assertion that there are actually more ways to be butch than there are ways to be masculine because when women appropriate the signs of masculinity "the element of travesty produces new significance and meaning."[97] Smith's account hints at the threat posed to masculine status when masculinity is enacted by the dildo-wielding dyke. For a woman to play at possessing the penis risks the copy exceeding the original. With her "cock mask," the butch can do everything that a "man" can and then some. The self-conscious parody of phallicism staged by Shaw's Stanley strips the original symbol of its privileged position and status. Given her blatant usurpation of masculine prerogative, Stanley overtly undercuts dominant notions of masculinity as well as the status of masculine desire. In addition, her/his masculine appearance lends Stanley greater visibility in straight society, and this greater visibility empowers the butch to frustrate the security with which men may be defined as masculine in that society.

Case thinks that Stanley's portrayal of "Man" reaches its height in the rape scene, which, Shaw relates, was the most difficult scene to script. According to Case, the play stresses Stanley's violent impulses as "specifically macho het-male, in its stereotypical representation"; although she does not say how it does this.[98] The point is a difficult one: how is the audience to know where Stanley's butch persona ends and masculine persona begins, particularly given that historically aggressiveness has been perceived as part of the butch role?[99] Blanche appears able to distinguish between Stanley the butch and Stanley as macho-het-male. Her/his wish for a bit of realism precipitates s/he and Stanley's acting out the rape scene as played by Brando and Leigh in the film of Williams' *Streetcar*. Yet, Blanche recognizes that the self-referential speech on gender-bending with which Stanley commences the scene is inconsistent with "real" straight masculinity: "You wouldn't talk this way if you were a real man," she responds.[100]

I continue to have reservations as to whether or not *Belle Reprieve* draws a clear enough distinction between butch masculinity and male masculinity. The play implies that Stanley's lesbian desire for Stella and Stella's for Stanley represents a disruptive force (unlike heterosexual desire) and hence, the allure of the two "women" must be different. But it is difficult to determine in what way these economies of desire in fact differ – how Stanley's desire for Blanche is "masculine" as opposed to her desire for Stella which is "butch." Notwithstanding Blanche's awareness, the audience might as easily interpret what is, after all, a finely differentiated point in the text, in the same way as Case. If Stanley the "Man's" act is perceived by the audience as normal in the sense that this is the way in which men are socialized to behave, what might be the social significance of a female subject acting in the same way? One possible answer is provided by Gabrielle Griffin in her study of lesbian images in women's writing. She puts forward the idea that images of lesbians are always presented in the "name of difference," a difference which relies on both a presence and an absence of the Other against whom the lesbian is defined and identified. Masculinity is the most significant point of comparison or reference for establishing difference for "lesbian." By taking on that other – the heterosexual male – Stanley assumes his symbolization and thereby, Griffin contends, s/he may destabilize the groundedness of this position.[101] By representing gender in excess, the discourse of butch/fem as articulated in the work of Split Britches, particularly in *Belle Reprieve*, undercuts the ground of gender-identity. Its camped-up version of masculinity and femininity exceeds gender's conventional markings. By replicating – and exceeding – the original or rather, the conventional modes of gender, Shaw and Weaver's butch/fem roles show that what is posited as the originary instance of the conventional is actually empty of signification. Butch/fem's camped-up repetition of gender's regulatory mechanism disrupts this mechanism's principle of coherence and then exposes, by hollowing it out, its fictitious make-up. Along with the other plays examined in this chapter, *Belle Reprieve* works to expose gender as an expression of certain sexed subjects as fallacious, instead demonstrating how gendered subjects are performative effects of gender's representation. The work of Split Britches problematizes the concept of a single feminine or masculine gender, suggesting that there are as many kinds of woman, as many genders as women and men can themselves imagine and embody. Hence, the plays contribute to the progressive feminist project of replacing the notion of Gender with a theory of genders.

# Conclusion: Toward a Progressive Feminist Politics – A House of Difference

By claiming to speak for all women, mainstream feminism seeks to enter women of subordinate groups into a narrative that affords them no space for expressing their own concerns or strengthening their particular sense of identity. There are, of course, identifiable similarities among women of different races, classes, and sexualities – the most significant being that all women feature as objects of representation in dominant discourse. However, such commonalities exist within a context of racial, class, and sexual differences among women. The controlling definition of difference in mainstream feminist theory – as that which hinders the effectiveness of the women's movement – itself precludes feminist movement; for it plays an integral role in maintaining the cultural authority of the category "Woman," which, in turn, sustains a hierarchical arrangement outside and inside the movement, whereby the voices of white heterosexual women predominate over those of black and lesbian women.   In order to move toward a model of feminism that may effectively contest the social and political factors that produce the power divisions between subcultural groups and the dominant – and among subcultural groups themselves – feminists must re-theorize difference so that it signifies something other than exclusion in feminist theory and practice.

bell hooks points out that when feminism is presented as a way to "develop shared identity and community," it holds little attraction or value for those women who already experience community.[1] A progressive feminist discourse might prove attractive to women who enjoy a sense of community within their specific ethnic/sexual groups in so far as it would not be based upon a specific feminine identity. The aim should not be to make the women's movement more inclusive by creating room within it for black and lesbian genders. Rather, a progressive feminism would emerge from the plurality of women's identities.

Underlying any feminist practice that supports the sameness/difference dichotomy, which positions all women against the difference of masculinity, lies the intention of making room for some women in pre-existing cultural and economic structures and the desire to maintain existing power relations among white, middle-class, heterosexual women and women who fall outside the normative construct "Woman." When feminist analyses are predicated upon a view of feminism as a movement directed primarily toward achieving gender equality, that is, equality between men and women, then any advances made will continue to benefit those women who currently hold a monopoly on femininity. Instead, progressive feminists should work to change the identity of feminism itself, its nature and scope, by re-framing both the issues it examines and the goals it seeks to achieve.

A progressive feminist discourse would avoid treating blackness and lesbianism as issues of otherness to whiteness and heterosexuality. Rather it would incorporate the analytical methods and critical tools needed for interrogating whiteness and heterosexuality, with a view to revealing how these discourses have the power to control the field of cultural meaning, to render lesbian and black genders as *always already* different. By challenging its own racial and sexual awareness, a progressive feminist analysis may hope to elude the ever-present danger of supporting and/or constructing representations of womanhood that prop up the systems of white supremacy and compulsory heterosexuality. An egalitarian and truly emancipatory feminist movement would also remain sensitive to the fact that even when attempting to act/write in a non-racist/heterosexist manner, individuals may unwittingly base their own sense of self on stereotypes and analogies that support various forms of social injustice. For this reason, a progressive feminism would have at its heart the recognition of how the very lack of awareness of racial/sexual identity can significantly reflect that identity.

Teresa de Lauretis argues that neither race nor gender, nor homosexual difference alone, can constitute individual identity and consequently, cannot form the basis for a theory and a politics of social change. Instead of a movement founded upon a concept of difference signifying the remainder left after abstraction, she recommends that feminists follow Audre Lorde's design for constructing a "house of difference." This would entail neither the denial of difference nor an attempt to derive security from any one difference. Lorde's "house of difference" represents a "conception of community not pluralistic, but at once global and local–global in its inclusive macro-political strategies, and local in its specific, micro-political strategies."[2] One of the preconditions for creating a house of difference is a recognition among feminists that there exists a plurality of feminine genders, each with its own particular set of cultural codes. Another important pre-condition is a critical understanding of how race, class, and sexuality form a nexus of oppression within and among different feminine genders. Until this change occurs, Ann Russo observes, our work as feminists will remain fragmented.[3]

Progressive feminists must be sensitive to the fact that although, theoretically, factors of race, class, gender, and sexuality may be treated distinctly, in reality, people often experience various forms of oppression simultaneously. Trinh T. Minh-Ha recognizes that "the pitting of anti-racist and anti-sexist struggles against one another allows some vocal fighters to dismiss blatantly the existence of either racism or sexism within their lines of action, *as if oppression only comes in separate, monolithic forms*" [emphasis mine].[4] When a woman suffers racial and sexual discrimination, she cannot afford to direct her energy toward struggling against either racial oppression or sexual oppression; she must, of course, struggle against both. Given one set of circumstances, it may prove advantageous to ally oneself with those who share one's experience of sexual oppression. Similarly, an individual might concentrate on the struggle against racial oppression given a different set of conditions. Where people locate themselves for resistance – a critical question for progressive feminists – will be contingent upon the specific struggle that women find most pressing at any particular historical moment.

While a progressive feminism would foster a commitment to women's ethnic/sexual particularity, at the same time it would undertake to establish and develop strategic alliances among women of diverse subcultural groups. In other words, we must respect each other's allegiance to cultural distinctiveness while expressing a willingness to cross boundaries, whether they be self-imposed boundaries or limits set by the terms of dominant discourse. Alison M. Jagger stresses the importance of progressive feminists theorizing together. This goal is a political one, and to achieve it, she argues, would represent a political move forward: "the construction of a systematic theoretical alternative to prevailing ways of interpreting the world is an achievement linked inseparably with a transformation of power relations."[5] It is important for subcultural groups to create accounts of themselves that illustrate their potential to disrupt or subvert the status quo. Jagger reminds us that it is equally important for women to produce counternormative ideologies that may serve as foundation to a new socio-political order. This new order would afford all women access to the discourse of subjecthood, without erasing, universalizing, or otherwise leveling the different ethnic, class, and sexual categories across which women are defined.

In *The Politics of Performance*, Baz Kershaw argues that radical work within the spheres of politics, society, and culture can be mutually supportive.[6] The category "Woman" is susceptible to change by political activity, and women's theatre can function as a viable and effective political enterprise for transfiguring this category and its meanings in society. John McGrath, who set up the radical theatre group 7:84, writes that, although the theater can never *cause* social change, it can articulate pressure towards one: "Above all, it can be the way people find their voice, their solidarity and their collective determination."[7] In *Finding Room on the Agenda for Love: A History of Gay Sweatshop*, Philip Osment explains how theatre has worked as an ideal space for exploring the politics of definition for gays and lesbians because it functions as a site where homosexual identities are constructed. Osment reveals how theatre has helped to constitute a positive transformation of gay and lesbian difference and has thereby helped to validate gay and lesbian identities.[8] Kimberley W. Benston argues a similar point in reference to black theatre. She notes that in addition to educating the black community, black theatre aims to embrace its audience in a collective affirmation of black values, styles, and goals.[9] In essence, black women's theatre, like gay and lesbian theatres, constitutes a space in which black women may produce counter-hegemonic narratives and supportive representations which they may draw upon to resist the negative effects of mainstream ideologies of femininity.

The value of theory to feminist movement is the way it denies any claim that there is one true interpretation of reality. It is easier to argue that women of subordinate groups must find new ways of seeing and representing themselves, of empowering themselves through self-definition, than it is actually to develop practical strategies through which they can do so. Nevertheless, to articulate and politicize women's perspectives on social reality, and to mobilize women around their own concerns, has been a key element in the production and performance of all kinds of women's theatre. Dramatic representations of femininity serve to reveal the multiplicity of feminine genders extant in society, as well as the fluidity of genders, and the historical instability of gender categories – whether dominant or subcultural constructions. These representations offer, by virtue of inhabiting what de Lauretis calls the "margins of hegemonic discourse," the terms of a different construction of gender.[10] They are not detached from feminist theory, but form part of the same cultural imaginary. A women's theatre of social engagement – one that is intentionally culturally interventionist – can help women remove the blinders of dominant ideology, and on this basis, such theatre constitutes part of a larger progressive feminist initiative. The demonstration in this book of the ways in which gender, race, class, and sexuality intersect has not been offered as an exercise in racism/hetero-sexism awareness training. But by providing a contextualized comparative analysis of the category "Woman" in terms of dominant and mainstream feminist theoretical and dramatic representations of femininity, the purpose has been to contribute another building block toward a progressive feminist "house of difference."

# Notes

---

## Introduction: Women and Representation

1   In the US, mainstream feminism denotes the movement which grew out of President Kennedy's Commission on the Status of Women (established 1961), the 1965 "rethinking conference" held by women members of SDS (Students for a Democratic Society) in 1965 and since which has been visible as a movement largely through the activities of groups such as NOW (National Organization for Women). In the UK, feminist ideology has developed against the trend of centralized feminist institutions (for reasons which will be identified in more detail later). The British feminist movement is not comprised of groups formally connected either by structural or organizational ties, and work among women's groups has historically been intermittent and isolated. However, beginning in the mid-eighties, UK women's groups began to adopt some of the operating procedures of the US movement, particularly the lobbying and electoral activities of NOW. While at the same time women's strength within the labor movement has continued to grow so that a profitable comparison can be made between the two movements.

2   Teresa de Lauretis, *Technologies of Gender: Essays on Theory, Film, and Fiction.* (Houndmills: Macmillan, 1987), 9.

3   Gayle Austin, *Feminist Theories for Dramatic Criticism* (Ann Arbor: The University of Michigan Press, 1990), 2–3.

4   Many women's theatre groups of the '60s and '70s emerged from actual CR groups or modeled their companies on the CR group process, with the audience acting as group members. For a detailed discussion of the role of CR in women's theatre, see chapter two of Charlotte Canning's *Feminist Theatres in the U.S.A.: Staging Women's Experiences* (London: Routledge, 1996).

5   Alice Walker, *In Search of Our Mothers' Gardens* (London: The Women's Press, 1984), 376.

6   Molefi Kete Asante, "Racism, Consciousness and Afrocentricity," in *Lure and Loathing: Essays on Race, Identity, and the Ambivalence of Assimilation,* ed. Gerald Early (London: Penguin, 1993), 140.

7   For a more detailed critique of Afrocentricity, see Sydney J. Lemelle's "The Politics of Cultural Existence: Pan-Africanism, historical materialism and

167

Afrocentricity," *Race & Class,* vol. 35, no. 1 (July–Sept. 1993): 93–112.

8    Henry Louis Gates Jr., "Talkin' that Talk," in *"Race" Writing and Difference,* ed. Henry Louis Gates (Chicago: The University of Chicago Press, 1986), 402.

9    Lorde quoted in Leslie Wahl Rabine's "A Feminist Politics of Non-Identity," *Feminist Studies,* vol. 14, no. 1 (1988): 11–32.

## 1   Representations of Motherhood

1    Minnie Bruce Pratt, "All The Women Caught in Flaring Light", in *Mother Journeys: Feminists Write About Mothering,* ed. Maureen T. Reddy (Minneapolis: Spinsters Ink, 1994), 2.

2    Jeffrey Weeks, *Coming Out: Homosexual Politics in Britain* (London: Quartet, 1979), 106–7.

3    The lesbian mother figures portrayed by Wandor, Daniels, and Lyssa are all representations of white lesbians. I was unable to locate any lesbian custody dramas written by black women or any which featured a black lesbian mother as protagonist. Hence, it must be noted that the conclusions drawn in chapter 1 are valid only in relation to white lesbian experience grounded predominantly in western European ideas about lesbianism.

4    While the principal concern of *Care and Control* is lesbian custody, it is far from a single-issue play. It establishes that male economic power is just as responsible for the obstacles women face in raising children as the contexts of sexism and heterosexism within which the women must perform their mothering roles. Gay or straight – Wandor asserts – women need access to secure, well-paid jobs and adequate publicly funded child-care provision if they are to mother successfully. Michelene Wandor, *Care and Control,* in *Strike While the Iron is Hot: Three Plays on Sexual Politics,* ed. Michelene Wandor (London: The Journeyman Press, 1980).

5    Sandra Freeman, *Putting Your Daughters on the Stage: Lesbian Theatre from the 1970s to the 1990s* (London: Cassell, 1997), 25.

6    The idea that lone women are unsuited to mothering continues to be promulgated for a number of reasons. In the early 1990s, single motherhood was a contentious and much publicized issue in British politics. At the 1993 Conservative Party Conference, the Home Secretary Michael Howard accused single mothers of failing to teach their children right from wrong. He pronounced them "less committed to their children," and "indirectly responsible for rising crime levels." However, it should be noted that heterosexual mothers are almost always awarded custody.

7    Kate Crutchley and Nancy Diuguid, introduction, in *Strike While the Iron is Hot: Three Plays on Sexual Politics,* ed. Michelene Wandor (London: The Journeyman Press, 1980), 64.

8    These words are only slightly adapted from an actual case transcript. Wandor, *Care and Control,* 102.

9    Of course, the dominant works to contain all forms of sexuality considered subversive. Britain's Section 28 (1992) being one example of how signifi-

cant controlling sexuality is deemed for the successful reproduction of dominant culture.

10 Adrienne Rich, "Compulsory Heterosexuality and Lesbian Existence," in *Desire: The Politics of Sexuality*, ed. Ann Snitow et al. (London: Virago, 1984).

11 Adrienne Rich, *Of Woman Born: Motherhood as Experience and Institution* (1976; London: Virago, 1977), 13.

12 Lynne Harne, "Lesbian Custody and the New Myth of the Father," in *Women's Studies: A Reader*, ed. Stevi Jackson et al. (London: Harvester/Wheatsheaf, 1993), 218.

13 Leah Fritz, *Dreamer's & Dealers. An Intimate Appraisal of The Women's Movement* (Boston: Beacon Press, 1979), 88.

14 Judith Butler, "Imitation and Gender Insubordination," in *Inside/Out: Lesbian Theories, Gay Theories*, ed. Diana Fuss (London: Routledge, 1991), 31.

15 Butler's theory corresponds to Monique Wittig's supposition, made in *The Straight Mind and Other Essays*, that lesbians cannot be considered women because they exceed the parameters of the binary opposition male/female and masculine/feminine. Monique Wittig, *The Straight Mind and Other Essays* (London: Harvester/Wheatsheaf, 1992).

16 Irigaray quoted in Margaret Whitford's *Luce Irigaray: Philosophy In The Feminine* (London: Routledge, 1991), 80.

17 Wandor, *Care and Control*, 112.

18 Leah Fritz, *Dreamers and Dealers*, 90.

19 Here Wandor directly reflects the attitude of the courts as exemplified by a House of Lords Judgement in 1976: "Changes in public attitude should not entitle the courts to relax in any degree the vigilance and severity with which they should regard the risk of children at critical ages being exposed or introduced to ways of life which may lead to severance from normal society, to psychological stresses and unhappiness and possibly even to physical experience which may *scar them for life* (emphasis mine)." Judgement reported in *Rocking the Cradle: Lesbian Mothers: A Challenge in Family Living*, ed. Gillian E. Hanscombe and Jackie Forster (London: Peter Owen, 1981), 67.

20 Wandor, *Care and Control*, 111.

21 Ibid., 111.

22 Valerie Jenness, "Coming out: Sexual identity and the categorization problem," in *Modern Homosexuality: fragments of gay and lesbian experience*, ed. Kenneth Plummer (London: Routledge, 1992), 66.

23 Gillian E. Hanscombe and Jackie Foster, *Rocking the Cradle*, 152.

24 Sarah Daniels, *Neaptide* (London: Methuen, 1986).

25 Sandra Freeman, *Putting Your Daughters on the Stage*, 159.

26 Lizbeth Goodman, *Contemporary Feminist Theatres: To Each Her Own* (London: Routledge, 1993), 130–1.

27 Anne Wollett and Ann Phoenix, "Issues Related to Motherhood," in *Women's Studies: A Reader*, ed. Stevi Jackson et al. (London: Harvester/Wheatsheaf, 1993), 217.

28 In this, Chodorow follows the lead of Melanie Klein. Like Klein's, Chodorow's project seeks to cleanse psychoanalytic discourse of Freudian

misogyny. However, by privileging the dominance of the maternal role, in actual fact, both women theoretically underwrite Freud's position

29 The edition quoted from here was published by The University of California Press, Berkeley in 1978.

30 Lynne Segal, *Is the Future Female?: Troubled Thoughts on Contemporary Feminism* (1987; London: Virago, 1988), 136.

31 Gayle Austin, *Feminist Theories for Dramatic Criticism*, 45.

32 Pauline Bart, "Review of Chodorow's The Reproduction of Mothering," in *Mothering: Essays in Feminist Theory*, ed. Joyce Trebilcot (Totowa: Rowman & Allanheld, 1984), 147 & 151.

33 See Sigmund Freud, "The Psychogenesis of a Case of Homosexuality in a Woman," *Penguin Freud Library*, trans. James Strachey (1920; London: Penguin Books, 1990).

34 Gillian E. Hanscombe and Jackie Forster, *Rocking the Cradle: Lesbian Mothers: A Challenge in Family Living* (London: Peter Owen, 1981), 88.

35 Lynne Harne and Rights of Women, *Valued Families: The Lesbian Mother's Legal Handbook* (London: The Women's Press, 1997), 5–7.

36 Nancy Chodorow, *The Reproduction of Mothering*, 33.

37 Daniels, *Neaptide*, 26.

38 Ibid., 20.

39 Ibid., 31.

40 Lizbeth Goodman, *Contemporary Feminist Theatres*, 30.

41 Daniels, *Neaptide*, 15.

42 Michel Foucault, *The History of Sexuality Volume 1: An Introduction*, trans. Robert Hurley (1978; New York: Vintage, 1980), 105.

43 Elizabeth V. Spelman, *Inessential Woman: Problems of Exclusion in Feminist Thought* (1988; London: The Women's Press, 1990), 123.

44 Mary Daly, *Gyn/Ecology: The Metaethics of Radical Feminism* (London: The Women's Press, 1979), 9, 315.

45 See also Daly's *Beyond God the Father: Toward a Philosophy of Women's Liberation* (Boston: Beacon, 1973) and Adrienne Rich's *On Lies, Secrets and Silence* (New York: Norton, 1979).

46 Daniels, *Neaptide*, 46–7.

47 Ibid., 47.

48 Ibid., 8.

49 Alison Lyssa, *Pinball, Plays By Women: Volume 4*, ed. Michelene Wandor (London: Methuen, 1985).

50 Alan Sinfield, *Gay and After* (London: Serpent's Tail, 1998), 103–4.

51 Ellen Lewin, "Negotiating Lesbian Motherhood: The Dialectics of Resistance and Accommodation," in *Mothering: Ideology, Experience, and Agency*, ed. Evelyn Nakano Glenn et al. (London: Routledge, 1994), 338.

52 Ibid., 349.

53 Andrew Sullivan, *Virtually Normal: An Argument About Homosexuality* (London: Picador, 1995).

54 The Rights of Women Lesbian Custody Group report that in general Australian courts consider lesbianism to be a deviant sexuality and one which must be hidden from children. They find the myths and prejudices

used against lesbian mothers in British courts to be prevalent in Australia as well and, in cases where lesbian mothers are granted custody, it is often by default; that is, the father is incapable of taking the children. Where custody is granted, the same harsh conditions usually prevail: women are denied the right to spend the night with their partners or to engage in any activity of a sexual nature in the presence of the children (including hand-holding or kissing) and the children's condition is often monitored by a state psychiatrist. See chapter 16, "Lesbian Custody Cases in Australia" in the *Lesbian Mothers' Legal Handbook* (London: The Women's Press, 1986), 176–80.

55   Alison Lyssa, afterward, *Pinball,* in *Plays by Women, vol. 4,* ed. Michelene Wandor (London: Methuen, 1985), 158.
56   Alan Sinfield, *Faultlines: Cultural Materialism and the Politics of Dissident Reading* (Oxford: Clarendon Press, 1992), 297.
57   Antonio Gramsci, *Selections from the Prison Notebooks of Antonio Gramsci,* ed. and trans. Quintin Hoare and Geoffrey Nowell Smith (1971; London: Lawrence & Wishart, 1986), 365.
58   Language at the simplest level can be understood as a response to signs with signs. Powerful social groups appropriate signs in ways that serve their interests. Consequently, the sign is an arena of struggle – among genders, races, and classes. In fact, signs such as "Woman" and "Mother" are multi-accentual sites within and through which struggles for various forms of social dominance are played out.
59   Lyssa, *Pinball,* 129.
60   Michel Foucault, *Language, Counter-Memory and Practice,* ed. Donald F. Bouchard and Sherri Simon (Ithaca: Cornell University Press, 1977), 33–5.
61   Judith Butler, *Gender Trouble: Feminism and the Subversion of Identity* (London: Routledge, 1990), 22–23.
62   Jonathan Dollimore, *Sexual Dissidence: Augustine to Wilde, Freud to Foucault* (Oxford: Clarendon Press, 1991), 66.
63   Feminist theories of language reveal that power relations between women and men inhere in discursive mechanisms. Cixous' model of patriarchal binary thought was one of the first to demonstrate women's subordinate location within discourse. She outlines how binary oppositions such as nature/culture, rational/irrational, and activity/passivity have as their underlying opposition male/female, with the female always presumed the powerless instance. Irigaray, too, notes that the feminine within discourse is defined as "lack, deficiency, or as imitation and negative of the subject."
64   Nancy Chodorow, *The Reproduction of Mothering,* 214.
65   See Lynne Harne and Rights of Women, *Valued Families.*
66   For specific cases, see Hanscombe and Forster's *Rocking the Cradle* and Ellen Lewin's "Negotiating Lesbian Motherhood: The Dialectics of Resistance and Accommodation," in *Mothering: Ideology, Experience, and Agency,* ed. Evelyn Nakano Glenn et al.
67   One of the most important initiatives has been The Rights of Women Lesbian Custody Project, recently re-named The Lesbian Parenting and the Law Project, founded in 1982. ROWLCP set up training workshops and

symposiums open to anyone with an interest in lesbian parenting rights; these gatherings served to disseminate non-biased research.

68  Gillian E. Hanscombe and Jackie Forster draw their conclusions from a project carried out at the Institute of Psychiatry in London in 1980, *Rocking the Cradle*, 85–6.

69  Fiona Tasker and Susan Golombok, "Children Raised by Lesbian Mothers: The Empirical Evidence," *Family Law* 21 (1991), 184–7.

70  Lynne Harne and Rights of Women, *Valued Families*, 10.

71  Madeline Colvin with Jane Hawksley, *Section 28: A Practical Guide to the Law and Its Implications* (London: National Council for Civil Liberties, 1989), 1.

72  Lynne Harne and Rights of Women, *Valued Families*, 127.

73  Ibid., 14.

74  Liberty, *Sexuality and the State: Human Rights Violations Against Lesbians, Gays, Bisexuals, and Transgendered People* (London: National Council of Civil Liberties, 1994), 41–3.

75  Lynne Harne and Rights of Women, *Valued Families*, 59.

76  Ibid., 83.

77  Ibid., 45.

78  Ibid., 49.

79  Ibid., 12.

80  Ibid., 86.

81  Lyssa, *Pinball*, 156.

## 2  OtherMothers

1  Quoted in Stephanie J. Shaw's "Mothering Under Slavery In The Antebellum South," in *Mothering: Ideology, Experience, and Agency*, ed. Evelyn Nakano Glenn et al. (London: Routledge, 1994), 237–8.

2  Elizabeth V. Spelman, *Inessential Woman*, 157.

3  The idea of a sex/gender system was first theorized by Gayle Rubin in her 1975 essay "The Traffic in Women: notes on the political economy of sex." Reprinted in *Women: The Longest Revolution: Essays on Feminism, Literature and Psychoanalysis* (London: Virago, 1984).

4  Lyssa, *Pinball*, 141.

5  Ibid., 144.

6  Uta Ranke Heinemann quoting from the medieval tract *The Hammer of Witches*. Historically, lesbians have been characterized as witches who are responsible for the breakdown of marital union, the family, and for the proliferation of "unnatural" intercourse. See Uta Ranke-Heinemann, *Eunuchs for the Kingdom of Heaven: Women, Sexuality and the Catholic Church*, trans. Peter Heinegg (New York: Penguin, 1990), 229–32.

7  Lyssa, *Pinball*, 155.

8  Ibid., 136.

9  Teresa de Lauretis, *Technologies of Gender*, 5.

10  Mae Gwendolyn Henderson, "Speaking in Tongues: Dialogics, Dialectics, and the Black Woman Writer's Literary Tradition," in *Reading Black,*

*Reading Feminist*, ed. Henry Louis Gates, Jr. (New York: Meridian, 1990), 119.

11   Donna Haraway, *Simians, Cyborgs and Women: The Reinvention of Nature* (London: Free Association Books, 1991), 145–6.

12   For purposes of analysis I apply these divisions to British culture with only occasional discriminations. (Note that in American race discourse the term black applies only to people of African descent, unlike in the UK where the term black may encompass people of Asian descent as well). Barbara Christian, "An Angle of Seeing: Motherhood in Buchi Emecheta's Joys of Motherhood and Alice Walker's Meridian," in *Mothering: Ideology, Experience, and Agency*, ed. Evelyn Nakano Glenn et al. (London: Routledge, 1994), 98.

13   Tracey Reynolds, "(Mis)representing the black (super)woman," in *Black British Feminism: A Reader*, ed. Heidi Safia Mirza (London: Routledge, 1997), 107.

14   Ibid., 102–3.

15   Grace Dayley, *Rose's Story*, *Plays by Women: Volume Four*, ed. Michelene Wandor (London: Methuen, 1985).

16   Solinger makes the case that a child's perceived "value" is central to its mother's fate. Black women's fertility is likened to an occupation – one which violates basic consumerist principles. They are said to offer bad value – black babies – for a high price, tax-payer supported welfare grants. Furthermore, in a new-take on the slave woman-breeder image, they are portrayed as animalistic – as breeding for profit – that is, to increase their income from state benefits.

17   Beverley Bryan, Stella Dadzie and Suzanne Scafe, *The Heart of the Race: Black Women's Lives in Britain* (1986; London: Virago, 1993), 102–3. Angela Davis describes a similar situation in the US. She reminds us of the compulsory sterilization laws passed by many states in the 1930s, which were designed to prevent "unfit" persons from reproducing. Although these laws are no longer in effect, the involuntary sterilization of black women remains all too commonplace. And the 1977 Hyde amendment, which ended government funding for abortion except in the cases of rape and risk of death or severe illness, carefully reserves the right of poor women to free sterilization. When it comes to black women, the line between abortion rights and the advocacy of abortion has always been blurred. While white women have had to fight for an individual woman's right to choose birth control, black women have had to fight against racist attempts at population control. Davis sees this as the reason why black women have been reluctant to support mainstream feminism's abortion-rights campaign, pointing out how "abortion for black women is often seen as a viable alternative to the problems of poverty, as if having fewer children could create more jobs, higher wages, better schools, etc. etc." Quoted from Angela Davis' *Women, Race and Class* (1981; London: The Women's Press, 1984), 214 & 220.

18   Dayley, *Rose's Story*, 58.

19   Ibid., 64.

20   Ibid., 65.

21   Elizabeth V. Spelman, *Inessential Woman*, 99.

22   Dayley, *Rose's Story*, 60.

23   Patricia Hill Collins, "Shifting the Center," in *Mothering: Ideology, Experience and Agency*, ed. Evelyn Nakano Glenn et al., 53.

24   Ann Phoenix, "Narrow definitions of culture: the case of early mother-hood," in *Women's Studies: A Reader*, ed. Stevi Jackson et al. (London: Harvester/Wheatsheaf, 1993), 212.

25   Patricia Hill Collins recognizes the same absence of difference in feminist sociological studies of mothering. See "Shifting the Centre," in *Mothering: Ideology, Experience and Agency*, ed. Evelyn Nakano Glenn et al.

26   Dayley, *Rose's Story*, 72.

27   Ibid., 57.

28   Zhana,"Mother/Daughter," *Sojourn*. ed. Zhana (London: Methuen, 1988), 67.

29   Ibid., 65.

30   This is also apparent in Lyssa's *Pinball*. Consider this speech by Archibald, Theenie's father:

> You expect me to welcome the female involvement society? Do you know what lies behind that balderdash? Every troublesome, unqual-ified, ungrammatical, pill popping dishmop of a housewife in this country, and every guttural, lisping tinpot god of a migrant desperate to settle here, thinks he . . . or she, is entitled to the freedom to dictate to everybody else.

The charge that women and immigrants collude in seeking to undermine social order or democracy, that they aspire to impose an inferior and fraudulent value system upon "everybody else," has long been standard right-wing rhetoric. The play reveals that what parades as democracy and social order can be, in fact, designed to stifle minority voices and thereby, to insure that the dominant can dictate its preferred way of life.

Though crude in its characterization of women and immigrants, Archibald's words, like Solomon and Kurt's, embody the sophisticated and complex interweaving of the discourses of race, gender and nation as well as of national and cultural identities. They help to illuminate how these constructs permeate one another and facilitate the rule of white men's law.

31   Elizabeth Brown-Guillory, *Their Place on the Stage: Black Women Playwrights in America* (New York: Greenwood Press, 1988), 135.

32   Breena Clarke and Glenda Dickerson, *Re/membering Aunt Jemima: A Menstrual Story, Contemporary Plays by Women of Color: An Anthology*, ed. Kathy A. Perkins and Roberta Uno (New York: Routledge, 1996).

33   "Artistic Statement by Breena Clarke," in *Contemporary Plays by Women of Color: An Anthology*, ed. Perkins and Uno, 34.

34   The mammy image serves as the basis for that of Aunt Jemima; therefore, I only occasionally discriminate between the two.

35   Sau-li C. Wong, "Diverted Mothering: Representations of Caregivers of Color in The Age of "Multiculturalism," in *Mothering: Ideology, Experience, and Agency*, ed. Evelyn Nakano Glenn et al. (London: Routledge, 1994), 69.

36  K. Sue Jewell, *From Mammy to Miss America and Beyond: Cultural Images and the Shaping of US Social Policy* (London: Routledge, 1993), 12 & 36.

37  "Artistic Statement by Breena Clarke," in *Contemporary Plays by Women of Color*, ed. Perkins and Uno, 34.

38  Adrienne Rich, *Of Woman Born*, 253.

39  Elizabeth V. Spelman, *Inessential Woman*, 158–9.

40  In nineteenth-century racist discourse, black women were represented as both non-sexual and over-sexed, depending on the expectations the dominant ideology sought to generate. The figure of Jezebel represented Mammy's over-sexed counterpart. Rich, while not denying the sexual nature of her "black mother," evokes the cultural image of the hypersexual black as a contrast to that of the sexually naïve white woman.

41  Alice Walker, *In Search of Our Mothers' Gardens* (London: The Women's Press, 1984), 374.

42  Dickerson and Clarke, *Re/membering Aunt Jemima*, 38.

43  Alice Walker, *In Search of Our Mothers' Gardens*, 376.

44  Dickerson and Clarke, *Re/membering Aunt Jemima*, 39.

45  Ibid., 43.

46  bell hooks, *Black Looks: Race and Representation* (London: Turnaround, 1992), 9.

47  Dickerson and Clarke, *Re/membering Aunt Jemima*, 37.

48  Ibid., 38.

49  At the turn of the century, The National Association of Colored Women took as their motto the phrase "Lifting As We Climb."

50  bell, hooks, *Yearning: Race, Gender and Cultural Politics* (London: Turnaround, 1991).

51  Patricia Hill Collins, *Black Feminist Thought: Knowledge, Consciousness, and the Politics of Empowerment* (New York: Routledge, 1991), 50.

52  Patricia Hill Collins, "Shifting the Center," in *Mothering: Ideology, Experience, and Agency*, ed. Evelyn Nakano Glenn et al., 48.

53  Dickerson and Clarke, *Remembering Aunt Jemima*, 37.

54  Motherwork is a term which Patricia Hill Collins employs in an effort "to soften the existing dichotomies in feminist theorizing about motherhood that posit rigid distinctions between private and public, family and work, the individual and the collective, identity as individual autonomy and identity growing from the collective self-determination of one's group." "Shifting the Center," in *Mothering: Ideology, Experience and Agency*, ed. Evelyn Nakano Glenn et al., 47–8.

55  Dickerson and Clarke, *Re/membering Aunt Jemima*, 43.

56  Ibid., 44.

57  Ibid., 45.

58  Among some segments of the black community, particularly in the black middle class, there resides a tendency to idealize the dominant mode of gender relations which idealizes the man as provider and the woman as housewife/mother. However, as Evelyn Brooks-Higginbotham points out, structural conditions of poverty, discrimination and segregation has prevented many of them from achieving more than a psychological alle-

giance to this idea. See *Coming To Terms: Feminism, Theory, Politics* (New York: Routledge, 1989), 130.

59  bell hooks, *Yearning, Race, Gender and Cultural Politics*, 36.

60  Patricia Hill Collins, *Black Feminist Thought*, 120, 129.

61  Shay Youngblood, *Shakin' The Mess Outta Misery* (Woodstock, Illinois: The Dramatic Publishing Company, 1994).

62  Youngblood, *Shakin' The Mess*, 7. Interestingly, the Big Mamas fit one definition of lesbian, that is, they are women-identified-women. Yet, besides the presence of Lily and Tom, a butch-feme couple, no other elements are present which might warrant categorizing this play as lesbian feminist drama.

63  Alice, Walker, *In Search of Our Mothers' Gardens*, 382.

64  Youngblood, *Shakin' The Mess*, 17.

65  An exception is radical feminism's idea of mother-right. Mother-right is a somewhat mystical belief that women's power stems from the womb and that women are to be revered because of their procreative ability. The downside of this idea is that it only inverts the male/female hierarchy rather than empowers women in their mothering roles. There is no popular equivalent in black feminist thought of mother-right.

66  Friday: New York: Delacorte, 1977; Arcana: Berkeley: Shameless Hussy Press, 1979.

   The views articulated in the above texts may be traced to Juliet Mitchell's essay, "Women: the Longest Revolution," published in *New Left Review* in 1966. This piece, which describes reproduction as a sad mimicry of production, rapidly became one of mainstream feminism's seminal compositions.

67  Dinnerstein's depiction of motherhood closely emulates Mitchell's argument that the child is an object or product for the mother which grows to threaten the woman's autonomy:

> The biological product – the child – is treated as if it were a solid product. Parenthood becomes a substitute for work, an activity in which the child is seen as an object created in the same way as a commodity is created by a worker. . . . The child as an autonomous person inevitably threatens the activity which claims to create it continually merely as a *possession* of the parent. Possessions are felt as extensions of the self. The child as a possession of supremely this. Anything the child does is therefore a threat to the mother herself who has renounced her autonomy through this misconception of her reproductive role. There are few more precarious ventures on which to base a life.

68  Dorothy Dinnerstein, *The Rocking of the Cradle* (1976; London: The Women's Press, 1987), 81, 111–12.

69  Youngblood, *Shakin' The Mess*, 45.

70  *Shain' The Mess* is also reminiscent of *Rose's Story* and *Re/Membering Aunt Jemima* in its ambivalence/negativity toward men.

71  Genevieve Fabre, *Drumbeats, Masks, and Metaphor: Contemporary Afro-American Theatre*, trans. Melvin Dixon (Cambridge, Mass.: Harvard University Press, 1983), 219–20.

Elaine Aston identifies orality as an important component of identity politics for black British women writers as well; for it provides a way of linking with the culture of the black Diaspora; see *An Introduction to Feminism and Theatre*, 91.

72 Alan Sinfield, *Literature, Politics and Culture in Postwar Britain* (Oxford: Basil Blackwell, 1989), 26.

73 Again, men do not figure as part of this network.

74 Alan Sinfield, *Literature, Politics and Culture in Postwar Britain*, 25.

75 Here, I adopt Ruth Frankenberg's interpretation of race where she considers race, like gender, to be "real" in the sense of its tangible and complex impact on individuals' sense of self, experiences, and life chances. *The Social Construction of Whiteness: White Women, Race Matters* (London: Routledge, 1993), 11.

76 Youngblood, *Shakin' The Mess*, 31.

77 Ibid., 7.

78 Ibid., 30.

79 Audre Lorde, *Sister Outsider: Essays & Speeches* (New York: The Crossing Press, 1984), 123.

80 Youngblood, *Shakin' The Mess*, 14.

81 See chapter two of Stephen Small's *Racialized Barriers: The Black Experience in the United States and England in the 1980s.* (London: Routledge, 1994).

## 3   Friedan's Daughters: Representations of "Woman" at Work

1 Alice Childress quoted in Elizabeth Brown-Guillory's *Their Place on the Stage*, 53.

2 As I mention in chapter 2, the idealized form of family life continues to be: Man as principal wage-earner with Woman as stay-at-home Wife and Mother plus children.

3 Naomi Wolf, *Fire with Fire: The New Female Power and How It Will Change the 21st Century* (London: Chatto & Windus, 1993).

4 Janice Doane and Devon Hodges, *Nostalgia and Sexual Difference: The Resistance to Contemporary Feminism* (London: Methuen, 1987), 9.

5 As defined in Betty Friedan's *The Feminine Mystique* (1963; London: Victor Gollancz, 1971).

6 Betty Friedan, *The Second Stage* (London: Michael Joseph, 1982), 33.

7 Friedan's second book like her first is blatantly heterosexist. Now, the second stage's "lavender menace" is responsible for a feminism that is no more than a "reactive reversal of the feminine mystique." She concludes that women who repudiate so much of women's identity must necessarily be self-hating and merely masking their hatred of their own sex by ostentatiously professing their love of women, *The Second Stage*, 324.

8 Betty Friedan, *The Feminine Mystique*, 342; *The Second Stage*, 101.

9 Betty Friedan, *The Second Stage*, 161, 264–9.

10 Ibid., 235.

11 Ibid., 343.

12 Sylvia Ann Hewlett, *A Lesser Life: The Myth of Women's Liberation* (New

York: William Morrow & Co.), 1986.

13 This includes a Harvard and Cambridge education, a lectureship at Barnard, and, at the time of writing, a term of years as head of the Economic Policy Council. Hewlett, in keeping with most of the women who touted an anti-feminist line, shared few commonalities with the domesticated women whose wonderful lives she extolled.

14 Hewlett, *A Lesser Life*, 51–65.

15 Ibid., 186, 189.

16 Julia Penelope, *Call Me Lesbian: Lesbian Lives, Lesbian Theory* (Freedom, California: The Crossing Press, 1992), 147.

17 Elaine Aston, *An Introduction to Feminism and Theatre* (London: Routledge, 1995), 65.

18 Wendy Wasserstein, *Uncommon Women and Others. The Heidi Chronicles and Other Plays* (1990; New York: Vintage Books, 1991).

19 Ibid., 34.

20 Wasserstein, *The Heidi Chronicles*, 193.

21 Elaine Aston, *An Introduction to Feminism and Theatre*, 66.

22 Helene Keyssar, "Drama and the Dialogic Imagination: *The Heidi Chronicles and Fefu and Her Friends,*" *Modern Drama* 34 (March 1991): 98–9.

23 Esther Cohen, "Uncommon Woman: an interview with Wendy Wasserstein," *Women's Studies* 15 (1988): 257–70, 261.

24 Helene Keyssar, "Drama and the Dialogic Imagination," 98.

25 Alan Sinfield, *Faultlines*, 291.

26 Wendy Wasserstein, *Isn't It Romantic, The Heidi Chronicles and Other Plays* (1990; New York: Vintage Books, 1991).

27 Ibid., 82.

28 Ibid., 106.

29 Ibid., 104.

30 Ibid., 144.

31 Ibid., 144.

32 Ibid., 143.

33 Ibid., 146.

34 Alan Sinfield, *Faultlines*, 74.

35 Alan Sinfield, *Literature, Politics and Culture*, 33.

36 Andrew Hacker, *Two Nations: Black and White, Separate, Hostile, and Unequal* (1992; New York: Ballantine Books, 1995), 157.

37 For example, in 1988 child benefit paid to women was frozen.

38 While right-wing scare-mongers issued dire warnings about bogus infertility epidemics among white middle-class women, they adroitly ignored the fact that infertility rates among young black women had been increasing since the 1960s. The racist nature of male concern over white female fecundity is illuminated in a host of commentaries by the Right. One example, Ben Wattenberg's book, *The Birth Dearth* (New York: Pharos Books, 1987), warned that "if people in free countries don't have enough babies, the US would lose its world power status . . . and *multiplying minorities would create ugly turbulence*" (emphasis mine).

39 Susan Faludi, *Backlash: The Undeclared War Against Women* (London: Chatto

& Windus, 1991).

40 Ibid., 25.
41 Wasserstein, *Isn't It Romantic*, 80 & 152–3.
42 Susan Faludi, *Backlash*, 33–4.
43 Ibid., 48.
44 One example cited by Faludi is government funding of research into infertility. If fertility was decreasing at an epidemic rate, why did the US government refuse to allocate research funds toward developing treatments? And why did British health authorities choose infertility treatment for rationing on the NHS and in some areas cut it completely? See Susan Faludi, *Backlash*, 49–51.
45 In the US, this included abolishing federal funding for birth control and sex education as well as abortion and attempting to subvert the discourse of abortion rights by substituting it with that of fetal rights. Some states even attempted to criminalize pregnant women by applying child abuse laws to the fetus. In Britain, In-Vitro fertilization was attacked on the grounds that it diminished the role of the father. And reports of virgin births provoked an hysterical response in the British tabloid press. *The Daily Mail* dismissed as feminist claptrap the idea that a woman could raise a child alone and denounced IVF as "a scheme which strikes at the very heart of family life." See Susan Faludi, *Backlash*, 461.
46 Janelle Reinelt, *After Brecht: British Epic Theater* (Ann Arbor: The University of Michigan Press, 1994), 81–2.
47 Elin Diamond, *Unmaking Mimesis: Essays on Feminism and Theater* (London: Routledge, 1997), 52.
48 Ibid., 52.
49 Lizbeth Goodman, *Contemporary Feminist Theatres*, 227.
50 Janelle Reinelt, *After Brecht*, 88–9.
51 Baz Kershaw, *The Politics of Performance: Radical Theatre as Cultural Intervention* (1992; London: Routledge, 1994), 33.
52 Richard Schechner, *Performance Theory* (London: Routledge, 1988), 39.
53 Baz Kershaw, *The Politics of Performance*, 33–4.
54 Christine Gledhill, "Pleasurable Negotiations," in *Female Spectators*, ed. E. Deidre Pribham (London: Verso, 1988), 70–2.
55 Caryl Churchill, *Top Girls* (London: Methuen, 1982).
56 Janet Brown, *Taking Center Stage: Feminism in Contemporary U.S. Drama* (London: The Scarecrow Press, 1991), 105.
57 Elaine Aston, *Caryl Churchill* (Plymouth: Northcote House, 1997), 39.
58 Merrill also sees Marlene as prototype, pointing out how Marlene's role is the only one performed by an actor with no other role. See her "Monsters and Heroines," in *Caryl Churchill: A Casebook*, ed. Phyllis R. Randall (New York: Garland Publishers, 1988).
59 Elaine Aston, *Caryl Churchill*, 41.
60 Although Joyce's animosity to Marlene's conservatism appears to be part of sisterly rivalry, there is evidence that Joyce envies Marlene for escaping her working class world, being able to choose the kind of work she does, the money that she earns, and the freedom that comes with money. The

tediously pedantic exchange in the final scene in some way frustrates Churchill's advocacy of a community-centered ethic of accountability. Joyce's politics do not appear to be something she has thought much about, especially given that her idea of political action is to spit when she sees a Rolls Royce. She seems to be merely reciting Left dogma: Marlene calls her "dadda's little parrot."

61  Lisa Merrill, "Monsters and Heroines," in *Caryl Churchill: A Casebook*, ed. Phyllis R. Randall, 88. Joseph Marohl also defines the central action of the play as employment. See his "De'realised Women: Performance and Identity in Churchill's Top Girls," in *Contemporary British Drama, 1970–90*, eds, Hersch Zeifman and Cynthia Zimmerman (New York: Macmillan, 1993), 314.

62  Marohl also refers to the way in which gender issues are displaced by Joyce's class-conscious politics, especially in the women's final exchange. Joseph Marohl, "De-realised Women," *Contemporary British Drama*, ed. Zeifman, et al., 321.

63  Michael Swanson, "Mother/Daughter Relationships in Three Plays by Caryl Churchill," *Theatre Studies* (1985–1986): 49–66, 54.

64  Churchill, *Top Girls*, 30.

65  Aston, *Caryl Churchill*, 40.

66  Helene Keyssar, "Drama and the Dialogic Imagination," *Modern Drama*, 95.

67  Keir Elam, *The Semiotics of Theatre and Drama* (1980; London: Routledge, 1988), 95.

68  Naomi Wolf, *Fire with Fire*, 52.

69  Audre Lorde, *Sister Outsider: Essays & Speeches* (New York: The Crossing Press, 1984), 112.

70  bell hooks, "Dissident Heat: Fire with Fire," in *Outlaw Culture: Resisting Representations* (New York: Routledge, 1994), 97.

71  Naomi Wolf, *Fire with Fire*, 15.

72  The case against this fallacy, especially common in the social sciences, is put by Bonnie Thornton Dill in her article "The Dialectics of Black Womanhood," *Signs* 4(3) (Spring 1979), 543–55.

73  bell hooks, *Black Looks*, 82.

74  Naomi Wolf, *Fire with Fire*, 276 & 279.

75  Ibid., 314.

76  Glenn C. Loury, "Free at Last? A Personal Perspective on Race and Identity in America," in *Lure and Loathing: Essays on Race, Identity and the Ambivalence of Assimilation*, ed. Early, 3.

77  Cassandra Medley, *Ma Rose, Women's Work: 5 New Plays from The Women's Project*, ed. Julia Miles (New York: Applause Theatre Book Publishers 1989).

78  bell hooks notes that the American class structure has always been shaped by the racial politics of white supremacy. The same can be said for American gender relations. *Feminist Theory from Margin to Center* (Boston: South End Press, 1984), 3.

79  Medley, *Ma Rose*, 47.

80  Ibid., 84.

81    bell hooks, *Talking Back: Thinking Feminist, Thinking Black* (Boston: South End Press 1989), 75.

82    Medley, *Ma Rose*, 86.

83    Elizabeth Brown-Guillory, *Their Place on the Stage*, 136.

84    In *Labour and Racism*, Annie Phizacklea and Robert Miles report a similar situation in the UK. They argue that there is a lower incidence of discrimination among black female applicants for jobs as compared to black men and that the gap in terms of job levels and earnings between white and blacks is much greater among men than women (London: Routledge & Kegan Paul, 1980, 9). And Small quotes a 1990 study by O'Hare et al which suggests that Phizacklea and Miles' findings were valid for the 1980s as well. See his *Racialised Barriers*, 52–3.

85    Andrew Hacker, *Two Nations*, 107.

86    Medley, *Ma Rose*, 87.

87    bell hooks, *Talking Back*, 81.

88    Kim Dowell, "Lines That Divide Black Women," in *Engaging Feminism: Students Speak Up & Speak Out*, ed. Jean O'Barr and Mary Wyer (Charlottesville: University Press of Virginia, 1992), 30.

89    Medley, *Ma Rose*, 79.

90    Ibid., 95.

91    Kristin Hunter Lattany, "Off-timing: Stepping to the Different Drummer," in *Lure and Loathing*, ed. Early, 171.

92    Medley, *Ma Rose*, 96.

93    Ruth Frankenberg, *The Social Construction of Whiteness: White women, race matters* (London: Routledge, 1993), 228.

94    bell hooks, *Talking Back*, 79.

95    Medley, *Ma Rose*, 77.

96    Kristin Hunter Lattany, "Off-Timing," in *Lure and Loathing*, ed. Early, 167.

97    Medley, *Ma Rose*, 74.

98    Ibid., 78.

99    Ibid., 88.

100   The ability of Rosa to pay for someone else to provide this kind of physical care also could be seen as a progressive alteration in the way black women are usually represented; that is, as ministering to the bodily needs of others.

101   Medley, *Ma Rose*, 112.

102   Ethel laments the loss of the "old time" and its "old ways": "Y'all talk about what ya'll will do but when it come to the doing, what you gonna do is you jaunt off to St. Thomas and – and every where else cross the planet ya'll go to. The family's so far-flung so till I don't know what." Medley, *Ma Rose*, 110.

103   Kristin Hunter Lattany, "Off-Timing," in *Lure and Loathing*, ed. Early, 172.

104   Ibid., 168.

105   bell hooks, "Keeping Close To Home," in *Talking Back*, 83.

106   Ruth Frankenberg, *The Social Construction of Whiteness*, 131.

107   Shelby Steele, *The Content of Our Character: A New Vision of Race in America* (New York: St. Martin's Press, 1990), 96.

108   Kristin Hunter Lattany, "Off-Timing," in *Lure and Loathing*, 171.

**4 "Woman" as Object**

1   Toril Moi, *Sexual/Textual Politics: Feminist Literary Theory* (London: Methuen, 1985), 148.
2   A good history of white women in the Civil Rights Movement, especially as it shows how white women used black womanhood as a model for resisting dominant images of appropriate behavior for women, is the second chapter of Sara Evans' *Personal Politics: The Roots of Women's Liberation in the Civil Rights Movement & The New Left* (New York: Vintage Books, 1980). See also Myra Marx Ferree and Beth B. Hess, *Controversy and Coalition: The New Feminist Movement* (Boston: Twayne Publishers, 1985)
3   Christine Delphy, *Close To Home: A Materialist Analysis of Women's Oppression*, trans. Diana Leonard (London: Hutchinson, 1984), 113–14.
4   Ruth Frankenberg, *The Social Construction of Whiteness*, 231.
5   Elizabeth V. Spelman, *Inessential Woman*, 166, 185, 215.
6   Ruth Frankenberg, *The Social Construction of Whiteness*, 228.
7   Ibid., 198.
8   Elaine Jackson, *Paper Dolls, 9 Plays By Black Women*, ed. Margaret B. Wilkerson (New York: New American Library, 1986).
9   See bell hooks' *Black Looks: Race and Representation*, Patricia Hill Collins' *Black Feminist Thought*, and K. Sue Jewell's *From Mammy to Miss America*.
10   Margaret B. Wilkerson, introduction, *9 Plays by Black Women*, ed. Margaret B. Wilkerson (New York: New American Library, 1986), 347.
11   Itabari Njeri, in his essay "Sushi and Grits: Ethnic Identity and Conflict in a Newly Multicultural America," quotes a number of studies which demonstrate the social and economic gap between light and dark skinned African Americans. Njeri suggests that colorism within the black community is as significant as one of the greatest socio-economic cleavages in America, that is, the chasm between the income and status of all blacks and whites. See *Lure and Loathing: Essays on Race, Identity and the Ambivalence of Assimilation*, ed. Gerald Early (New York: Penguin Books, 1993).
12   The way that Margaret-Elizabeth and Lizzie identify with dominant white culture can be compared to that of the female viewer's relationship to the male protagonist on-screen. As first described by Laura Mulvey, the female viewer, by identifying with the leading male role, thereby participates in her own objectification. See Mulvey's "Visual Pleasure and Narrative Cinema," *Screen* 16 (Autumn 1975): 6–18.
13   Patricia Hill Collins, *Black Feminist Thought*, 170–1.
14   Gloria J. Joseph, "White Promotion, Black Survival" in *Common Differences: Conflicts in Black and White Feminist Perspectives*, ed. Gloria J. Joseph and Jill Lewis (New York: Anchor Books, 1981), 28.
15   bell hooks, *Outlaw Culture: Resisting Representations* (New York: Routledge, 1994), 174.
16   bell hooks, *Black Looks*, 65–6.
17   Jezebel represents the bad-black-girl cultural image of black women. K. Sue Jewell describes Jezebel as "a mulatto or fair-complexioned Africa-American female, who possesses features that are considered European."

She is a worldly seductress who reinforces cultural stereotypes regarding the hypersexuality of black women. See Jewell's *From Mammy to Miss America*, 46–7.

18 As described by Foucault in *The Order of Things: An Archaeology of the Human Sciences* (New York: Vintage Books, 1973).

19 Jackson, *Paper Dolls*, 391.

20 Lisa Jones play, *Combination Skin*, addressed in chapter 5, which explores the tragic mulatto archetype as constructed in fiction and film, demonstrates how common it remains for black women to "whiten" their appearance. The current methods include color contact lens, skin peels over bleaching creams, hair weaves over straighteners, plus a range of cosmetic surgical procedures on offer.

21 *Paper Dolls* supports Sue Ellen Case's observation in *Feminism and Theatre* as to the black actress being relegated to the same role in theatre and film production as her counterpart in society, both of which reflect the same race and class bias. The roles generally accorded to black women are marginal ones, "ensuring relative invisibility and bringing paltry financial reward." See *Feminism and Theatre*, 101.

22 Addell Austin Anderson, "Paper Dolls: Playthings That Hurt," in *Upstaging Big Daddy: Directing Theatre as if Gender and Race Matter*, ed. Ellen Donkin and Susan Clement (Ann Arbor: The University of Michigan Press, 1992), 277–8.

23 Jackson, *Paper Dolls*, 383.

24 Gayle Austin, *Feminist Theories for Dramatic Criticism*, 91.

25 Jacques Derrida, *Writing and Difference*, trans. Alan Bass (Chicago: The University of Chicago Press, 1978), 246.

26 Judith Butler, *Gender Trouble*, 30.

27 Kathleen Collins, *The Brothers, 9 Plays by Black Women*, ed. Margaret B. Wilkerson (New York: New American Library, 1986).

28 The Edwards' men share the women's disassociation from the various black movements transpiring around them. For instance, Franklin resents being asked to speak in the Assembly after King's assassination because it draws attention to his race (he is the Assembly's only black member), hating "the race stuff politics locks him into." Collins, *Paper Dolls*, 335.

29 Evelyn Brooks-Higginbotham recounts how during reconstruction, even though both black men and women had to work, they idealized white sex–gender roles, with the man as economic provider and the woman as domestic helpmate. See her essay "The Problems of Race in Women's History" in *Coming to Terms: Feminism, Theory, Politics* (New York: Routledge, 1989), 130. hooks argues that blacks' psychological allegiance to these conservative gender roles was unquestionably reinforced after the Second World War, as blacks were not immune to the sexual politics of the fifties which socialized all men and women into believing that a woman's place was in the home. See hooks' *Ain't I A Woman: Black Women and Feminism* (London: Pluto Press, 1982), 177.

30 Collins, *Paper Dolls*, 324.
It should be noted that colorism is not only a black American phenomena.

It is not unusual for Anglo-African women, particularly those whose parents are from the Caribbean, to speak of the importance placed upon "good hair" and "good coloring" by their own parents. Women of Caribbean ancestry also recount that in Caribbean culture people who failed to marry light were often derogated. See Debbie Weekes' "Shades of Blackness: Young Black Female Constructions of Beauty" in *Black British Feminism: A Reader*, ed. Heidi Safia Mirza (London: Routledge, 1997), 118–19.

31   bell hooks, *Black Looks*, 94.

32   Ruth Frankenberg, *The Social Construction of Whiteness*, 192–6, 228–9.

33   Carol Lee Bacchi, *Same Difference: Feminism and Sexual Difference* (Sydney: Allen & Unwin, 1990), 208.

34   Robin Morgan, *Going Too Far: The Personal Chronicle of a Feminist* (New York: Vintage Books, 1978), 169.

35   Morgan's explanation elides the category of the psychic as it ignores the element of fantasy in pornography. Anti-censorship feminists argue that ideology is precisely what most fantasy does not express. In "Pornography and fantasy: Psychoanalytic perspectives," Elizabeth Cowie contends that what pornography represents is not the object of desire but a scenario in which certain wishes are presented. See *Sex Exposed: Sexuality and the Pornography Debate*. ed. Lynne Segal and Mary McIntosh (London: Virago, 1992), 139. For example, the typical pornographic narrative portrays the uncontrollably sexually desiring female who is always visibly sexually satisfied by means of the male's larger-than-life and always erect penis. In "Sweet Sorrows, painful pleasures: Pornography and the perils of heterosexual desire," Lynne Segal also contends that pornographic fantasy has no straightforward connection with what would be presumed to be its real-life enactment, unless it is a stylized enactment such as S/M, which is under the fantasizer's control. Further, she argues that pornographic narratives demonstrate how pornography is not a means for men to achieve power over women, but, in fact, proof that men lack power over women. See *Sex Exposed*, 71 & 76.

36   Lynne Segal, "Feminist Sexual Politics and the Heterosexual Predicament," in *New Sexual Agendas*, ed. Lynne Segal (Houndmills: Macmillan, 1997), 79.

37   Avedon Carol, *Nudes, Prudes and Attitudes: Pornography and Censorship* (Cheltenham: New Clarion Press, 1994).

38   Dworkin and MacKinnon make no effort to account for lesbian or male-on-male rape.

Lesbian–feminist Sheila Jeffreys makes a similar argument in *Anti-Climax: a Feminist Perspective on the Sexual Revolution* (North Melbourne, Victoria: Spinifex, 1990), positing heterosexual desire as eroticized power difference.

39   Linda Gordon and Ellen Dubois, "Seeking Ecstasy on the Battlefield: Danger and Pleasure in Nineteenth Century Feminist Sexual Thought," *Feminist Review*, nos 13–15 (1983): 42–51, 43.

40   Andrea Dworkin, *Intercourse* (New York: The Free Press, 1988).

41   Anna Coote and Beatrix Campbell, *Sweet Freedom: The Struggle for Women's*

*Liberation* (Oxford: Basil Blackwell, 1982), 227.

42  Andrea Dworkin, *Womanhating* (New York: E.P. Dutton, 1974), 23.

43  Andrea Dworkin, *Our Blood: Prophecies and Discourses on Sexual Politics* (London: The Women's Press, 1982), 12 & 83.

44  MacKinnon's "dominance theory" is set out in *Feminism Unmodified* (Cambridge, Mass.: Harvard University Press, 1987).

45  Andrea Dworkin, *Intercourse*, 139.

46  Carol Smart, "Unquestionably a moral issue: Rhetorical devices and regulatory imperatives," in *Sex Exposed: Sexuality and the Pornography Debate*, eds. Lynne Segal and Mary McIntosh (London: Virago, 1992), 189.

47  Avedon Carol, *Nudes, Prudes and Attitudes*, 50–1.

48  However, Merck notes that Dworkin and McKinnon's definition of pornography as stated in the Ordinance was incorporated by the Labour MP Dawn Primarolo in her 1989 Location of Pornographic Material Bill.

    See Many Merck, "From Minneapolis to Westminster," in *Sex Exposed: Sexuality and the Pornography Debate*, ed. Lynne Segal and Mary McIntosh (London: Virago, 1992), 54–5.

49  Andrea Dworkin, "Feminism: An Agenda" and "Pornography Is A Civil Rights Issue," in *Letters From A War Zone* (1988; New York: Lawrence Hill Books, 1993).

50  Judith Butler, *Bodies That Matter: On The Discursive Limits of "Sex"* (London: Routledge, 1993), 181–2.

    Angela P. Harris, "Race and Essentialism in Feminist Legal Theory," in *Representing Women: Law, Literature and Feminism*, ed. Susan Sage Heinzelman and Zipporah Batshaw Wiseman (Durham: Duke University Press, 1994), 114–15.

52  Adrienne Rich, "Compulsory Heterosexuality and lesbian existence," *Signs*, vol. 5, no. 4 (1980): 631–60.

53  See *The Persistent Desire: A Femme-Butch Reader*, ed. Joan Nestle (Boston: Alyson Publications, 1992) and Lillian Faderman's *Odd Girls and Twilight Lovers: A History of Lesbian Life in Twentieth-Century America* (London: Penguin, 1994).

54  Hazel V. Carby, *Reconstructing Womanhood: The Emergence of the Afro-American Woman Novelist* (Oxford: Oxford University Press, 1987), 18.

55  Eve Lewis, *Ficky Stingers, Plays by Women*, vol. 6, ed. Mary Remnant (London, Methuen, 1987).

56  Susan Brownmiller, *Against Our Will: Men, Women and Rape* (New York: Penguin Books, 1975).

57  The inference I draw is supported when before Terry rapes "Woman", he calls her an old dog, and when after being raped, "Woman" refers to feeling suffocated and "breathing hot pond," *Ficky Stingers*, 123.

58  Eve Lewis, *Ficky Stingers*, 125.

59  According to sexually conservative feminists, sex and murder are fused in the male psyche. In keeping with this idea, the level of physical violence in the play never lets us forget that men have the power to literally crush women.

60  Avedon Carol, *Nudes, Prudes, and Attitudes*, 148.

61    Charlotte Canning, *Feminist Theatres in the U.S.A.: Staging Women's Experiences* (London: Routledge, 1996), 170.

62    Lewis, postscript, *Ficky Stingers*, 126.

63    Jill Dolan, *The Feminist Spectator as Critic* (Ann Arbor: The University of Michigan Press, 1988), 114.

64    However, using a Brechtian influenced feminist theorization of the body in performance may allow "Woman" to occupy the space Diamond calls "looking-at-being-looked-at-ness" or simply "looking-ness," which could frustrate the power of the male gaze because this position involves the body as paradoxically available for analysis and identification and allows it to be within represenatation without being fixed by it. This position acknowledges no fourth wall; thus, as Dolan comments, the actor/subject is theoretically free to look back. See Elin Diamond's *Unmaking Mimesis*, 52 and Jill Dolan's *The Feminist Spectator as Critic*, 114.

65    Lewis, *Ficky Stingers*, 122.

66    In light of my comments on the reactionary nature of Dworkin's political agenda, I would note the following. In *Nostalgia and Sexual Difference: The Resistance to Contemporary Feminism*, Janice Doane and Devon Hodges point out that in conservative ideology the attachment of feminine sexuality to pleasure and power is considered to be a mark of the decay of society (New York: Methuen, 1987), 56–7. It is also a typical complaint of backlash literature. It is interesting that a feminist playwright would copy a position held by those who consider feminism threatening to the status quo and whose aim is to authenticate the traditional place of woman, and it demonstrates once again the dangers to feminism of Dworkin and MacKinnon's allegiance to stereotypical gender categories.

67    Lynne Segal, "Sweet sorrows, painful pleasures: Pornography and the perils of heterosexual desire," in *Sex Exposed: Sexuality and the Pornography Debate* ed. Lynne Segal and Mary McIntosh (London: Virago, 1991), 77.

68    Eve Lewis, *Ficky Stingers*, 123.

69    Ibid., 124.

70    Ibid., 125.

71    Lynne Segal, "Feminist Sexual Politics," in *New Sexual Agendas*, ed. Lynne Segal (Houndmills: Macmillan, 1997), 89.

72    Ine Vanwesenbeeck, "The Context of Women's Power(lessness) in Heterosexual Interactions," *New Sexual Agendas*, ed. Lynne Segal (Houndmills: Macmillan, 1997), 171.

73    Judith Butler, *Gender Trouble*, 126.

74    Youngblood, in *Shakin' The Mess*, also makes reference to rape as a tool used to control what whites deem "inappropriate" behavior for blacks. Daughter's mother is gang-raped because the white youths believe she has been acting too white, that is, too free in her movements.

       Robbie McCauley, *Sally's Rape, Moon Marked & Touched By Sun: Plays By African-American Women*, ed. Sydne Mahone (New York: Theatre Communications Group, 1994).

75    McCauley, *Sally's Rape*, 220.

76    Slavery was not merely an economic institution. Darlene Clark Hines iden-

tifies white male control of black women as sexual beings, including their institutionalized rape, as that which shored up the patriarchal dimension of the system. See "'In the Kingdom of Culture': Black Women and the Intersection of Race, Gender and Class," in *Lure and Loathing: Essays on Race, Identity and the Ambivalence of Assimilation*, ed. Early, 341.

77 A typical example of white feminist inattention to the way that rape and race have been historically connected is the "Take Back the Night" campaign (known as Reclaim The Night in Britain). These marches, first launched in the US by the group "Women Against Violence Against Women," were a significant part of the 1980s feminist campaign to expose heteropatriarchal culture as a *rape-culture*. However, the events, primarily directed by white activists, in many cases inadvertently pointed to black culture as a rape culture by virtue of parading through the poorest districts, which also happened to be predominantly black neighborhoods. The organizers simply failed to think through the implications of where they chose to march, and black women were reluctant to take part in an event which could bolster the myth of the black rapist.

78 Nellie V. McKay, "Alice Walker's 'Advancing Luna – and Ida B. Wells' A Struggle Toward Sisterhood," in *Rape and Representation*, ed. Lynn A. Higgins and Brenda R. Silver (New York: Columbia University Press, 1991), 254.

79 "Identity, Skin, Blood, Heart," in *Yours in Struggle: three feminist perspectives on anti-Semitism and racism*, ed. Elly Bulkin, Minne Bruce Pratt, Barbara Smith (New York: Long Haul Press, 1984), 40.

80 Lynne Segal, *Is The Future Female?: Troubled Thoughts on Contemporary Feminism* (London: Virago, 1988), 102.

81 Davis, Angela, *Women, Race & Class* (London: The Women's Press, 1982), 182.
   White obsession with black sexual bestiality has its roots in a nineteenth-century brand of racism as does white's history of sexual terrorism against blacks. Here it was the case that one group projected onto another their own unacknowledged violent impulses in order to affirm a set of moral values which they wished to believe were their own.

82 Davis' analysis covers Shulamith Firestone's *The Dialectic of Sex: The Case for Feminist Revolution*, Jean McKellar's *Rape: The Bait and the Trap*, and Diana Russell's *The Politics of Rape: The Victim's Perspective*.

83 The myth of the bad black woman (think of Castle's image of Margaret-Elizabeth in *Paper Dolls*) is analogous to the image of the rapist-as-black-man and both have been used to justify violence against the black community and sexual violence against black women in particular. This is not to say that there can be any facile equation of racial and sexual discrimination and/or violence, nor do I mean to suggest that rape encompasses some form of masculine alliance that overlays racial divisions. However, this myth has been used as a justification for white male attacks on black women in retaliation for supposed black male sexual crimes against "their" women as well as for the lynching of black men.

84 Jill Lewis, "The Subject of Struggle: Feminism and Sexuality," in *Common*

*Differences: Conflicts in Black and White Feminist Perspectives*, ed. Gloria J. Joseph and Jill Lewis (New York: Anchor Books, 1981), 252.

85  Some other cultural institutions to which feminists have applied the metaphor of rape are the government, the media, marriage and the nuclear family.

86  McCauley, *Sally's Rape*, 231.

87  Ibid., 223.

88  Ibid., 237.

89  Charlotte Canning, *Feminist Theatres in the USA*, 41–8.

90  McCauley does not comment on the make-up of the audience.

91  *Ficky Stingers* also draws a link between the linguistic domination of women by men with women's sexual domination through force. In "Words, Words, Words," Deborah Cameron writes: "in the context of addressing someone, words are deeds" See *The War of the Words: The Political Correctness Debate*, ed. Sarah Dunant (London: Virago, 1994), 26. When "Woman" pulls over to offer her friends a lift, "Man" asks "Who's that cunt?" to which she replies "Its this cunt." "Man" greets "Woman" as a cunt because in the world of the play "Woman" is equated to a fucking-machine. That "Woman" accepts this arguably crude reference to women's genitalia as a designation of herself illustrates how she assesses herself in masculine terms. It soon becomes apparent from her speech that "Woman" views other women as well through the eyes of "Man." She participates in dialogue with him which degrades other women, referring to them as silly bitches and discussing the relative merits of their "tits." In order that she might be accepted and approved, she tries to act like one of the boys, for instance, laughing at "Man's" sexist jokes and his two-timing her girlfriend with another friend. Through engaging in this sexist banter, she publicly affirms the heteropatriarchal value system. And prior to her being raped, it seems that she genuinely acquiesces in it. Initially, being accepted by men is more important to her than being accepted by her women friends because she sees women as unimportant and thus, their approval is value-less. As opposed to McCauley, Lewis suggests that women may speak a masculine language or not speak at all.

92  McCauley, *Sally's Rape*, 226.

93  Deborah K. Chappel, "Racism Goes Underground," in *Engaging Feminism: Students Speak Up & Speak Out*, ed. Jean O'Barr & Mary Wyer, 76.

94  Nellie V. McKay, "Alice Walker's Advancing Luna," in *Race and Representation*, ed. Higgins & Silver, 250–1. That society, and particularly the criminal justice system, is more likely to listen to white women victims of assault and respond positively when the alleged assailant is black is borne out by the number of black men who are in prison for raping black women as opposed to black or white men who rape black women (black-on-black rape accounts for two-thirds of rapes committed by black men). The rates for arrest and conviction of black men are disproportionate for rape. Sentences for black-on-white rape are also more severe than for black-on-black or white-on-black rape.

## 5  "Woman" as Subject: Negotiating Multiple Identities

1   Cheryl L. West, "I Ain't the Right Kind of Feminist," in *Third World Women and the Politics of Feminism*, eds. Chandra Talpade Mohanty, Ann Russo, Lourdes Torres (Bloomington: Indiana University Press, 1991), n.p.

2   Robert Young, *Colonial Desire: Hybridity in Theory, Culture and Race* (London: Routledge, 1995).

3   Ibid., 21–2.

4   Homi K. Bhabha, "Signs Taken for Wonders," in *The Post-Colonial Studies Reader*, ed. Bill Ashcroft, Gareth Griffiths, Helen Tiffin. 1995 (London: Routledge, 1997), 35.

5   Hall quoted in Young, *Colonial Desire*, 24.

6   Ibid., 24–5.

7   Stuart Hall, "New Ethnicities," in *The Postcolonial Studies Reader*, ed. Ashcroft et al., 223–7.

8   By "slightly" I allude to the way in which individual consciousness is a combination of the self-regulating agent of humanist desire – the idea of the conscious mind belonging to the individual – and "a decentered network of desire." Jonathan Dollimore quoting Terry Eagleton in *Sexual Dissidence*, 71.

9   This denotation of subject position resembles Bhabha's theory of the third space in terms of its politicization through its link to hybridity. It is the third space, Bhabha suggests, that carries the burden of cultural meaning and which constitutes the discursive conditions of enunication that ensure that the meaning and symbols of culture have no primordial unity or fixity; in other words, it is in the third space that signs can be appropriated by subordinate groups and read anew. See *The Location of Culture* (1994; London: Routledge, 1997), 37–9.

10  This is not to say that any individual/group can entirely create a subject space. Much of what we refer to as our subjectivity is constructed by external social, political, and economic forces and in a sense, fixed upon us. However, that identity is to a degree imposed does not render us powerless to alter our socio-cultural standpoints. Foucault asserts that freedom does not necessarily lie in discovering or being able to determine who we are, but rather in rebelling against those ways in which we are already defined, categorized and classified – Foucault quoted in Jana Sawicki's *Disciplining Foucault: Feminism, Power and the Body* (New York: Routledge, 1991), 27. Therefore, if identity is an effect of how we are defined, categorized, and classified, then we possess at least a modicum of power to modify it.

11  When discussing the connection between political and personal notions of identity, it is necessary to address the issue of essentialism versus antiessentialism," as identity is often held to include the idea of unity or essence. Diana Fuss warns against always taking essentialism to be "a problem or a mistake," for one may deploy or activate essentialism as readily as one may fall or lapse into it. See *Essentially Speaking: Feminism, Nature & Difference* (London: Routledge, 1989), 32. Her point is that essen-

tialism is not inherently reactionary; it may have some strategic interventionary value. "Essentialism when put into practice by the dispossessed themselves can be powerfully displacing and disruptive," she writes (99). The question in relation to essentialism should be one of permissibility, and the permissibility of engaging in essentialism must be framed by the subject-position from which one speaks.

12   Jayne O. Ifekwunigwe, "Diaspora's daughters, Africa's orphans?: On lineage, authenticity and 'mixed race' identity," in *Black British Feminism: A Reader*, ed. Heidi Safia Mirza (London: Routledge, 1997), 127.

The term "metisse," the feminine form of a French African word meaning someone who by virtue of parentage holds two world views, is preferred by Ifekwunigwe over mixed-race or bi-racial in an attempt to move away from a discourse of race based on the premise of skin color.

13   Ibid., 141.
14   Ruth Frankenberg, *The Social Construction of Whiteness*, 55 & 98.
15   Trinh T. Minh-Ha, "She, the Inappropriate/d Other." *Discourse* 8 (Fall–Winter 1986–87). See also Minh-Ha's introduction to this special issue.
16   Akousa, Jayne O. Ifekwunigwe, "Diaspora's Daughters," in *Black British Feminism*, ed. Mirza, 136.
17   hooks writes that "most folks in this society do not want to openly admit that 'blackness' as sign primarily evokes in the public imagination of whites (and all other groups who learn that one of the quickest ways to demonstrate one's kinship within a white supremacist order is by sharing racist assumptions) hatred and fear." See *Black Looks*, 10.
18   Lisa Jones, *Combination Skin, Contemporary Plays by Women of Color*, ed. Kathy A. Perkins and Roberta Uno (London: Routledge, 1996).
19   Jones, *Combination Skin*, 215–16.
20   Ibid., 222.
21   Ibid., 219.
22   Ruth Frankenberg, *The Social Construction of Whiteness*, 240.
23   Jones, *Combination Skin*, 218.
24   Ibid., 227.
25   Ibid., 227–8.
26   Ibid., 220.
27   Ibid., 222.
28   Ibid., 220.
29   Ibid., 220–1.
30   Ruth Frankenberg, *The Social Construction of Whiteness*, 142.
31   Jones, *Combination Skin*, 219.
32   Ibid., 225.
33   Ibid., 225–6.
34   In "Diaspora's Daughters," Jayne O. Ifekwunigwe notes that it is common among many families with one black parent and one white for white cultural codes to be reified at the expense of black referents – even in cases where both parents are present. See *Black British Feminism*, ed. Mirza, 140.
35   Judith Butler, *Bodies That Matter*, 39.

36   In contrast to the reaction of Specimen Two's father, historically, there seems to be a greater willingness among black people to incorporate children of mixed-race, whether they are the products of force or choice, than among white. Unlike the difficulties one can face being black and middle-class (See Medley's *Ma Rose* and Collins' *The Brothers* in chapter 4), according to Akousa's account, people of black and white heritage do not meet with too much difficulty in gaining acceptance within the black community provided that they do not make too great an effort to "black-wash" themselves. Akousa suggests that the black community's borders are more porous on the issue of race than the white community's. John Solomos, Bob Findlay, Simon Jones and Paul Gilroy, authors of "The Organic crisis of British Capitalism and race: the experience of the seventies," recall the long history in white culture of breeding for the race. This is the idea that white women should produce only pure white offspring. Those who bore mulattos, it was argued, failed in their duty to the race by polluting it with inferior blood; see *The Empire Strikes Back: Race and racism in 70s Britain* (London: Routledge in Association with the Centre for Contemporary Cultural Studies University of Birmingham, 1992, 2nd edn), 71. Unlike the case of Specimen Two, it appears that a mixed-race child stands more chance of being rejected by her white relations than her black.
37   Genevieve Fabre, *Drumbeats, Masks and Metaphor*, 218.
38   Jackie Kay, *Chiaroscuro, Lesbian Plays*, ed. Jill Davis (London: Methuen, 1987).
39   Robert Young, *Colonial Desire*, 25.
40   Jackie, Kay, afterward, *Chiaroscuro,* 82. Kay explores her own hybrid identity and the experience of being a black child in a predominantly white country (Scotland) in *The Adoption Papers*, first broadcast on BBC Radio 3 in 1990. The play is printed in Judith Baxter's *Four Women Poets* (Cambridge: Cambridge University Press, 1995).
41   Jill Dolan, "Breaking the Code: Musings on Lesbian Sexuality and the Performer," *Drama Review* 32 (1989): 146–52, 151. Jill Davis is quoted as also holding this view in Goodman's *Contemporary Feminist Theatres*, 140.
42   Anna Lee, "A Black Separatist," in *Radical Feminism,* ed. Anna Koedt, Ellen Levine and Anita Rapone (1973; New York: Quadrangle Books, 1981), 84.
43   Genevieve Fabre, *Drumbeats, Masks and Metaphor*, 221.
44   Sandra Freeman, *Putting Your Daughters on the Stage*, 32.
45   Kay, *Chiaroscuro*, 64.
46   Ibid., 79–80.
47   Ibid., 59.
48   Ibid., 49.
49   Jeffrey Weeks, "Questions of Identity," in *The Cultural Construction of Sexuality*, ed. Pat Kaplan (London: Tavistock Publications, 1987), 47.
50   James T. Sears, *Growing Up Gay in the South: race, gender, and journeys of the spirit* (London: Harrington Park Press, 1991), 139.
51   Kay, *Chiaroscuro*, 64.
52   Ibid., 78.
53   Jewelle Gomez and Barbara Smith, "Talking About It: Homophobia in the

Black Community," *Feminist Review* 34 (1990), 47–55, 54.

54 Kay, *Chiaroscuro*, 73.

55 Ibid., 72.

56 Minnie Bruce Pratt, "Identity, Skin, Blood, Heart," in *Yours in Struggle*, ed. Elly Bulkin et al., 39.

57 Kay, *Chiaroscuro*, 67.

58 Ibid., 68.

59 Homi K. Bhabha, *The Location of Culture*, 9.

60 Kay, *Chiaroscuro*, 65.

61 Ibid., 76.

62 Kay, afterward, *Chiaroscuro*, 82–3.

63 Audre Lorde, *Sister Outsider*, 31.

## 6 Infiltrating "Woman": Butch/Fem Lesbian Subjectivities

1 Lois Weaver, "Sheila Dances with Sheila," in *butch/femme: Inside Lesbian Gender*, ed. Sally R. Munt (London: Cassell, 1998), 71–2.

2 Primarily, this chapter will focus upon butch and fem roles as they are constructed within a white, working class / middle-class context as these are the identities encompassed within the group Split Britches and its play-texts.

3 In *The Feminist Spectator as Critic*, Jill Dolan argues that the lesbian subject offers the most radical position from which to subvert representation: personally, artistically, and spectatorially (Ann Arbor: The University of Michigan Press, 1988), 119. Here, Dolan refers primarily to postmodern forms of lesbian theatre. She adds that this kind of lesbian theatre works to appropriate the subject position by creating a new economy of desire between women.

4 Virtually without exception, butches and fems are identified in relation to one another, as if the one requires the other to exist. Nevertheless, as Gayle Rubin recognizes, "to define 'butch' as the object of femme desire, or 'femme' as the object of butch desire presupposes that butches do not desire or partner with other butches, and that femmes do not desire or partner with other femmes"; see "Of Catamites and Kings: Reflections on Butch, Gender, and Boundaries," in *The Persistent Desire: A Femme-Butch Reader*, ed. Joan Nestle (Boston, Alyson Publications, 1992), 471. Just as butch and fem roles cannot be elided in the social realm, they cannot be elided in the psychic. Each occupies a unique position in material relations as well as a distinctive place in representation.

5 Gramsci provides a worthwhile recipe for theoretical enterprises: "one can construct, on a specific practice, a theory which, by coinciding and identi-fying itself with the decisive elements of the practice itself, can accelerate the historical process that is going on . . . " In other words, theory must not be envisaged as either primary to or ancillary to practice; to the contrary, theoretical proposals must take into account that theoretical constructs inhabit the same cultural imaginary as do representations of mass culture; see *Selections From The Prison Notebooks Of Antonio Gramsci*, ed. and trans.

Quintin Hoare and Geoffrey Nowell Smith (1971; London: Lawrence and Wishart, 1986), 365.

6   Judith Roof, *A Lure of Knowledge: Lesbian Sexuality and Theory* (New York: Columbia University Press, 1991), 242.

7   Sheila Jeffreys, "Butch and Fem: Now and Then," in *Not A Passing Phase*, ed. Lesbian History Group (London: The Women's Press, 1989), 175.

8   For example, see Amber Hollibaugh and Cherie Moraga's "What We're Rollin' around in Bed With: Sexual Silences in Feminism: A Conversation toward Ending Them," *Heresies* 12 (1981): 58–62); Lyndall MacCowan's "Re-collecting History, Renaming Lives: Femme Stigma and the Feminist Seventies and Eighties," in *The Persistent Desire*, ed. Nestle; Joan Nestle's "Sexual Courage in the 1950s," *A Restricted Country* (1988; London: Pandora Press, 1996); and Joan Nestle's "The Fem Question," in *The Persistent Desire*, ed. Nestle.

9   Jeanne Cordova, "Butches, Lies, and Feminism," in *The Persistent Desire*, ed. Joan Nestle, p. 288.

10  Sheila Jeffreys, "Butch and Fem," in *Not A Passing Phase*, ed. Lesbian History Group, 179. Catherine R. Stimpson subscribes to a similar view; she calls butch/fem the "ironic tragedy" of homosexuality because it keeps the stereotypes of masculine and feminine spinning; see *Where the Meanings Are: Feminism and Cultural Spaces* (London: Methuen, 1988), 59.

11  For example, see the accounts in "A Celebration of butch-femme identities in the Lesbian community" in *The Persistent Desire*, ed. Nestle.

12  Mykel Johnson, "Butchy Femme," in *The Persistent Desire*, ed. Nestle, 396.

13  Jacques Derrida, *Writing and Difference*, trans. Alan Bass (1967; London: Routledge, 1991), 25.

14  Michel Foucault, "The Order of Discourse," in *Untying the Text: A Post-Structuralist Reader*, ed. Robert Young (London: Routledge & Kegan Paul, 1981), 48–9.

15  Introduction to "Lipstick Vogue: The Politics of Drag," *Radical America*, vol. 22 (1988), 35.

16  Sue-Ellen Case, introduction, *Split Britches: Lesbian Practice/Feminist Performance* (London: Routledge, 1996), 1.

17  Lizbeth Goodman, *Contemporary Feminist Theatres*, 140.

18  Peggy Shaw, Deborah Margolin, Lois Weaver, *Beauty and The Beast*, *Split Britches: Lesbian Practice/Feminist Performance*, ed. Sue Ellen-Case (London: Routledge, 1996).

19  For the sake of brevity, Deborah Margolin's role of Rabbi Hitchcock Rabin/Father will not be treated unless it directly impacts upon the production of the butch/fem dynamic.

20  Joan Nestle, "The Fem Question," in *Pleasure and Danger*, ed. Carole S. Vance (London: Routledge, 1984), 236.

21  Shaw, Margolin, Weaver, *Beauty and The Beast*, 81.

22  Ibid., 82.

23  Sue-Ellen Case, "Toward a Butch-Femme Aesthetic," in *Making A Spectacle: Feminist Essays on Contemporary Women's Theatre*, ed. Lynda Hart (Ann Arbor: University of Michigan Press, 1989), 295–7.

24 Shakespeare, *Romeo and Juliet, The Warwick Shakespeare*, ed. J.E. Crofts (London: Blackie and Son Ltd., 1963), 27.

25 Shaw, Margolin, Weaver, *Beauty and The Beast*, 68.

26 Alan Sinfield, *The Wilde Century: Effeminacy, Oscar Wilde and the Queer Moment* (London: Cassell, 1994), 202–3.

27 Jonathan Dollimore, *Sexual Dissidence*, 285.

28 Ibid., 323.

29 Sue-Ellen Case, "Toward a Butch-Femme Aesthetic," in *Making a Spectacle*, ed. Hart, 283.

30 Wendy Holloway, "Gender Difference and The Production of Subjectivity," in *Changing the Subject: Psychology, Social Regulation, and Subjectivity*, ed. Julian Henriques, Wendy Holloway et al. (London: Methuen, 1984), 236.

31 Jane Gallup, *Thinking Through The Body* (New York: Columbia University Press, 1988), 113.

32 Naomi Schor, "Dreaming Dissymetry: Barthes, Foucault, and Sexual Difference," in *Men in Feminism*, ed. Alice Jardine and Paul Smith (London: Methuen, 1987), 110.

33 Judith Butler, *Gender Trouble*, 30.

34 Jacques Derrida, *Of Grammatology*, trans. Gayatri Chakravorty Spivak (1967; Baltimore: Johns Hopkins University Press, 1976), 24.

35 Jonathan Dollimore, *Sexual Dissidence*, 87–8.

36 Sue-Ellen Case, "Toward a Butch-Femme Aesthetic," in *Making a Spectacle*, ed. Hart, 296–7.

37 The Hepburn/Tracy dialogue also shows how a woman chooses her butch/fem identity just as she chooses her lesbian identity: its a personal and political choice. Whereas in Jeffrey's concept of lesbianism, butch, fem, and lesbian function as essentialist terms.

38 Madeline Davis, "Epilogue, nine years later," in *The Persistent Desire*, ed. Joan Nestle, pp. 270–1.

39 Sigmund Freud, "The Psychogenesis of a Case of Homosexuality in a Woman," *The Penguin Freud* Library, vol. 9, trans. James Strachey (1920; London: Penguin Books, 1990), 397.

40 Similarly, the fem's desire for another woman cannot be accounted for within the terms of heterosexual logic as articulated by Lacan in so far as Lacan can only entertain the female as the object of a male audience.

41 Roof, who also recognizes this point, provides an excellent reading of the masculine bias which underlies Freud's theory of female homosexuality; see chapter 4 of *A Lure of Knowledge*.

42 Havelock Ellis quoted in Mary Louise Adams' *Cherchez Les Femmes: On the Invisibility of the "Feminine" Invert in Lesbian History*, Paper 16 (Canterbury: University of Kent, n.d), 14–15.

43 George Chauncey Jr., "From Sexual Inversion to Homosexuality: Medicine and the Changing Conceptualization of Female Deviance," *Salmagundi* 58–9 (1982–3): 114–46, 126–7.

44 Amber Hollibaugh and Cherie Moraga, "What We're Rollin Around in Bed With: Sexual Silences in Feminism," *Heresies* 12 (1981): 58–62.

45  Mykel Johnson, "Butchy-Femme," in *The Persistent Desire*, ed. Nestle, 397–8.

46  Deborah Margolin, Peggy Shaw, Lois Weaver, *Upwardly Mobile Home, Split Britches: Lesbian Practice/Feminist Performance*, ed. Sue Ellen Case (London: Routledge, 1997).

47  The play aims to make visible the poverty of the 1980s. The three women represent those who were left out of Reagan's economic miracle – which the play reveals as fiction.

48  Margolin, Shaw, Weaver, *Upwardly Mobile Home*, 88.

49  Sandra Lee Bartky, "Foucault, Femininity and the Modernization of Patriarchal Power," in *Feminism & Foucault: Reflections on Resistance*, ed. Irene Diamond and Lee Quincy (Boston: Northeastern University Press, 1988), 78.

50  Sue-Ellen Case quoting from Elin Diamond's "Mimesis, Mimicry and the True-Real," introduction, *Split Britches*, ed. Case, 23.

51  Margolin, Shaw, Weaver, *Upwardly Mobile Home*, 91.

52  She defines the butch as "the hero of open expression, the only woman who could openly say she was a lesbian in a very clear concrete way." Jewelle Gomez, "A Celebration of Butch-Femme Identities in the Lesbian Community," in *The Persistent Desire*, ed. Nestle, 454–63.

53  Joan Riviere developed her theory of womanliness as a masquerade from analyses of particular types of intellectual women. According to Riviere, while these women realized "complete feminine development" in that they married, bore children, and capably exercised domestic duties, at the same time, they excelled professionally, that is, at masculine pursuits. Forming the center of Riviere's essay "Womanliness as a Masquerade" is the case of a woman who complained that she would experience anxiety after giving a public address. To alleviate this anxiety, she would seek complementary attention from the men in her audience; she sought both reassurance about her intellectual competence and her sexual attractiveness. Riviere analyzed the woman's behavior as follows: this woman's flirtatious manner was an "unconscious attempt to ward off the anxiety which would ensue on account of the reprisals she anticipated from the father-figures after her intellectual performance. The exhibition in public of her intellectual proficiency . . . signified an exhibition of herself in possession of the father's penis, having castrated him." Therefore, she adopted a mask of womanliness in order to "hide [her] possession of masculinity and to avert the reprisals expected if she was found to possess it." Joan Riviere, "Womanliness as a Masquerade," in *Formations of Fantasy*, ed. Victor Burgin, James Donald and Cora Kaplan (London: Methuen, 1986), 37–8.

54  Sue-Ellen Case, "Toward a Butch-Femme Aesthetic," in *Making a Spectacle*, ed. Hart, 291.

55  Joan Riviere, "Womanliness as a Masquerade," in *Formations of Fantasy*, ed. Burgin et al., 38.

56  Stephen Heath, "Joan Riviere and the Masquerade," *Formations of Fantasy*, ed. Burgin et al., 50.

57  Ibid., 57.

58    Margolin, Shaw, Weaver, *Upwardly Mobile Home*, 92.

59    Ibid., 93.

60    Ibid., 107.

61    Esther Newton, *Mother Camp: Female Impersonators in America* (New Jersey: Prentice-Hall, 1972), 100–5.

62    Note the difference between Newton's definition of camp and Susan Sontag's; see *A Susan Sontag Reader* (New York: Farrar, 1982). Sontag's notion of camp as a depoliticized or apolitical sensibility, as a "a certain mode of aestheticism," is the most widely known and, among traditional literary critics, the most widely accepted. The problems with her definition have been amply documented by lesbian and gay writers. Briefly, while giving mention to camp's affiliation with homosexuality, Sontag nevertheless proffers an anaesthetized version of camp, one which evacuates camp of its historically gay specificity and robs it of its dissident qualities in an attempt to assimilate camp to an elitist sense of "good taste."

63    Sue-Ellen Case, "Toward a Butch-Femme Aesthetic." in *Making a Spectacle*, ed. Hart, 291.

64    Elizabeth Lapovsky Kennedy and Madeline Davis, "'They Was No One To Mess With': The Construction of the Butch Role in the Lesbian Community of the 1940s and 1950s," in *The Persistent Desire*, ed. Nestle, 75.

65    Ibid., 62. The findings of Kennedy and Davis are reflected in many of the personal accounts documented in *Inventing Ourselves: Lesbian Life Stories* (Hall Carpenter Archives: Lesbian Oral History Group. London: Routledge, 1991). Their findings are also backed up by the accounts in *What a Lesbian Looks Like: Writings by Lesbians on their Lives and Lifestyles* (National Gay and Lesbian Survey. London: Routledge, 1992).

66    Peggy Shaw, Deborah Margolin, Lois Weaver, *Split Britches: A True Story, Split Britches*, ed. Case.

67    Lillian Faderman, *Odd Girls And Twilight Lovers: A History of Lesbian Life in Twentieth-Century America* (New York: Columbia University Press, 1991), 167.

68    Jeffrey Weeks, *Coming Out: Homosexual Politics in Britain from the Nineteenth Century to the Present* (1977; London: Quartet Books, 1979), 49–50.

69    Arlene Stein, "All Dressed Up, But No Place To Go? Style Wars and the New Lesbianism," in *The Persistent Desire*, ed. Nestle, 434.

70    For example, Jeanne Cordova, a working class Butch, asserts that "it is not our job to redefine who we are; it is merely our job to discover who we are—and make a safe-land for our reality;" see "Butches, lies, and feminism," in *The Persistent Desire*, ed. Nestle, 291.

71    Lyndall MacCowan, "Re-collecting history, renaming lives: Femme stigma and the feminist seventies and eighties," in *The Persistent Desire*, ed. Nestle, 316.

72    Lillian Faderman, *Odd Girls and Twilight Lovers*, 263–4.

73    Arlene Stein, "All Dressed Up," in *The Persistent Desire*, ed. Nestle, 434–5.

74    Laura Jackson, interview, *Inventing Ourselves: Lesbian Life Stories*, Hall Carpenter Archives, Lesbian Oral History Group (1989; London: Routledge, 1991), 126.

75 Arlene Stein, "All Dressed Up," in *The Persistent Desire*, ed. Nestle, 435.
76 Bette Bourne, Paul Shaw, Peggy Shaw, Lois Weaver, *Belle Reprieve, Split Britches: Lesbian Practice/Feminist Performance*, ed. Sue-Ellen Case (London: Routledge, 1996).
77 Lizbeth Goodman, *Contemporary Feminist Theaters*, 141.
78 Sue-Ellen Case, introduction, *Split Britches*, ed. Case, 29.
79 Peggy Weaver quoted by Case, introduction, *Split Britches*, ed. Case, 28.
80 Bourne, Shaw, Shaw, Weaver, *Belle Reprieve*, 158.
81 Ibid., 158.
82 Esther Newton, *Mother Camp*, 105–7.
83 Kate Davy, "Reading Past the Heterosexual Imperative: Dress Suits To Hire," *Drama Review*, vol. 33 (1988): 153–70.
84 Leo Bersani, "Is the Rectum a Grave?" *October* 41–44 (1987–88): 195–277, 208. See also Oscar Montero's "Lipstick Vogue: The Politics of Drag," *Radical America* 22 (1988): 37–41; and see Carole-Anne Tyler's "Boys Will be Girls: The Politics of Gay Drag," in *Inside/Out*, ed. Fuss.
85 Sue-Ellen Case, "Toward a Butch-Femme Aesthetic," in *Making a Spectacle*, ed. Hart, 292.
86 Alan Sinfield, *The Wilde Century*, 200.
87 Kate Davy, "Reading Past the Heterosexual Imperative," 153 & 162.
88 Alan Sinfield's comments are taken from a work in progress.
89 Bourne, Shaw, Shaw, Weaver, *Belle Reprieve*, 155.
90 Ibid., 157.
91 Diana Fuss, "Imitation and Gender Insubordination," in *Inside/Out*, ed. Fuss, 28.
92 Bourne, Shaw, Shaw, Weaver, *Belle Reprieve*, 172.
93 Ibid., 172–3.
94 Ibid., 169.
95 Barbara Smith, "The Dance of Masks," in *The Persistent Desire*, ed. Nestle, 430.
96 Smith's statement also complicates Freud's idea that lesbians suffer from a rudimentary masculinity complex.
97 Gayle Rubin, "Of Catamites and Kings: Reflections on Butch, Gender, and Boundaries," in *The Persistent Desire*, ed. Nestle, 469.
98 Sue-Ellen Case, introduction, *Split Britches*, ed. Case, 28.
99 For a discussion of how fems equate butch aggressiveness with erotic desire and pleasure, see Elizabeth Lapovsky Kennedy and Madeline D. Davis' *Boots of Leather, Slippers of Gold: The History of a Lesbian Community* (New York: Routledge, 1993), 197ff.
100 Bourne, Shaw, Shaw, Weaver, *Belle Reprieve*, 180.
101 Gabrielle Griffin, *Heavenly Love? Lesbian Images in Twentieth-Century Women's Writing* (Manchester: Manchester University Press, 1983), 181–2.

**Conclusion: Toward a Progressive Feminist Politics – A House of Difference**

1 bell hooks, *Feminist Theory From Margin to Center*, 27.
2 Teresa de Lauretis, "Sexual Indifference and Lesbian Representation,"

*Theatre Journal* vol. 40. (1988), 164.

3    Ann Russo, "We Cannot Live Without Our Lives: White Women, Antiracism, and Feminism," in *Third World Women and the Politics of Feminism*, ed. Chandra Talpade Mohanty, Ann Russo, Lourdes Torres (Bloomington: Indiana University Press, 1991), 303.

4    Trinh T. Minh-Ha, "Writing Postcoloniality and Feminism," in *The Post-Colonial Studies Reader*, ed. Ashcroft, et al., 268.

5    Alison M. Jagger, *Feminist Politics and Human Nature* (New Jersey: Rowman & Littlefield, 1988),388.

6    Baz Kershaw, *The Politics of Performance*, 165.

7    John McGrath quoted in Kershaw, *The Politics of Performance*, 165.

8    Philip Osment, "Finding Room on the Agenda for Love: A history of Gay Sweatshop," in *Gay Sweatshop: Four Plays and a Company*, ed. Philip Osment (London: Methuen, 1989).

9    Kimberley W. Benston, "The Aesthetic of Modern Black Drama: From Mimesis to Methexis," in *The Theater of Black Americans, Volume 1*, ed. Errol Hill (New Jersey: Prentice-Hall, 1980), 77.

10    De Lauretis, *Technologies of Gender*, 18.

# Bibliography

Adams, Mary Louise. "Cherchez Les Femmes: On the Invisibility of the 'Feminine' Invert in Lesbian History." Paper 16 Canterbury: University of Kent, n.d.

Anderson, Addell Austin. "Paper Dolls: Playthings That Hurt." *Upstaging Big Daddy: Directing Theatre as if Gender and Race Matter*. Ed. Ellen Donkin and Susan Clement. Ann Arbor: The University of Michigan Press, 1982, 277–89.

Asante, Molefi Kete. "Racism, Consciousness and Afrocentricity." In Early, 127–43.

Ashcroft, Bill, Gareth Griffiths, and Helen Tiffin, Ed. *The Postcolonial Studies Reader*. 1995. London: Routledge, 1997.

Aston, Elaine. *An Introduction to Feminism and Theatre*. London: Routledge, 1995.

——. *Caryl Churchill*. Plymouth: Northcote House, 1997.

Austin, Gayle. *Feminist Theories for Dramatic Criticism*. Ann Arbor: The University of Michigan Press, 1990.

Bacchi, Carol Lee. *Same Difference: Feminism and Sexual Difference*. Sydney: Allen & Unwin, 1990.

Bart, Pauline. "Review of Chodorow's The Reproduction of Mothering." *Mothering: Essays in Feminist Theory*. Ed. Joyce Trebilcott. Totowa: Rowman & Allanheld, 1984.

Bartky, Sandra Lee. "Foucault, Femininity and the Modernization of Patriarchal Power." *Feminism & Foucault: Reflections on Resistance*. Ed. Irene Diamond and Lee Quincy. Boston: Northeastern University Press, 1988, 61–86.

Benston, Kimberley W. "The Aesthetic of Modern Black Drama: From Mimesis to Methexis." *The Theater of Black Americans, Volume 1*. Ed. Errol Hill. New Jersey: Prentice-Hall, 1980, 61–78.

Bersani, Leo. "Is the Rectum a Grave?" *October* 41–4 (1987–8): 195–277.

Bhabha, Homi K. *The Location of Culture*. London: Routledge, 1994.

——. "Signs Taken for Wonders." In Ashcroft et al., 29–35.

Boris, Eileen. "The Power of Motherhood: Black and White Activist Women Redefine The 'Political.'" *Mothers of a New World: Maternalist Politics and the Origins of the Welfare State*. Ed. Seth Koven and Sonya Michel. London: Routledge, 1983, 213–45.

Bourne, Bette, Paul Shaw, Peggy Shaw and Lois Weaver. *Belle Reprieve*. In Case, *Split Britches*, 149–84.

Breines, Wini. *Young, White and Miserable: Growing Up Female in the Fifties*. Boston: Beacon Press, 1992.

Brooks-Higginbotham, Evelyn. *Coming to Terms: Feminism, Theory, Politics*. New York: Routledge, 1989.

Brown-Guillory, Elizabeth. *Their Place on the Stage: Black Women Playwrights in*

*America*. New York: Greenwood Press, 1988.

Brown, Janet. *Taking Center Stage: Feminism in Contemporary U.S. Drama*. London: The Scarecrow Press, 1991.

Brownmiller, Susan. *Against Our Will: Men, Women and Rape*. New York: Penguin Books, 1975.

Bryan, Beverley, Stella Dadzie and Suzanne Scafe. *The Heart of the Race: Black Women's Lives in Britain*. 1986. London: Virago, 1993.

Burgin, Victor, James Donald and Cora Kaplan. *Formations of Fantasy*. London: Methuen, 1986.

Butler, Judith. *Gender Trouble: Feminism and the Subversion of Identity*. London: Routledge, 1990.

——. *Bodies That Matter: On the Discursive Limits of 'Sex.'* London: Routledge, 1993.

——. "Imitation and Gender Insubordination." In Fuss, *Inside/Out*, 13–31.

Cameron, Deborah. "Words, Words, Words." *The War of the Words: The Political Correctness Debate*. Ed. Sarah Dunant. London: Virago, 1994, 15–34.

Canning, Charlotte. *Feminist Theaters in the U.S.A.: Staging Women's Experiences*. London: Routledge, 1996.

Carby, Hazel V. *Reconstructing Womanhood: The Emergence of the Afro-American Woman Novelist*. Oxford: Oxford University Press, 1987.

Carol, Avedon. *Nudes, Prudes and Attitudes: Pornography and Censorship*. Cheltenham: New Clarion Press, 1994.

Case, Sue-Ellen. *Feminism and Theatre*. New York: Methuen, 1988.

——. "Toward a Butch-Femme Aesthetic." *Making A Spectacle: Feminist Essays On Contemporary Women's Theatre*. Ed. Lynda Hart. Ann Arbor: University of Michigan Press, 1989, 283–99.

——, Ed. *Split Britches: Lesbian Practice/Feminist Performance*. London: Routledge 1996.

——. Introduction. In Case, *Split Britches*, 1–34.

Chappel, Deborah K. "Racism Goes Underground." In O'Barr and Wyer, 75–6.

Chauncey Jr., George. "From Sexual Inversion to Homosexuality: Medicine and the Changing Conceptualization of Female Deviance." *Salmagundi* 58–9 (1982–3): 114–46.

Chodorow, Nancy. *The Reproduction of Mothering: Psychoanalysis and the Sociology of Gender*. Berkeley: The University of California Press, 1978.

Christian, Barbara. "An Angle of Seeing: Motherhood in Buchi Emecheta's Joys of Motherhood and Alice Walker's Meridian." In Glenn et al., 95–120.

Churchill, Caryl. *Top Girls*. London: Methuen, 1982.

Clarke, Breena and Glenda Dickerson. *Re/membering Aunt Jemima: A Menstrual Story*. In Perkins and Uno, 35–45.

Clarke, Breena. "Artistic Statement by Breena Clarke." In Perkins and Uno, 32–4.

Cohen, Esther. "Uncommon Woman: An Interview with Wendy Wasserstein." *Women's Studies* 15 (1988): 257–70.

Collins, Kathleen. *The Brothers*. In Wilkerson, 299–345.

Collins, Patricia Hill. *Black Feminist Thought: Knowledge, Consciousness, and the Politics of Empowerment*. New York: Routledge, 1991.

——. "Shifting the Center." In Glenn et al., 45–65.

Colvin, Madeline with Jane Hawksley. *Section 28: A Practical Guide to the Law and Its Implications*. London: National Council for Civil Liberties, 1989.

Coote, Anne and Beatrix Campbell. *Sweet Freedom: The Struggle for Women's Liberation*. Oxford: Basil Blackwell, 1982.

Cordova, Jeanne. "Butches, Lies and Feminism." In Nestle, *The Persistent Desire*, 272–92.

Cowie, Elizabeth. "Pornography and Fantasy: Psychoanalytic Perspectives." In Segal and McIntosh, 132–52.

Crutchley, Kate and Nancy Diuguid. Introduction. In Wandor, *Strike While the Iron is Hot*, 63–4.

Daly, Mary. *Gyn/Ecology: The Metaethics of Radical Feminism*. London: The Women's Press, 1979.

——. *Beyond God the Father: Toward a Philosophy of Women's Liberation*. Boston: Beacon Press, 1973.

Daniels, Sarah. *Neaptide*. London: Methuen, 1986.

Davis, Angela. *Women, Race & Class*. 1981. London: The Women's Press, 1984.

Davis, Jill, Ed. *Lesbian Plays*. London: Methuen, 1987.

Davis, Madeline. "Epilogue: Nine Years Later." In Nestle, *The Persistent Desire*, 270–1.

Davy, Kate. "Reading Past the Heterosexual Imperative: Dress Suits To Hire." *Drama Review* 33 (1988): 153–70.

Dayley, Grace. *Rose's Story*. In Wandor, *Plays by Women*, 55–78.

de Lauretis, Teresa. *Technologies of Gender: Essays on Theory, Film and Fiction*. 1987. London: Macmillan, 1989.

——. "Sexual Indifference and Lesbian Representation." *Theatre Journal* 40 (1988): 155–77.

Delphy, Christine. *Close To Home: A Materialist Analysis of Women's Oppression*. London: Hutchinson, 1984.

Derrida, Jacques. *Writing and Difference*. Trans. Alan Bass. Chicago: The University of Chicago Press, 1978.

——. *Of Grammatology*. Trans. Gayatri Chakravorty Spivak. 1967. Baltimore: Johns Hopkins University Press, 1976.

Diamond, Elin. *Unmaking Mimesis: Essays on Feminism and Theater*. London: Routledge, 1997.

Dill, Bonnie Thornton. "The Dialectics of Black Womanhood." *Signs* 4(3) (Spring 1979): 543–55.

Dinnerstein, Dorothy. *The Rocking of the Cradle and The Ruling of the World*. 1976. London: The Women's Press, 1987.

Doane, Janice and Devon Hodges. *Nostalgia and Sexual Difference: The Resistance To Contemporary Feminism*. London: Methuen, 1987.

Dolan, Jill. *The Feminist Spectator as Critic*. Ann Arbor: The University of Michigan Press, 1988.

——. "Breaking the Code: Musings on Lesbian Sexuality and the Performer." *Drama Review* 32 (1989): 146–52.

Dollimore, Jonathan. *Sexual Dissidence: Augustine To Wilde, Freud to Foucault*. Oxford: Clarendon Press, 1991.

Dowell, Kim. "Lines That Divide Black Women." In O'Barr and Wyer, 30.

Dworkin, Andrea. *Intercourse*. New York: The Free Press, 1988.

——. *Womanhating*. New York: E.P. Dutton, 1974.

——. *Our Blood: Prophecies and Discourses on Sexual Politics*. London: The Women's Press, 1982.

——. *Letters From A War Zone*. 1988. New York: Lawrence Hill Books, 1993.

Early, Gerald, Ed. *Lure and Loathing: Essays on Race, Identity, and the Ambivalence of Assimilation*. London: Penguin, 1993.

Eisenstein, Zillah R. *The Color of Gender: Reimaging Democracy*. Berkeley:

University of California Press, 1994.

Elam, Keir. *The Semiotics of Theatre and Drama*. 1980. London: Routledge, 1988.

Evans, Sara. *Personal Politics: The Roots of Women's Liberation in the Civil Rights Movement & the New Left*. New York: Vintage Books, 1980.

Fabre, Genevieve. *Drumbeats, Masks, and Metaphor: Contemporary Afro-American Theatre*. Trans. Melvin Dixon. Cambridge, Massachusetts: Harvard University Press, 1983.

Faderman, Lillian. *Odd Girls and Twilight Lovers: A History of Lesbian Life in Twentieth-Century America*. London: Penguin, 1994.

Faludi, Susan. *Backlash: The Undeclared War Against Women*. London: Chatto & Windus, 1991.

Ferguson, Ann. *Blood at the Root: Motherhood, Sexuality, and Male Dominance*. New York: Unman Hyman/Routledge, 1989.

Ferree, Myra Marx and Beth B. Hess. *Controversy and Coalition: The New Feminist Movement*. Boston: Twayne Publishers, 1985.

Flax, Jane. "Mother-Daughter Relationships: Psychodynamics, Politics and Philosophy." *The Future of Difference*. Ed. Hester Eisenstein and Alice Jardine. New Jersey: Rutgers University Press, 1994, 20–40.

Foucault, Michel. *The History of Sexuality Volume 1: An Introduction*. Trans. Robert Hurley. 1978. New York: Vintage, 1980.

——. *Language, Counter-Memory and Practice*. Ed. Donald F. Bouchard and Sheri Simon. Ithaca: Cornell University Press, 1977.

——. *The Order of Things: An Archaeology of the Human Sciences*. New York: Vintage Books, 1973.

——. *Discipline and Punish: The Birth of the Prison*. London: Allen Lane, 1977.

——. "The Order of Discourse." *Untying the Text: A Post-Structuralist Reader*. Ed. Robert Young. London: Routledge & Kegan Paul, 1981, 48–78.

Frankenberg, Ruth. R. *The Social Construction of Whiteness: White Women, Race Matters*. London: Routledge, 1993.

Freeman, Sandra. *Putting Your Daughters on the Stage: Lesbian Theatre from the 1970s to the 1990s*. London: Cassell, 1997.

Freud, Sigmund. "The Psychogenesis of a Case of Homosexuality in a Woman." *Penguin Freud Library*. Trans. James Strachey. 1920. London: Penguin Books, 1990.

Friedan, Betty. *The Feminine Mystique*. 1963. London: Victor Gollancz, 1971.

——. *The Second Stage*. London: Michael Joseph, 1982.

Fritz, Leah. *Dreamer's and Dealers: An Intimate Appraisal of the Women's Movement*. Boston: Beacon Press, 1979.

Fuss, Diana. *Essentially Speaking: Feminism, Nature & Difference*. London: Routledge, 1989.

——, Ed. *Inside/Out: Lesbian Theories, Gay Theories*. London: Routledge, 1991.

Gallup, Jane. *Thinking Through the Body*. New York: Columbia University Press, 1983.

Gates Jr., Henry Louis. "'Talkin' That Talk." *'Race' Writing and Difference*. Ed. Henry Louis Gates Jr. Chicago: The University of Chicago Press, 1986, 402–9.

Gledhill, Christine. "Pleasurable Negotiations." *Female Spectators*. Ed. E. Deidre Pribham. London: Verso, 1988, 64–89.

Glenn, Evelyn Nakano, Grace Chang and Linda Rennie Forcie, Ed. *Mothering: Ideology, Experience, Agency*. London: Routledge, 1994.

Gomez, Jewelle and Barbara Smith. "Talking About It: Homophobia in the Black

Community." *Feminist Review* (1990): 47–55.

Gomez, Jewelle (Panel Discussion). "A Celebration of Butch-Femme Identities in the Lesbian Community." In Nestle, *The Persistent Desire,* 454–63.

Goodman, Lizbeth. *Contemporary Feminist Theatres: To Each Her Own.* London: Routledge, 1993.

——. *Reader in Gender and Performance.* London: Routledge, 1998.

Gordon, Linda and Ellen Dubois. "Seeking Ecstasy on the Battlefield: Danger and Pleasure in Nineteenth Century Feminist Sexual Thought." *Feminist Review,* no 13–15 (1983): 42–51.

Gordon, Dr. Vivian. *Black Women: Feminism and Black Liberation: Which Way?* 1987. Chicago: Third World Press, 1991.

Gramsci, Antonio. *Selections from the Prison Notebooks of Antonio Gramsci.* Ed. and Trans. Quintin Hoare and Geoffrey Nowell Smith. 1971. London: Lawrence & Wishart, 1986.

Griffin, Gabrielle. *Heavenly Love? Lesbian Images in Twentieth-Century Women's Writing.* Manchester: Manchester University Press, 1983.

Hacker, Andrew. *Two Nations: Black and White, Separate, Hostile, and Unequal.* 1992. New York: Ballantine Books, 1995.

Hall, Stuart. "New Ethnicities." In Ashcroft et al., 223–7.

Hanscombe, Gillian E. and Jackie Forster. *Rocking The Cradle: Lesbian Mothers: A Challenge in Family Living.* London: Peter Owen, 1981.

Haraway, Donna. *Simians, Cyborgs and Women: The Reinvention of Nature.* London: Free Association Books, 1991.

Harding, Sandra and Hintikka Merrill, Ed. *Discovering Reality: Feminist Perspectives On Epistemology, Metaphysics, Methodology, and the Philosophy of Science.* Dordrecht: Reidel Publishing, 1983.

Harne, Lynne. "Lesbian Custody and the New Myth of the Father." In Jackson, 217–20.

—— and Rights of Women. *Valued Families: The Lesbian Mothers' Legal Handbook.* London: The Women's Press, 1997.

Harris, Angela P. "Race and Essentialism in Feminist Legal Theory." *Representing Women: Law, Literature and Feminism."* Ed. Susan Sage Heinzelman and Zipporah Batshaw Wiseman. Durham: Duke University Press, 1994, 106–46.

Heath, Stephen. "Joan Riviere and The Masquerade." In Burgin et al., 45–61.

Heinemann, Uta Ranke. *Eunuchs For The Kingdom of Heaven: Women, Sexuality and the Catholic Church.* Trans. Peter Heinegg. New York: Penguin, 1990.

Henderson, Mae Gwendolyn. "Speaking in Tongues: Dialogics, Dialectics, and The Black Woman Writer's Literary Tradition." *Reading Black, Reading Feminist.* Ed. Henry Louis Gates, Jr. New York: Meridian, 1990, 116–42.

Hennessy, Rosemary. *Materialist Feminism and The Politics of Discourse.* New York: Routledge, 1993.

Hewlett, Sylvia A. *A Lesser Life: The Myth of Women's Liberation.* New York: William Morrow & Co., 1986.

Higgins, Lynn A. and Brenda A. Silver, Ed. *Rape and Representation.* New York: Columbia University Press, 1991.

——. "Introduction: ReReading Rape." In Higgins and Silver, 1–11.

Hines, Darlene Clark. "In the Kingdom of Culture: Black Women and the Intersection of Race, Gender and Class." In Early, 337–51.

Hollibaugh, Amber and Cherie Moraga. "What We're Rollin' Around in Bed With: Sexual Silences in Feminism." *Heresies* 12 (1981): 58–62.

Holloway, Wendy. "Gender Difference and The Production of Subjectivity." *Changing the Subject: Psychology, Social Regulation, and Subjectivity*. Ed. Julian Henriques and Wendy Holloway. London: Methuen, 1984, 105–25.

hooks, bell. *Black Looks: Race and Representation*. London: Turnaround, 1992.

——. *Yearning, Race, Gender and Cultural Politics*. London: Turnaround, 1991.

——. *Outlaw Culture: Resisting Representations*. New York: Routledge, 1994.

——. *Talking Back: Thinking Feminist, Thinking Black*. Boston: South End Press, 1989.

——. *Ain't I A Woman: Black Women and Feminism*. London: Pluto Press, 1982.

Ifekwinugwe, Jayne O. "Diaspora's Daughters, Africa's Orphans?: On Lineage, Authenticity, and 'mixed-race' identity." In Mirza, 127–52.

Jackson, Elaine. *Paper Dolls*. In Wilkerson, 349–423.

Jackson, Laura. Interview. Hall Carpenter Archives: Lesbian Oral History Group. *Inventing Ourselves: Lesbian Life Stories*. London: Routledge, 1991, 119–34.

Jackson, Stevi, Ed. *Women's Studies: A Reader*. London: Harvester/Wheatsheaf, 1993.

Jagger, Alison M. *Feminist Politics and Human Nature*. New Jersey: Rowman & Littlefield, 1988.

Jeffreys. Sheila. *Anti-Climax: A Feminist Perspective on the Sexual Revolution*. North Melbourne, Victoria: Spinifex, 1990.

——. "Butch and Fem: Now and Then." *Not A Passing Phase*. Ed. Lesbian Herstory Group. London: The Women's Press, 1989.

Jeness Valerie. "Coming Out: Sexual Identity and the Categorization Problem." *Modern Homosexuality: Fragments of Gay and Lesbian Experience*. Ed. Kenneth Plummer. London: Routledge, 1992, 65–74.

Jewell, K. Sue. *From Mammy to Miss America and Beyond: Cultural Images & The Shaping of U.S. Social Policy*. London: Routledge, 1994.

Johnson, Mykel. "Butchy Femme." In Nestle, *The Persistent Desire*, 395–8.

Jones, Lisa. *Combination Skin*. In Perkins and Uno, 217–29.

Jones, Simon and Paul Gilroy. "The Organic Crisis of British Capitalism and Race: The Experience of the Seventies." *The Empire Strikes Back: Race and Racism in 70s Britain*. London: Routledge in association with the Centre for Contemporary Cultural Studies University of Birmingham,1992, 2nd edn, 9–32.

Joseph, Gloria J. "Black Mothers and Daughters: Their Roles and Functions in American Society." In Joseph and Lewis, 76–111.

——. "White Promotion, Black Survival." In Joseph and Lewis, 20–40.

Joseph, Gloria J. and Jill Lewis, Ed. *Common Differences: Conflicts in Black and White Feminist Perspectives*. New York: Anchor Books, 1981.

Kaplan, Cora. *Sea Changes: Essays on Culture and Feminism*. 1986. London: Verso, 1990.

Kay, Jackie. *Chiaroscuro*. In Jill Davis, 57–81.

——. Afterword. In Jill Davis, 82–3.

——. *The Adoption Papers. Four Women Poets*. Ed. Judith Baxter. Cambridge: Cambridge University Press, 1995, 34–58.

Kennedy, Elizabeth Lapovsky and Madeline D. Davis. *Boots of Leather, Slippers of Gold: The History of a Lesbian Community*. New York: Routledge, 1993.

——. "They Was No One To Mess With: The Construction of the Butch Role in the Lesbian Community of the 1940s and 1950s." In Nestle, *The Persistent Desire*, 62–80.

Kershaw, Baz. *The Politics of Performance: Radical Theatre as Cultural Intervention.* London: Routledge, 1994.

Keyssar, Helene. *Feminist Theatre.* Houndmills: Macmillan, 1984.

——. "Drama and the Dialogic Imagination: 'The Heidi Chronicles' and 'Fefu and Her Friends.'" *Modern Drama* 34 (March 1991): 88–106.

Lattany, Kristin Hunter. "Off-timing: Stepping to the Different Drummer." In Early, 163–74.

Lee, Anna. "A Black Separatist." *Radical Feminism.* Ed. Anne Koedt, Ellen Levine and Anita Rapone. 1973. New York: Quadrangle Books, 1981.

Lemelle, Sydney J. "The Politics of Cultural Resistance: Pan-Africanism, Historical Materialism and Afrocentricity." *Race & Class* 35 no 1 (July–Sept. 1993): 93–112.

Lewin, Ellen. "Negotiating Lesbian Motherhood: The Dialectics of Resistance and Accommodation." In Glenn et al., 333–54.

Lewis, Eve. *Ficky Stingers. Play By Women Volume 6.* Ed. Mary Remnant. London: Methuen, 1987, 117–27.

Lewis, Jill. "The Subject of Struggle: Feminism and Sexuality." In Joseph and Lewis, 232–71.

Lorde, Audre. *Sister Outsider: Essays & Speeches.* New York: The Crossing Press, 1984.

Loury, Glenn C. "Free at Last? A Personal Perspective on Race and Identity in America." In Early, 1–12.

Lyssa, Alison. *Pinball.* In Wandor, *Plays By Women,* 121–55.

——. Afterword. In Wandor, *Plays By Women,* 156–9.

MacGowan, Lyndall. "Re-collecting History, Renaming Lives: Femme Stigma and the Seventies and Eighties." In Nestle, *The Persistent Desire,* 299–330.

McCauley, Robbie. *Sally's Rape. Moon Marked & Touched By Sun: Plays By African-American Women.* Ed. Sydne Mahone. New York: Theatre Communications Group, 1994, 211–38.

McKay, Nellie V. "Alice Walker's 'Advancing Luna – and Ida B. Wells': A Struggle Toward Sisterhood." In Higgins and Silver, 248–62.

MacKinnon, Catherine. *Feminism Unmodified.* Cambridge, Massachusetts: Harvard University Press, 1987.

Margolin, Deborah, Peggy Shaw and Lois Weaver. *Upwardly Mobile Home.* In Case, *Split Britches,* 87–118.

Marohl, Joseph. "'De'realised Women: Performance and Identity in Churchill's Top Girls." *Contemporary British Drama, 1970–90.* Eds. Hersch Zeifman and Cynthia Zimmerman. New York: Macmillan, 1993, 308–21.

Medley, Cassandra. *Ma Rose. Women's Work: 5 New Plays From The Women's Project.* Ed. Julia Miles. New York: Applause Theatre Book Publishers, 1989.

Merck, Mandy. "From Minneapolis to Westminster." In Segal and McIntosh, 50–62.

Merrill, Lisa. "Monsters and Heroines: Caryl Churchill's Women." *Caryl Churchill: A Casebook.* Ed. Phyllis R. Randall, 71–89.

Minh-Ha, Trinh T. "Introduction. She, the Inappropriate/d Other." *Discourse: Journal for Theoretical Studies in Media and Culture* 8 (Fall–Winter 1986–7): 1–9.

——. "Difference: A Special Third World Women Issue." *Discourse: Journal for Theoretical Studies in Media and Culture* 8 (Fall–Winter 1986–7): 11–37.

Mirza, Heidi Safia, Ed. *Black British Feminism: A Reader.* London: Routledge, 1997.

Mohanty, Chandra Talpade, Ann Russo, and Lourdes Torres, Ed. *Third World Women and the Politics of Feminism*. Bloomington: Indiana University Press, 1991.

Moi, Toril. *Sexual/Textual Politics: Feminist Literary Theory*. London: Methuen, 1985.

Montero, Oscar. "Lipstick Vogue: The Politics of Drag." *Radical America* 22 (1988): 37–41.

Morgan, Robin. *Going Too Far: The Personal Chronicle of a Feminist*. New York: Vintage Books, 1978.

Mulvey, Laura. "Visual Pleasure and Narrative Cinema." *Screen* 16 (Autumn 1975): 6–18.

National Gay and Lesbian Survey. *What a Lesbian Looks Like: Writings by Lesbians on their Lives and Lifestyles*. London: Routledge, 1992.

Nestle, Joan, Ed. *The Persistent Desire: A Femme-Butch Reader*. Boston: Alyson Publications, 1992.

——. *A Restricted Country*. 1988. London: Pandora Press, 1996.

——. "The Fem Question." *Pleasure and Danger*. Ed. Carole S. Vance. London: Routledge, 1984, 232–41.

Newton, Esther. *Mother Camp: Female Impersonators in America*. New Jersey: Prentice-Hall, 1972.

Njeri, Itabari. "Sushi and Grits: Ethnic Identity and Conflict in a Newly Multicultural America." In Early, 13–40.

O'Barr, Jean and Mary Wyer, Ed. *Engaging Feminism: Students Speak Up & Speak Out*. Charlottesville: University Press of Virginia, 1992.

Osment, Philip. "Finding Room on the Agenda for Love: A History of Gay Sweatshop." *Gay Sweatshop: Four Plays and a Company*. Ed. Philip Osment. London: Methuen, 1989.

Penelope, Julia. *Call Me Lesbian: Lesbian Lives, Lesbian Theory*. Freedom, California: The Crossing Press, 1992.

Perkins, Kathy A. and Roberta Uno, Ed. *Contemporary Plays by Women of Color: An Anthology*. New York: Routledge, 1996.

Phizacklea, Annie and Robert Miles. *Labour and Racism*. London: Routledge & Kegan Paul, 1980.

Posener, Jill. *Any Woman Can*. London: Methuen, 1987.

Pratt, Minnie Bruce. "All The Women Caught in Flaring Light." *Mother Journeys: Feminists Write About Mothering*. Ed. Maureen T. Reddy. Minneapolis: Spinsters Ink, 1994, 2–3.

——. "Identity, Skin, Blood, Heart." *Yours In Struggle: Three Feminist Perspectives On Anti-Semitism and Racism*. Ed. Elly Bulkin, Minnie Bruce Pratt, Barbara Smith. New York: Long Haul Press, 1984, 11–63.

Purkiss, Diane. "Women's Rewriting of Myth." *The Feminist Companion to Mythology*. Ed. Carolyne Larrington. London: Pandora Press, 1992, 441–57.

Rabillard, Sheila, Ed. *Caryl Chuchill: Contemporary Re-Visions*. Canada: Blizzard Press, 1999.

Rabine, Leslie Wahl. "A Feminist Politics of Non-Identity." *Feminist Studies* 14 (1) (1988): 11–32.

Reinelt, Janelle. *After Brecht: British Epic Theater*. Ann Arbor: The University of Michigan Press, 1994.

Reynolds, Tracey. "(Mis)representing the black (super)woman." In Mirza, 97–112.

Rich, Adrienne. "Compulsory Heterosexuality and Lesbian Existence." *Powers of Desire: The Politics of Sexuality*. Ed. Ann Snitow and Christine Stansell, London: Virago, 1984, 217–28.

——. *Of Woman Born: Motherhood as Experience and Institution*. 1976. London: Virago, 1977.

——. *On Lies, Secrets and Silence*. New York: Norton, 1979.

Rights of Women Lesbian Custody Group. *Lesbian Mothers' Legal Handbook*. London: The Women's Press, 1986.

Riviere, Joan. "Womanliness as a Masquerade." In Burgin et al., 35–44.

Roof, Judith. *A Lure of Knowledge: Lesbian Sexuality and Theory*. New York: Columbia University Press, 1991.

Rubin, Gayle. *Women: The Longest Revolution: Essays on Feminism, Literature, And Psychoanalysis*. London: Virago, 1984.

——. "Of Catamites and Kings: Reflections on Butch, Gender, and Boundaries." In Nestle, *The Persistent Desire*, 266–82.

Russo, Ann. "We Cannot Live Without Our Lives: White Women, Antiracism, and Feminism." In Mohanty et al., 297–314.

Sawicki, Jana. *Disciplining Foucault: Feminism, Power and the Body*. New York: Routledge, 1991.

Schechner, Richard. *Performance Theory*. London: Routledge, 1988.

Schor, Naomi. "Dreaming Dyssymetry: Barthes, Foucault, and Sexual Difference." *Men In Feminism*. Ed. Alice Jardine and Paul Smith. London: Methuen, 1987, 98–110.

Sears, James T. *Growing Up Gay in the South: Race, Gender and Journeys of the Spirit*. London: Harrington Press, 1991.

Segal, Lynne. *Is the Future Female?: Troubled Thoughts on Contemporary Feminism*. London: Virago, 1988.

——, Ed. *New Sexual Agendas*. Houndmills: Macmillan, 1979.

—— and Mary McIntosh, Ed. *Sex Exposed: Sexuality and the Pornography Debate*. London: Virago, 1992.

——. "Sweet Sorrows, Painful Pleasures: Pornography and the Perils of Heterosexual Desire." In Segal and McIntosh, 65–91.

——. "Feminist Sexual Politics and The Heterosexual Predicament." In Segal, *New Sexual Agendas*, 77–89.

*Sexuality and the State: Human Rights Violations Against Lesbians, Gays, Bisexuals And Transgendered People*. London: Liberty: National Council for Civil Liberties, 1994.

Shakespeare. *Romeo and Juliet. The Warwick Shakespeare*. Ed. J. E. Crofts. London: Blackie and Son Ltd., 1963.

Shaw, Peggy, Deborah Margolin and Lois Weaver. *Beauty and The Beast*. In Case, *Split Britches*, 59–86.

——. *Split Britches: A True Story*. In Case, *Split Britches*, 35–58.

Shaw, Stephanie J. "Mothering Under Slavery in the Antebellum South." In Glenn et al., 237–58.

Sinfield, Alan. *Gay and After*. London: Serpent's Tail, 1998.

——. *Faultlines: Cultural Materialism and the Politics of Dissident Reading*. Oxford: Clarendon Press, 1992.

——. *Literature, Politics and Culture in Postwar Britain*. Oxford: Basil Blackwell, 1989.

——. *The Wilde Century: Effeminacy, Oscar Wilde and the Queer Moment*. London: Cassell, 1994.

Small, Stephen. *Racialized Barriers: The Black Experience in the United States and*

*England in the 1980s*. London: Routledge, 1994.

Smart, Carol. "Unquestionably A Moral Issue: Rhetorical Devices and Regulatory Imperatives." In Segal and McIntosh, 184–99.

Smith, Barbara. "The Dance of Masks." In Nestle, *The Persistent Desire*, 426–30.

Sontag, Susan. *A Susan Sontag Reader*. New York: Farrar, 1982.

Spelman, Elizabeth V. *Inessential Woman: Problems of Exclusion in Feminist Thought*. 1988. London: The Women's Press, 1990.

Steele, Shelby. *The Content of Our Character: A New Vision of Race in America*. New York: St. Martin's Press, 1990.

Stein, Arlene. "All Dressed Up, But No Place To Go? Style Wars and the New Lesbianism." In Nestle, *The Persistent Desire*, 431–9.

Stimpson, Catherine R. *Where the Meanings Are: Feminism and Cultural Spaces*. London: Methuen, 1988.

Sullivan, Andrew. *Virtually Normal: An Argument About Homosexuality*. London: Picador, 1995.

Swanson, Michael. "Mother/Daughter Relationships in Three Plays by Caryl Churchill." *Theatre Studies* (1985–6): 49–66.

Tasker, Fiona and Susan Golombok. "Children Raised by Lesbian Mothers: The Empirical Evidence." *Family Law* 21 (1991): 184–7.

Terborg-Penn, Rosalyn. "Discontented Black Feminists: Prelude and Postscript to the Passage of the Nineteenth Amendment." *Decades of Discontent: The Women's Movement, 1920–40*. Ed. Lois Scharf and Joan H. M. Jensen. Westport, Connecticut: Greenwood Press, 1983.

Tyler, Carole-Anne. "Boys Will be Girls: The Politics of Gay Drag." In Fuss, *Inside/Out*, 32–70.

Vanwesenbeeck, Ine. "The Context of Women's Power(lessness) in Heterosexual Interactions." In Segal, *New Sexual Agendas*, 171–9.

Walker, Alice. *In Search of Our Mothers' Gardens*. London: The Women's Press, 1984.

Wandor, Michelene. *Care and Control. Strike While The Iron is Hot: Three Plays On Sexual Politics*. Ed. Michelene Wandor. London: The Journeyman Press, 1980.

——, Ed. *Plays by Women, Vol. 4*. London: Methuen, 1985.

Wasserstein, Wendy. *The Heidi Chronicles and Other Plays*. New York: Vintage Books, 1991.

——. *Uncommon Women and Others*, 1–72.

——. *Isn't It Romantic* 73–154.

——. *The Heidi Chronicles*, 155–249.

Wattenberg, Ben. *The Birth Dearth*. New York: Pharos Books, 1987.

Weaver, Lois. "Sheila Dances with Sheila." *Butch/Femme: Inside Lesbian Gender*. Ed. Sally R. Munt. London: Cassell, 1998, 67–73.

Weeks, Jeffrey. *Coming Out: Homosexual Politics in Britain, from the Nineteenth Century to the Present*. London: Quartet, 1979.

——. "Questions of Identity." *The Cultural Construction of Sexuality*. Ed. Pat Kaplan. London: Tavistock Publications, 1987, 31–51.

West, Cheryl L. "I Ain't the Right Kind of Feminist." In Mohanty, et al., n.p.

Whitford, Margaret. *Luce Irigaray: Philosophy In The Feminine*. London: Routledge, 1991.

Wilkerson, Margaret B., Ed. *9 Plays By Black Women*. New York: New American Library, 1986.

——. Introduction. In Wilkerson, 13–28.

Williams, Raymond. *Problems in Materialism and Culture*. London: Verso, 1980.

Wittig, Monique. *The Straight Mind and Other Essays*. London: Harvester /Wheatsheaf, 1992.

Wolf, Naomi. *Fire with Fire: The New Female Power and How It Will Change the 21st Century*. London: Chatto & Windus, 1993.

Wollett, Anne and Ann Phoenix. "Issues Related to Motherhood." In Jackson, 216–17.

Wong, Sau-li C. "Diverted Mothering: Representations of Caregivers of Color in The Age of Multiculturalism." In Glenn et al., 67–94.

Young, Robert. *Colonial Desire: Hybridity in Theory, Culture and Race*. London: Routledge, 1995.

Youngblood, Shay. *Shakin' The Mess Outta Misery*. Woodstock, Illinois: The Dramatic Publishing Company, 1994.

Zhana. "Mother/Daughter." *Sojourn*. Ed. Zhana. London: Methuen, 1988, 59–73.

# Index